2698

FROM THE LIBRARY OF
Donn Starry

William Orlando Darby

William Orlando Darby
A Military Biography

By
Michael J. King

1981
Archon Books

© Michael J. King 1981

First published 1981 as an Archon Book,
an imprint of The Shoe String Press, Inc.,
Hamden Connecticut 06514

All rights reserved
Printed in the United States of America

Library of Congress Cataloging in Publication Data

King, Michael J
  William Orlando Darby, a military biography.

  Bibliography: p.
  Includes index.
  1. Darby, William Orlando. 2. United States. Army. 1st Ranger Battalion—History. 3. United States. Army. 3d Ranger Battalion—History. 4. United States. Army. 4th Ranger Battalion—History. 5. World War, 1939-1945—Campaigns—Africa, North. 6. World War, 1939-1945—Campaigns—Italy. 7. World War, 1939-1945—Regimental histories—United States—1st Ranger Battalion. 8. World War, 1939—1945—Regimental histories—United States—3d Ranger Battalion. 9. World War, 1939—1945—Regimental histories—United States—4th Ranger Battalion. 10. Generals—United States—Biography. 11. United States. Army—Biography.
  I. Title.
  E745.D37K56   940.54'12'730924 [B]   80-21162
  ISBN 0-208-01867-0

*In memory of my parents
George and Virginia King*

Contents

Maps and Tables ix
Preface 1

    I   The Young Darby 5
   II   The Foundation and Organization of the
         Rangers 27
  III   North Africa 41
  IV   Sicily 73
   V   From Salerno to the Winter Line 99
  VI   Anzio and Cisterna di Littoria 139
 VII   The War Department and the Tenth
         Mountain Division 163
VIII   Epilogue 177

Abbreviations 189
Notes 191
The Sources 197
Index 211

Maps and Tables

1. Organization of the First Ranger Battalion at Carrickfergus
2. Allied Invasion of North Africa
3. Center Task Force Invasion Sites showing Arzew
4. Port of Arzew showing Sites of Tactical Importance
5. Ranger Battle Sites in Tunisia
6. Organization of Ranger Force
7. Sicily showing Allied Landing Sites and Principal Locations
8. Allied Invasion of Italy
9. Salerno Landings showing Sites of Greatest Military Importance
10. Maiori and Chiunzi Pass showing Most Important High Ground
11. Sites of Importance in the Drive on Naples
12. Ranger Battle Sites on the Winter Line showing High Ground Important to Ranger Operations.
13. Military Situation in Italy at the Time of the Landing at Anzio.
14. Anzio and Sites of Greatest Military Importance
15. Sites of Importance in the Rangers' Battles for Cisterna
16. Northeastern Italy showing Principal Cities and Sites of Importance during Darby's Assignment to the 10th Mountain Division

Preface

Brig. Gen. William Orlando Darby, 1933 graduate of the United States Military Academy and World War II combat leader, is best known as the organizer and commander of the First, Third and Fourth Ranger Battalions. These battalions, commonly known as Darby's Rangers, were commanded by Darby during most of their existence.

While training at the U.S. Army Ranger School at Fort Benning, Georgia, in the spring of 1963, I became interested in World War II Ranger operations and the role which Darby had played in organizing the first Ranger battalions. I was disappointed, however, to find that very little regarding Darby or his Rangers had been published. In fact, only two items were widely available at the time I began my research. One, a general history of American Ranger units from the time of the French and Indian War through the Korean War, was found in a thirteen-page appendix to *FM 21-50: Ranger Training and Ranger Operations*, a Department of the Army field manual. It was too brief to be of real value. The other, a book titled *The Spearheaders*, was written by former World War II Ranger James Altieri. It concentrated upon the organization and early operations of the First, Third and Fourth Ranger Battalions and contained numerous references to Darby. Although it was very well written and informative, it was a highly personal account of the actions described and covered Ranger operations in Sicily and Italy too lightly to answer the questions I was asking.

Two additional books came into print while I was doing my research, but both proved to be deficient. *Military Elites* by Roger A. Beaumont mentions the Rangers only briefly, placing them within the larger context of elite fighting units of many nations. Sadly, what little treatment Beaumont gives to the Rangers is superficial and tainted by error. Contrary to Beaumont's belief, the Rangers who took part in the Dieppe raid did not return to England "unscathed," nor was Darby a brigadier general at the time of his death. James Ladd's *Commandos and Rangers of World War II* is a much more reliable source of information about the Rangers, but also deals with them too briefly. The First, Third and Fourth Ranger Battalions are mentioned on only 21 of the book's 275 pages.

As a biography of Darby, this book is intended to tell only a part of the Rangers' story. The Second, Fifth and Sixth Ranger Battalions are not included in it. The Second and Fifth Ranger Battalions were activated at Camp Forrest, Tennessee, in April and September of 1943 respectively and fought in Normandy, northern France, the Rhineland, the Ardennes, and central Europe. The Sixth Ranger Battalion was activated in January of 1941 at Fort Lewis, Washington, as the Ninety-eighth Field Artillery Battalion. It was redesignated the Sixth Ranger Infantry Battalion in September of 1944 and fought in New Guinea and the Philippines. These battalions were separate units and were never commanded by Darby or joined with his battalions under a common headquarters, although they were born of the same concept and some of their men had served under Darby.

In undertaking this project, I sought to answer two questions. The first was, how did Darby manage to rise to the rank of brigadier general by the age of thirty-four? Although his final promotion was posthumous, it was a true and not an honorary promotion, for a recommendation that he be made a brigadier general had been prepared for presidential approval shortly before his death in combat. Answering this question

Preface

involved an examination of Darby's personal qualities, the means by which he climbed the army's promotion ladder, and the nature of the system within which he rose.

The second question I sought to answer was, why were the Rangers so often used to perform missions which could have been given to conventional infantry, instead of being given missions suited to their own unique training and background? The conclusions reached concerning the Rangers' misemployment helps to explain why other elite fighting units, such as the British commandos, were similarly misused, thereby casting additional light on the question of the place, or very suitability, of such units in modern mass armies.

While many aspects of Darby's personal life are touched upon in this biography, it is intended to be first and foremost a study of a soldier's life. Consequently, I have emphasized only those elements of Darby's personal life which, in my opinion, had an impact on his military career or his development as a soldier.

This biography could never have been written without the help of hundreds of men and women who corresponded with me or allowed themselves to be interviewed.

There were also those who assisted me at the several archives and other collections which I visited, and whose names do not appear in the bibliography. These were: Mr. Raymond F. Alm of Oak Lawn, Illinois, who helped put me in touch with numerous members of the Ranger Battalions Association of World War II; Mr. William Avery of the Washington National Records Center at Suitland, Maryland; Mrs. Leona Bolden of the National Personnel Records Center at Saint Louis, Missouri; Mr. Mal J. Collett, director of the Archives-Museum at The Citadel, Charleston, South Carolina; the late Mr. Ervin J. Gorecki of Chicago, Illinois, who provided me with army field manuals of World War II; Mr. Louis F. Lisko, historian of the Ranger Battalions Association of World War II, of Brackenridge, Pennsylvania; Mr. Stanley P. Tozeski, chief of the United States Military Academy Archives at West Point, New York; and Miss

Hannah Zeidlik of the U.S. Army Center of Military History, formerly known as the Office of the Chief of Military History, at Washington, D.C. Technical factors and expenses have made it impractical to footnote every item which could have been footnoted. I have thus limited footnotes to only those items, such as the assignment of Ranger missions, which are pivotal or controversial. All sources which have been used, however, are listed in the bibliography.

Special gratitude is due the late Brig. Gen. William O. Darby's sister, Mr. Doris Nell Watkins of Cleveland, Mississippi, who authorized me to use her brother's West Point and army personnel files.

Finally, I am indebted to my wife Cheryl, who assisted in the preparation of the manuscript of this book, and my late mother Virginia, who freed my wife for such work through her frequent babysitting.

I
The Young Darby

Visitors to the United States National Cemetery at Fort Smith, Arkansas, enter through black iron gates swung open on white cement gateposts. On the right is the cemetery's red brick administration building. Two hundred feet ahead lies a circular lawn with a white flagpole at its center. Beyond lie the dead, identified by rows of white tabletlike markers. Uniformity is occasionally broken by clusters of distinctive monuments atop the few small knolls which announce the presence of once-distinguished men. An oversized monument of polished grey granite stands out on a lightly wooded knoll two hundred feet beyond the flagpole. Its inscription reads:

> WILLIAM O. DARBY
> ARKANSAS
> BRIG. GENERAL U.S. ARMY
> WORLD WAR II
> BORN IN FORT SMITH ARK. FEB. 8, 1911
> GRADUATE U.S.M.A. JUNE 1933
> ASSISTANT COMDR. 10TH MOUNTAIN DIV.
> DIED IN PO VALLEY ITALY APR. 30, 1945
> ORGANIZED FIRST RANGER BN.
> CO RANGER FORCE—TUNISIA SICILY ITALY 1942-1944
> COMDR. 179TH INFANTRY 45TH DIVISION
> 1944 1945 POD WDGS

William O. Darby was the second of three children of Percy and Nell Darby of Fort Smith, Arkansas. Their eldest child, Thelma May, was born in September of 1905 and died of vaguely diagnosed causes before reaching the age of twenty-one. A second daughter, Doris Nell, was born several years after Thelma's death.

There was nothing in the Darby family background to suggest that Billy, as he was called during his childhood and youth, would become a soldier. Indeed, if his future was to be determined by his background, he might well have become a musician for he came from a family in which music played a central part. His father played the clarinet and saxophone and had organized the Darby Orchestra, a group of about thirty musicians who played at public gatherings and in the pavilion of the Electric Park, an amusement center built by the Fort Smith Light and Traction Company. In addition to performing out-of-doors, the Darby Orchestra furnished musical accompaniment for silent movies. This led to the orchestra's failure, for when sound came to the screen the orchestra's services were no longer needed. Fortunately, Percy Darby was also in the printing business and his family was not economically dependent upon the orchestra. He had begun as a printer in the Darby and Bly Printing Company, but the partnership dissolved under friendly circumstances in the 1920s and he established the Darby Printery in Fort Smith's business district. Although Percy was unable to build his life solely around music, he passed his love of it on to his son. Billy learned to play the clarinet and saxophone like his father.

The family into which Billy had been born was also religious, for the Darbys had made the First Methodist Church, a large neoclassical building near the center of town, one of the centers of their lives. Percy was a member of the men's Bible study group, and Nellie was the secretary of the women's group. When Billy was old enough, he joined the church-sponsored Boy Scout troop. As well as adding focus to the Darbys' family life, the church helped to combine their musical inclinations with the practice of their religion. Percy and his family usually arrived at church long before Sunday services so they could enjoy the music.

While no one as yet foresaw that young Darby would become a soldier, friends and family reflected upon his childhood antics in later years and retrospectively saw them as typical of the soldier he became. Indeed, his early activities reveal a willful and confident personality, realistic enough to know when not to risk probable failure but headstrong enough to overcome obstacles and objections and to succeed where success was possible, even though it might mean challenging authority. On one Memorial Day, for example, when Billy was eight or nine years old, he and his cousin Bill Hogan decided to travel the circuit of Fort Smith's National Cemetery without touching the ground by walking along the top of its stone fence. The boys got off to a good start, but when they were about halfway around Bill lost his balance and fell off. Billy told him to go back to where they had begun and start over. Bill did, but when he reached the point where he had fallen he found the cemetery caretaker ordering them both off the fence. Bill Hogan obeyed but young Darby rejoined that he was as close to the end of the fence as to the beginning, and went on his way to complete the circuit.

In doing things his own way, Billy sometimes revealed an ability to lead. When his mother asked whom he wanted at his twelfth birthday party, he said that he wanted only Bill Hogan and two friends, Paige Mulholland and Kellum Woodruff. Nell Darby did not think that three guests would make much of a party, but Billy insisted that they were all the guests he wanted. The main event of the day came after the party when Billy took his guests to an open storm sewer and claimed that he could lead them out of town through the sewer system. All three followed him into the sewer but rising water and fear sent Bill Hogan and Kellum Woodruff up to the street after they had gone about a quarter of a mile. Billy made it to the edge of town, as he said he could, with Paige Mulholland.

Although Billy's self-will frequently led him into mischief, it was an innocent mischief and the expression of an energetic and adventurous curiosity. This same curiosity gave him a desire for book learning.

Billy received his first few years of primary education at the Belle Grove School but transferred and graduated from Prince Rogers, later known as the Peabody School. A minor episode which occurred while Billy was in grade school was a typical expression of his serious attitude toward studies. When Billy was nine, his uncle Edgar Darby married Lena Godt, the daughter of a Fort Smith sand contractor. Because the wedding took place on a weekday, his parents told him to take the day off from school. He refused, saying that going to school was more important than seeing a wedding.

Edgar and Lena did not have children but treated their nieces and nephews as though they were their own. During their visits to Percy Darby's home, Aunt Lena formed the impression that Billy was the studious type because he always seemed to be reading. He was, in fact, an avid reader. In addition to subscribing to *Boy's Life*, *American Boy*, and *Popular Mechanics*, Billy read books which emphasized struggle or adventure, frequently staged within the context of a morality tale. Books from the Horatio Alger, Rover Boys, Tom Swift, Tom Slade, Billy Whiskers, and Zane and Jane Grey series found their way into his library. He also read more serious material. Virgil and Minta Tumblin, who were next-door neighbors and close friends of the Darbys, owned *The Book of Knowledge*, a multivolume encyclopedia. Whenever one of the volumes was missing, the Tumblins' daughter Ruth, who was three years younger than Billy, automatically knew that he was the one who had borrowed it.

In light of Billy's voracious appetite for reading, it is not surprising that the desire for a military career was first planted in his mind through the written word. When Billy was about ten, Aunt Pearle Bachle, his mother's sister, gave him a subscription to *Mentor* magazine. When *Mentor* carried a series glamorizing cadet life at West Point, Billy aspired to share in that life.[1] It was the opportunity to extend the adventurousness of his youth into adulthood.

Not all of young Darby's life was adventure, reading, and aspiration; he also had to accept adult responsibilities. Unfortunately, Percy Darby was not a very successful businessman or money manager, and when Billy was old enough it became necessary for him to help his family financially. For three of his high school years, he spent Saturdays and summers working as a stock and delivery boy at a local grocery store.

Whether attributable to a galvanizing effect caused by his sister Thelma's recent death, or to a natural maturing of his personality, Billy's activities at the Fort Smith Senior High School were serious and demonstrated his growing capacity for leadership. As a junior, he was business manager of the student newspaper, *The Grizzly*; a member of the student council; and had a minor role in the class play, *The Lucky Break*. During his senior year, Billy was advertising manager of the school annual, *The Bruin*; was vice-president of his school's chapter of the National Honor Society; and continued his dramatic activities by taking a lead part in the senior play, *The Enchanted Cottage*.

Though seldom accurate, class prophecies are interesting when they portray their subjects as seen by their peers. The class prophecy found in the 1929 *Bruin* is particularly interesting because of its unique treatment of young Darby. The writer of the prophecy, a girl, falls asleep and meets in the dream that follows "a magnificent-looking male, dressed in gorgeous clothing." "Woman," the mysterious figure says, "to you I give one wish. This is because you have the Holy characteristic, Nerve. No one else has ventured this far or even looked upon me." Her wish is to learn what the future holds for each member of her graduating class. The apparition grants her wish by presenting the class prophecy and, upon finishing, is recognized as Billy. "How did you become so powerful?" the dreamer asks him. "I studied every night for ten minutes on Prof. Smith's booklet, 'Let Me Make You a Genius,'" Billy answers. "Let me sell you one? Only 10¢ the copy, ten for $1..."

This fanciful portrayal of Billy had a resemblance to reality. If the class prophetess thought him "a mignificent-looking male," she was in agreement with the school's female consensus. The high forehead, penetrating blue eyes, and firm mouth and jaw that would characterize Billy's good looks later in life were already prominent; even some of his women teachers found him attractive. The imaginary Billy's recognition of nerve as "the Holy characteristic," and the importance he gave to diligent study were in harmony with his adventurousness and love of reading. There was also significance in Billy's offer to sell the booklet to which he claimed to owe success. Some who knew Billy when he had grown to manhood later said that if he had not gone into the army he would have been a great salesman. Herman W. Dammer, Darby's executive officer when he became commander of the First Ranger Battalion, commented that "he could tell you that black was white and before long he'd convince you that he was right." Even while young, Billy, possessed the quality of persuasiveness necessary for effective leadership.

The class prophetess was not the only person to foresee greatness for young Darby; he foresaw it, or at least hoped for it, himself. In a piece he wrote for the 1929 *Bruin* titled "Why Write An Essay," he stated that he saw no reason for writing an essay. His conclusion was revealing: "Let those who will and wish write them, but force me not. Alexander the Great at one time conquered all the known world. Where, pray tell, is a volume of his essays to be found? If perchance he did write essays they must have been poor ones for they have never reached print. Let us take Napoleon Bonaparte, Frederick the Great, Maria Theresa, Catherine de Medici, Thomas Edison and Colonel Charles Lindbergh—again I ask you, where are their essays? Why, then, since I am to become great, should I have to tax my soul with the writing of essays?"

But most aspirants to greatness have had to overcome

The Young Darby

obstacles in their quest, and Billy was no exception. His first obstacle—his father—was easily overcome. Percy had hoped that the Darby Printery would someday be known as Darby and Son, but he put his son's desire to go to West Point above his own dreams and did not hold Billy back. Billy's natural reluctance to leave his parents lost much of its force when his mother gave birth to Doris Nell; at least he would not have to leave his parents alone. So great was his happiness at Doris's birth, and so frequent his visits to his mother and sister in the hospital, that the nurses jokingly asked him if he was the father. His happiness may have been caused as much by the freedom the new birth gave him as by the birth itself.

Once Billy gained familial approval to go to West Point, he had to win an appointment and pass the academy's entrance physical. He accomplished both by the proverbial hairsbreadth.

In 1929, 2 cadets could be appointed from each congressional district, 4 from each state at large, and 122 from the nation at large. Billy sought the nomination of his congressman, the Democrat Otis Wingo, who represented Arkansas's Fourth Congressional District. Ironically, Aunt Pearle, who had been responsible for first arousing Billy's interest in a military career, also helped to gain his nomination to West Point. A court reporter by profession, she had become acquainted with Wingo through her work. She persuaded him to include Billy in his nominations and he submitted Billy's name as a second alternate candidate.[2] In early December, the War Department notified Billy that he had been recommended for appointment but, as a second alternate candidate, his selection was contingent upon the disqualification of both the principal and first alternate candidates. Thus, he would go to West Point only if the two nominees who had priority over him did not graduate from high school, failed the physical examination, or were otherwise unable or unwilling to meet the academy's entrance requirements. Improbable as it was, both the principal and first alternate candidates failed to qualify. Billy had only to pass the entrance physical to win his appointment.

Billy took his entrance physical on 5 March 1929 at Army and Navy General Hospital, Hot Springs National Park, Arkansas. Records of the examination show him to have been five feet, nine inches tall and to have weighed 144 pounds. A tendency to gain weight shared by both his parents had not yet begun to affect him. For the most part, young Darby's medical history and physical examination were unexceptional. The last barrier to appointment seemed about to fall until Darby's pulse was taken. His pulse rate two minutes after exercise was above minimum requirements and his examiners concluded: "He is disqualified for service in the United States Army, and we do therefore recommend that he be REJECTED...."[3]

Fortunately for both Darby and the army, rules and regulations are sometimes relaxed in favor of the individual when there is reason to believe that both the individual and the army will benefit thereby. In Darby's case, the same examiners who found him unqualified when measured against objective and impersonal standards requested that the requirement governing pulse rate be waived, noting that he was "well muscled, healthy, and seemed desirable for appointment." On 22 March the Surgeon General's Office gave its approval.[4] Darby was on his way to West Point and his aspirations were on their way to realization.

West Point

West Point required its incoming fourth classmen or plebes, the equivalent of freshmen in a civilian college, to take about two months of preparatory training during the summer preceding their first academic year. This training, known as "Beast Barracks" in cadet slang, was physically, mentally, and psychologically demanding and was designed to accustom the new cadets to functioning under pressure.

Darby thus reported to the academy on 1 July 1929. During "Beast Barracks," he and his fellow classmen were quartered separately from the corps of cadets, many of whom were on summer leave. During the first month they were instructed in drill, military courtesy, guard duty, marksmanship, and other subjects normally studied by recruits. During the second month the new cadets joined the corps for guard and ceremonies, although they continued to be quartered separately, and were given additional training in guard duty, infantry techniques, methods of study, swimming, dancing, hygiene, and customs of the service. At the end of summer, the fourth classmen were fully incorporated into the corps of cadets. All cadets of all classes were assigned to companies according to height in order to present a uniform appearance at formations and parades. Darby, who was of medium height, was assigned to Company "D."

Darby's roommates, or "wives" as they were known in cadet slang, were John Baird Shinberger of Norfolk, Virginia, and George Wood Beeler of Seattle. The two men were dissimilar from each other and from Darby, and the three together presented a contrasting mix of personalities. Shinberger, or "Shinny" as he was called, was a hard worker but no scholar, and would graduate from West Point near the bottom of his class. A Sunday school teacher while at the academy, he would become an Episcopal priest as the result of a covenant he made with God when he was severely wounded during World War II. Beeler, who would build a reputation as a man who got things done during his four years at the academy, would graduate near the top of his class and die later in his career of a brain tumor.

As a fourth classman, Darby studied mathematics, English, French, tactics, and military topography and graphics. He was a good but not outstanding student, and finished his first year ranking 198th in order of merit in his class of 377. Darby found competition on the Hudson stronger than it had been in Arkansas and academic distinction remained beyond his grasp. Happily, such distinction was not essential for the military places greater value on an officer's effectiveness than on his ability to engage in abstract intellectualization. Darby's drive and intensity showed itself elsewhere, such as in the area of conduct where he stood 35th in his class. He received forty-nine demerits the first year, all for minor offenses such as having his uniforms hung in improper order, being late for formation and, on one occasion, having a black thread on his absence card. Of course, all was not study and discipline. Darby balanced his military and academic training by playing intramural soccer, serving as hop manager, and singing in the cadet choir. True to his musical background and talents, he remained a member of the choir for the duration of his West Point days.

With the end of classes in June, Darby became a third classman. New third classmen did not return home for the summer, but lived instead in a tent camp near the barracks and took part in field training. Like his classmates, Darby would have to wait until the summer of 1931 to visit his home and family.

In the fall, Darby found his course of studies as a third classman similar to that of the previous year. He took second-year courses in mathematics, French, English, tactics, and military topography and graphics, and added to them physics and European history. His best year academically, he finished it ranking ninety-third in order of merit.

Darby's nonacademic activities during his second year were varied. In addition to continuing to sing in the choir and serve as hop manager, he was a stage hand for the "Hundredth Night" annual show and a staff member of *Bugle Notes*. *Bugle Notes*, unofficially known as "The Plebe Bible," was an annually published handbook that explained the history of West Point and the customs and traditions of the corps of cadets. Darby balanced his indoor activities with limited participation in athletics, playing intramural football in the fall and baseball in the spring.

Darby's academic efforts and leadership were not unrewarded. He was made acting corporal during the school year and was promoted to cadet corporal on the final day of classes, 11 June 1931, ranking fifty-fourth on a "make list" of 146.

Upon returning to West Point after summer leave, Darby waded into his second classman's curriculum. It was a technical course of study consisting of mechanics—which included hydraulics, aerodynamics, and surveying—chemistry, electrical engineering, Spanish, tactics, and military topography and graphics. He complemented his studies by continuing to sing on the cadet choir, serve on the staff of *Bugle Notes*, and be hop manager, and he began a new activity by serving as assistant editor of the academy's *YMCA Handbook*. His annual athletic effort went into track and lacrosse. It was an active year and not Darby's best academically; he finished it ranking 187th in order of merit in a class of 350.

It worked well for Darby that cadet rank was not awarded according to order of merit; leadership ability was considered more important. Thus, on 10 June 1932, he was promoted to cadet captain, passing over the ranks of cadet sergeant, first sergeant, and lieutenant, as did all captains appointed that June. It was a close call, though, as he ranked last on a "make list" of fifteen. Furthermore, his new rank was provisional and he had to demonstrate his right to wear his chevrons during summer training at Fort Monroe, Virginia, and Fort Bragg, North Carolina. Darby's cadet captaincy was confirmed at retreat on 26 August 1932 when new orders were read. He had advanced to eighth place on a "make list" of eighteen.

Cadet captains were either assigned to the corps staff or given command of one of the companies. As was appropriate to Darby's kinetic temperament, he was made a company commander. Although he probably would have preferred to remain in "D" Company, he was assigned to command "I" Company, becoming responsible for its discipline, interior administration, and general efficiency. The transfer of a commander into a company from outside was somewhat unusual, as most were promoted from within. In the case of "I" Company, however, an appointment from outside was necessary because none of its own members had been selected for promotion to cadet captain. In fact, it was a difficult company to handle and had caused one company commander to be "busted" and another to be transferred. Even *The Howitzer* of 1933, West Point's annual, jocosely described the company as being composed of "renegades" and "misfits." In spite of, or more probably because of, its character and reputation, the men of "I" Company were proud to be in it and their collective pride gave the unit a unique esprit. Having a streak of the maverick himself, Darby understood his company's peculiarities and ran it with a minimum of friction and without appearing to work very hard at it. There was no need to "bust" or transfer Darby.

Darby's success at rising within the corps of cadets was the almost inevitable result of his natural leadership ability, confident mental attitude, and strong, healthy presence. His fellow cadets certainly thought he looked like a soldier. To Lyle W. Bernard, Darby seemed to wear a uniform "like it had been poured on" and was always "neat as a pin." To Edward S. Ehlen, he seemed to have stepped out of the proverbial bandbox, while William F. Ryan thought he always looked as though he had stepped out of a shower. Beverly D. Jones, reminiscing forty-five years later, could not recall having ever seen Darby unkempt or sloppy in his dress or grooming. Of course, the army has an abundance of men who give the appearance of soldiers but are sorely lacking in substance. Darby was not among them. Indeed, both Lyle W. Bernard and George Van Way thought Darby possessed "innate" leadership abilities which enabled him to rise without giving the appearance of effort. To John A. Cleveland, Jr., it seemed that Darby was the kind of leader who made his followers want to please him—the hallmark of true leadership. To Cleveland's knowledge, Darby never treated anyone harshly or spoke unkindly to or about anyone. What impressed Walter A. Downing most was that Darby never spoke up or down to anyone, but addressed everyone as an equal. He also listened to what a person had to say and gave him a feeling of importance.

Darby's casual, natural style of leadership was well complemented by his engaging personality, an attribute which would later be given prominent mention in his efficiency reports. To James O. Boswell, he seemed to enjoy life and smile a great deal, while Harold C. Donnelly remembered him mostly for a sunny disposition and an infectious laugh. Harold K. Johnson, who would survive Japanese imprisonment following the fall of Bataan and eventually rise to become army chief of staff, thought Darby a "courteous, gracious individual," but one in whom "the instinct for fun bubbled, awaiting an opportunity for release." Edward D. Marshall, who became a close friend of Darby's while at West Point, took part in one episode in which Darby indulged just that instinct. The two were on a disappointing double blind date in New York City when they passed through the campus of Columbia University, which had a large granite ball at its center. Not wanting to throw good time after bad, Darby and Marshall put their unsuspecting dates on top of the ball and abandoned them, taking the subway downtown.

Darby's sense of humor sometimes led him to tell tall tales which only the most credulous would believe, and of which historians ought to beware. Poking fun at his own Arkansas background, for example, he once told his classmates that his family was so large and poor that his father fed them slop at a pig trough. No one took the pig trough seriously, but the story did leave some with the impression that he came from a large, poor family. Darby told other equally humorous but untrue stories about himself while at West Point and in the army. Some of these have sadly become accepted at face value and continue to be told—probably because they are too good not to repeat.

Because of the time and energy absorbed by his command responsibilities, and possibly because of his occasionally lighthearted attitude, Darby did less well academically as a first classman than at any other time at West Point. This is not to say that he did poorly in the absolute sense—his marks ranged from a second term grade of 75 percent in economics and government to an 89 percent in military hygiene—but by the relative standard of order of merit he finished the year ranking

233rd in a class of 346. Other subjects he took that year were law, ordnance, tactics, and military art and engineering. As a result of academic pressures and command responsibilities, he limited his nonessential activities to the cadet choir and the editorships of both *Bugle Notes* and the *YMCA Handbook*.

Darby graduated on 13 June 1933 with a Bachelor of Science degree and a commission as a second lieutenant in the field artillery. He ranked 177th in a class of 346, near the middle of his class and almost midway between Beeler and Shinberger. Although he had been well liked, he had not been outstanding academically or athletically and, except for his demonstration of leadership ability, most of his achievements had been undistinguishable from those of his fellows. Few of his classmates anticipated his future success. If Darby still had faith in his own destiny, he would have to wait almost a decade to see the beginning of its realization. Most of the duties which he would perform between graduation from West Point and the outbreak of World War II would be routine and unremarkable and, if for no other purpose, are worth recounting to demonstrate that even those who aspire to greatness must frequently bide their time.

With the Army in the 1930s

Following a graduation leave of seventy-four days, Darby arrived at Fort Bliss, Texas, where he was assigned to the First Battalion, Eighty-second Field Artillery, a unit of the First Cavalry Division. The battalion was the only horse artillery unit in the army, and drew considerable pride from that fact. Horse artillery differed from horse-drawn artillery in that all its officers and men were mounted. It was, in short, the cavalry's artillery.

Unit pride, however, could not compensate for the unfavorable political and economic realities which were eating away at the army's effectiveness. The martial spirit of the war against the kaiser had passed into history and been replaced by the antimilitary sentiments of businessmen and reform liberals. Military expenditures were condemned as wasteful, men in uniform criticized as economically unproductive, and the values and customs of the services considered incompatible with democratic ideals. In a reaction to imagined militarism, the army was legislated into impotence. Although the National Defense Act of 1920 had authorized a regular army of 288,000 men, Congress authorized a reduction to 125,000 by 1922, and to less than 119,000 after 1927.

These already grave problems were compounded during the Depression. The War Department added to the military duties of the First Cavalry Division responsibility for operating the Arizona-New Mexico District of the Civilian Conservation Corps and providing the headquarters and cadre for CCC members. The Eighty-second was involved in this nonmilitary work to such an extent that at one time all its officers were detached to the CCC except the commander, adjutant, and one officer for each of the four batteries. Three of the latter, however, were inexperienced second lieutenants. About eighty enlisted men were also assigned to temporary duty with the CCC. Fortunately, when Darby arrived at Fort Bliss in October, all but eight officers and fifty enlisted men had returned to the Eighty-second and the 435-man unit was again beginning to resemble a military organization.

Antimilitary feelings in Congress and the economic difficulties of the age also led to the army of the Depression era being equipped with obsolescent weapons. In 1933, the year Hitler came to power, the Eighty-second was still armed with the French 1897 model 75mm gun. In its day the gun had been revolutionary; it was the first artillery piece in the world with a successful hydro-pneumatic recoil system. When it was fired, the carriage remained stationary; it could thus be fired in rapid succession without having to be relaid on target. Although the gun had won deserved praise during World War I, its collimator sight and the absence of a hand-spike made it unsatisfactory for firing at the rapidly moving targets likely to be encountered on the modern battlefield.

Darby's first assignment was that of assistant executive of Battery "A." The following year, he became battery reconnaissance officer and performed the extra duties of supply officer. He continued in this role until 1 July 1943 when he became commanding officer of the First Cavalry Division Camp Detachment in Cloudcroft, New Mexico. By early November he was back with the Eighty-second.

The adventurous instincts of Darby's youth were still with him in young manhood, however, and after almost two and a half years of routine duties he decided to look for something more exciting. On 23 February 1935 he wrote to the Adjutant General's Office requesting that he be detailed to the Army Air Corps for flight training. About a month later a disappointed Darby was notified that his request had been disapproved because a previous physical had revealed eye imbalance and a history of sleepwalking. These defects were considered to be permanent and irremediable. Although 1935 did not bring the changes Darby had hoped for in his career, it did see him gain experience on the battalion staff as communications officer.

Darby's next assignment was as commanding officer of the 250th Motor Transport Company of the First Cavalry Division Quartermaster Train, a duty which he performed until the spring of 1936 when he returned to the Eighty-second Field Artillery as assistant communications officer. On 13 June, three years after his graduation from West Point, Darby was promoted to first lieutenant. He continued to serve as assistant communications officer until 12 February 1937 when he became commanding officer of Headquarters Battery.

In the summer of 1937, Darby went on leave with orders to report to the Field Artillery School at Fort Sill, Oklahoma. There he underwent the regular field artillery course from 1 September 1937 to mid-June of the following year, impressing the faculty as being a diligent worker who was especially suited to troop duty. Although he was on orders to join the Eighty-

The Young Darby

fourth Field Artillery at Fort Riley, Kansas, following graduation, he sought a change of pace and requested service in the Philippines or Hawaii. He failed to obtain either, however, and after graduation and a leave of more than two months reported to the Eighty-fourth.

This unit had been organized during World War I, demobilized in December 1918, and reactivated in mid-1936. Thus, when Darby reported to the Eighty-fourth on 1 September 1938, it was virtually new. If he hoped for different experiences, however, he did not find them at Fort Riley. The Eighty-fourth had been reactivated as horse artillery, the same type of unit as the Eighty-second, and Darby's duties were almost identical to those he had performed at Fort Bliss. He was probably well pleased in October of 1939 when he was notified that he was being reassigned to the Eightieth Field Artillery at Fort Lewis, Washington.

Darby joined the recently activated Battery "B" of the First Battalion of the Eightieth on 17 October 1939. Although his assignment as battery executive officer was very similar to the one he had just left, his unit was not. The battalion's mobility was provided by motor vehicles rather than horses, and it had three 155mm howitzer batteries and one 75mm antitank battery. The highlight of Darby's service with the battalion came during May and June of 1940 when it went to Camp Beauregard, Louisiana, to take part in the famous Louisiana, or Sabine area, maneuvers. The maneuvers were well covered by the press and are best remembered for having revealed a poor state of training that drew sharp criticism from both military and civilian circles. In July, Darby's performance and ability "to get the maximum response from his men and at the same time keep them smiling," a leadership quality which would later be one of his hallmarks, was rewarded with command of a battery. His new role was short-lived, however, for early the following month he received orders to join the Ninety-ninth Field Artillery at Fort Hoyle, Maryland, on 20 August. Of all the units he served with during peacetime, the Ninety-ninth would have the greatest influence on the way he would fight the war.

Ninety-ninth Field Artillery (Pack)

The Ninety-ninth was a pack unit—an unusual organization that used mules to carry its partially disassembled 75mm howitzers over terrain too rough for motor vehicles. On 1 June 1940, when the Ninety-ninth was first organized, there were only three pack artillery units in the army. One of these, the First Battalion, Second Field Artillery, was stationed in the Canal Zone; another, Battery "A," Twenty-third Field Artillery, was in the Philippines; and the third, the Fourth Field Artillery, was at Fort Bragg, North Carolina.

Darby found the Ninety-ninth in the same state he had found the Eightieth—going through the throes of organization. The first day of June had seen the activation of the Ninety-ninth's First Battalion at Fort Hoyle and its Second Battalion at Fort Lewis. On 31 July a Headquarters and Headquarters Battery were activated at Fort Hoyle, to accommodate an anticipated reorganization of the Ninety-ninth along regimental lines. It was a reorganization that never took place. On 16 December the unit was redesignated the Ninety-ninth Field Artillery Battalion, and its Second Battalion was transferred to the newly activated Ninety-eighth Field Artillery Battalion.

Lt. Col. George P. Hays, the Ninety-ninth's commander, was an outstanding soldier. Born in China of missionary parents in 1892, Hays was commissioned early during World War I and served as an artillery liaison officer with the Third Division, seeing action at Chateau-Thierry, Champagne-Marne, Aisne-Marne, St. Mihiel, and the Meuse-Argonne. A first lieutenant during the Second Battle of the Marne, he won the Medal of Honor for restoring contact among Allied units after a German artillery bombardment had disrupted communications. Riding from unit to unit on horseback, Hays had seven mounts shot from under him and was severely wounded.

On 4 September 1940, Darby began his tour with the Ninety-ninth as commander of the unit's Battery "A." The satisfaction of taking command of a firing battery was soon followed by another; on 1 October Darby was promoted to captain with a date of rank of 9 September. Darby continued to command the battery until mid-January of 1941 when he left temporarily to participate in a training operation in Puerto Rico, known as fleet landing exercise number seven.

This was a joint army-navy operation involving the First Division, the U.S. Fleet's Atlantic Squadron, and east coast units of the Fleet Marine Force. The commander of the Atlantic Squadron had overall responsibility for the exercise, and the commanding general of First Army was responsible for the army's role. The objectives of the exercise were considerable. In addition to testing previously developed procedures governing joint action, the exercise was designed to train army and navy units in planning and executing joint operations; to provide an opportunity for the funtioning of a joint staff; to train divisional units (combat teams) in embarking, disembarking and landing in the face of opposition; and, if time permitted, to train in defensive operations against a hostile landing.

The actual operation was not as extensive as the level of participating headquarters suggested. Only about twenty-two hundred troops took part, and a shortage of landing craft limited the number of men who could be landed simultaneously to twelve hundred.

The first week of training, which extended from 27 January through 1 February, was devoted to practicing debarkation techniques, the formation of boat waves and boat groups, the beaching and unloading of small landing craft, and the clearing of beaches. Although there was no opposition to interfere with the landings, they proceeded slowly and revealed numerous deficiencies in training. The umpires all agreed that there was general slowness in clearing the beach, that there was a lack of liaison between successive landing waves on the beach, and that parties of troops halted at the edge of the sand instead of moving inland and taking cover. Subsequent landings were better. On 6 February the debarkation went very well, much improvement was noted in clearing the beach, the attack was pushed vigorously and troops made maximum use of cover and proper tactical dispositions for the advance. In spite of heavy seas on 10 February, a debarkation into small landing craft showed marked improvement. The operations of 12 and 13 February were characterized by the most realistic approach to the tactical situation which had yet been attained by company commanders and platoon leaders. The landing was well carried out, and the speed with which the boats were unloaded was the best which had been observed. A coordinated attack was especially well executed.

Darby returned to his duties at Fort Hoyle after the Puerto Rican exercise and continued to serve under Hays until 21 May, when the latter was transferred. Hays would later command Darby in Italy.

In the second week of July, Darby was on the move again. Having gained amphibious training worth sharing while in Puerto Rico, he was sent to Fort Bragg to assist in the preparation of the Fourth Field Artillery Battalion (Pack) and the Ninety-seventh Field Artillery Battalion (Pack) for training with Carib Force in the New River area of North Carolina. Once there, they and other units, including the Ninety-ninth, were to conduct intensive training in landing operations and shore training in order to attain, by 25 July 1941, the proficiency required to execute landings in force against organized opposition.

The landing exercises in which Darby participated involved elements of the army's First Division and the First Marine Division. Both services demonstrated a lack of planning, proficiency, and equipment. Communications equipment was inadequate to handle the heavy radio traffic generated during the exercise, a shortage of lighters led to only half the vehicles on board ship being debarked, tanks were not debarked at all, and personnel debarkation was delayed because of the small size of the shore and beach parties. The forces that landed found that the supplies made available to them were insufficient for an operation of more than three days' duration, and shortages of engineer equipment made it impossible for them to organize a realistic beach defense. Furthermore, insufficient numbers of umpires and controllers and the absence of troops representing an enemy encouraged the landing forces to ignore the tactical situation and perform their duties without caution or urgency. Darby returned to Fort Hoyle in mid-August.

It is difficult to determine the precise influence all of Darby's peacetime training had upon his conduct of Ranger operations during the war. Although he eventually participated in four major landings with the Rangers, they took place after he had taken additional amphibious training with the British commandos. All that can be said with certainty about Darby's Puerto Rican and North Carolinian training is that it reflected poorly upon the United States's military preparedness, and showed him how not to conduct amphibious operations.

More can be said about his exposure to the new 4.2-inch or "four-deuce" mortar. While at Fort Hoyle, Darby participated in a comparison firing of the 75mm pack howitzer and the 4.2-inch mortar and was favorably impressed with the advantages of the mortar which fired a heavier shell, with a larger bursting radius, a greater distance than the howitzer.[5] Because the 4.2-inch mortar was originally designed for firing smoke and phosphorous rounds, it was officially termed a "chemical mortar" and assigned to chemical battalions. Early during World War II, unimaginative commanders would be slow to use the 4.2-inch mortar in routine support of infantry because its name suggested a specialized purpose. Darby, who knew better from experience and who had a strong appreciation of firepower because of his artillery background, would make frequent and effective use of the weapon in Sicily and Italy.

The training and new developments to which Darby was exposed while assigned to the Ninety-ninth Field Artillery were far more progressive and useful than what he had learned during his previous assignments.

In early November Darby received orders relieving him from duty with the Ninety-ninth and transferring him to Hawaii. For reasons that have not been recorded, these orders were formally rescinded on 5 January 1942 and new ones were issued. Darby was directed to leave Fort Hoyle and travel to New York City where he was to report to Maj. Gen. Russell P. Hartle, commanding general of the Thirty-fourth Infantry Division, no later than 7 January. Upon reporting, he was appointed Hartle's aide-de-camp.[6]

During the months of Darby's service with the Ninety-ninth, the United States had drawn closer to war. Conscription was approved by Congress in September of 1940, and American troops occupied Greenland in April of 1941 and Iceland in July. The Atlantic Charter came into being in August. Early in 1941 the United States sent Maj. Gen. James E. Chaney to London as an "observer." In May he was joined by a Special Observers Group. After Pearl Harbor, American troops were sent to Great Britain in strength, and Darby was among the first to go.

II
The Foundation and Organization of the Rangers

Northern Ireland

On 10 January 1942, a thirty-six-man advance party of the United States V Army Corps, commanded by Maj. Gen. Edmond H. Leavey, arrived in Belfast, Northern Ireland. Five days later Hartle, Darby, and leading elements of the Thirty-fourth Infantry Division sailed for Belfast out of Brooklyn. They arrived on 26 January, and on the following day Hartle assumed command of USANIF (United States Army Northern Ireland Forces) and V Army Corps (Reinforced), and Leavey became his chief of staff. Headquarters, USANIF and V Army Corps (Reinforced) opened officially at 1000 on 28 January at Wilmont, an estate about seven miles southwest of Belfast.

Darby put his personality to good use while he was Hartle's aide. He was smoother and more personable than Hartle, who was not very congenial, and took some of the social burden off his shoulders. But in spite of his external conviviality, Darby was unhappy; he had not asked to be Hartle's aide and would have preferred duty with a tactical unit. He intimated his disappointment to Leavey and asked if Leavey could help get him assigned to such a unit. Although Leavey was unable to be of immediate help, events were transpiring at higher headquarters which would give Darby, with Leavey's assistance, the opportunity to leave his present assignment for one far more suitable and promising.

During the last week of April, Gen. Mark W. Clark, who was then chief of staff of Army Ground Forces, summoned Col. Lucian K. Truscott, Jr., from Fort Bliss, Texas, to Washington, D.C. After arriving in Washington, Truscott learned from Clark and Maj. Gen. Dwight D. Eisenhower, who was then chief of the Operations Division of the War Department (ODWD), that he was to head a group of American officers who would join the staff of Britain's Lord Louis Mountbatten, chief of combined operations. This was part of a broad program conceived by Gen. George C. Marshall, army chief of staff, which would require a number of American officers to join various British headquarters to gain practical staff experience by participating in the planning of combat operations, and to facilitate British and American understanding of each other's staff procedures.

The nature of Truscott's mission was more clearly defined during a subsequent meeting with Marshall, who explained that Allied planners expected to launch an invasion of German-occupied Europe during the spring of 1943. He was gravely concerned because, unless something was done to give American forces combat experience before the invasion, they would have to land green. Marshall knew that the British were planning to conduct an increasing number of raids against the continent as the time of the invasion drew nearer, and he wanted as many Americans as possible to participate in the raids so they might be returned to their units prior to the invasion. A few combat-experienced men in each assault unit would partially compensate for the general lack of such training. Truscott's task was "to arrange for this participation and for the dissemination of this battle experience among the assault units."

Prior to Truscott's departure, Eisenhower furnished him with a letter of instructions which outlined his task in writing and put its several aspects into perspective. According to the letter, his mission was:

Firstly, to study the planning, organization, preparation, and conduct of combined operations, especially of the commando type, and to keep ODWD informed about developments in training, techniques, and equipment which pertained to such operations.

Secondly, to initiate plans for the participation of American troops in these operations to the fullest extent possible as a means of gaining combat experience, and to plan and coordinate the training of detachments specially formed for such participation.

Thirdly, to provide information and recommendations relative to the training, techniques, and equipment involved in these and related operations, and to assist HQ AGF (Headquarters, Army Ground Forces) in planning, organizing, and conducting training in similar operations within the United States.

And fourthly, to promote a spirit of Anglo-American teamwork in every way possible.[1]

Truscott was further instructed to keep in mind at all times that the principal objective of the program was to provide actual combat experience for as many Americans as possible. He was to retain existing American command and administrative organizations to the greatest extent that he could, and keep new organizations and installations to a minimum. His official communication with WD (the War Department), AGF, AAF (the Army Air Force), and SOS (Service of Supply) would be through the CG USAFBI (commanding general, United States Army Forces British Isles). Truscott was also directed to keep the CG USAFBI and appropriate members of his staff informed of developments, and advise them in matters concerning the training of and participation by American troops in the planned operations. Eisenhower prepared a letter containing similar information for Maj. Gen. James E. Chaney, CG USAFBI.

Truscott arrived in London on 17 May and began work on his project. Two factors, however, dictated that few Americans would gain the desired combat experience. The first was the small number of Americans in the United Kingdom. The Thirty-fourth Infantry Division had begun moving to Northern Ireland in mid-January and would not complete its relocation until the end of May. The First Armored Division began to arrive early in May and would continue to arrive through June. These two divisions would be the only American ground troops in the British Isles for several months. The second factor was that the COHQ (Combined Operations Headquarters) had only planned five raids for the summer of 1942. Only one of the raids was expected to require more than four hundred ground troops, but there were about forty-five hundred commandos and a large number of conventional British and Canadian units wanting to participate in them.

Other considerations would force changes in the organization of those Americans who were supposed to participate in the raids. The commandos had been organized to fit the limitations and characteristics of British landing craft and naval support. For example, a commando platoon was equal to the number of men who could fit aboard an ALC (assault landing craft), a commando troop could fit aboard two ALCs, and a Commando could be carried by a flotilla.[2] Truscott reasoned that since the Americans would be under control of COHQ and would use British landing craft and naval support, they should be organized like the commandos. On 26 May, the day on which Truscott was promoted to brigadier general, he submitted a proposal to Marshall that an American unit be organized along commando lines on a provisional basis pending the War Department's completion of appropriate TO&Es (tables of organization and equipment). Authorization from the War Department arrived by cable two days later.

Truscott then drafted a letter of instructions which directed Hartle to organize the Commandolike unit as soon as possible. The letter was approved by USAFBI on 31 May, and Truscott delivered it to Hartle in person the following day. Truscott's draft then became the basis for a subject letter titled "Commando Organization" which was dated 1 June, addressed to the CG USANIF, and officially written by command of Major

General Chaney. This letter both directed and gave guidance for the organization of an American "commando unit for training and demonstration purposes" which was to be "the first step in a program specifically directed by the Chief of Staff for giving actual battle experience to the maximum number of personnel of the American Army." The men joining the unit would be trained by the British and would participate in combat operations under British control. After receiving training and exposure to combat, "as many men as practicable" would return to their original organizations "and their places filled by other selected men."[3] The new unit was thus intended to be more of a school than a command. It differed from other schools in that combat was part of its curriculum.

Chaney's letter provided guidelines to be followed in the selection of personnel. Only "fully trained soldiers of the highest possible type" would be sought. Officers and NCOs would have to possess "qualities of leadership of a high order, with particular emphasis upon initiative, judgment and common sense." All men were to have "natural athletic ability, physical stamina," and "be without physical defects." Although no age limit was established, it was pointed out that members of the British Commandos averaged twenty-five years old. Men joining the New American unit would have to be capable of the maximum exertion and endurance expected from a man of that age. Certain military and civilian skills were especially desirable. Among these were self-defense, weaponry, scouting, mountaineering, seamanship, small boat handling, demolition, and knowledge of railway engines. Men who were familiar with public utilities such as power plants and radio stations and would, therefore, know how to disable them most effectively, were also sought.

The unit would be of battalion size and organized in Northern Ireland at a site to be chosen by Hartle. While in Northern Ireland, the unit would be attached to the Special Services Brigade (British) for training and tactical control, but the Thirty-fourth Infantry Division would be responsible for its administration and supplies. American equipment would be used and American doctrines and methods retained as much as possible.

Choosing an officer to organize the new battalion was one of Hartle's most immediate tasks. On the Sunday morning after he found out about the battalion, Hartle attended church services in Belfast with Leavey and Darby. While they were being driven into the city, Hartle spoke to Leavey about the importance of having a good man to put in command of the unit and asked for recommendations. Seizing the opportunity to help Darby get transferred to a tactical unit, Leavey replied, "Why don't you give the job to Bill?" When Hartle turned to Darby and asked what he thought of Leavey's suggestion, Darby responded predictably and the assignment was made.[4] Darby had been serving as Truscott's guide during the latter's visit to Northern Ireland and had impressed him very favorably. Truscott saw Darby as he had been portrayed in recent efficiency reports: "outstanding in appearance, possessed of a most attractive personality," and "keen, intelligent, and filled with enthusiasm." He concluded that Hartle had acted wisely in choosing Darby to organize the new battalion.

A name for the unit remained to be found. While in Washington, Truscott had discussed the possibility of organizing American units similar to the Commandos with Eisenhower. Eisenhower told him that if such units were organized, they should be named something other than Commandos because that name was so strongly identified with the British. Truscott chose "Rangers" because that name had been borne by a number of American units before, during, and after the American Revolution, which had displayed "high standards of individual courage, initiative, determination, ruggedness, fighting ability, and achievement." The new unit thus came to be designated the First Ranger Battalion.

Organizing the Rangers

On 7 June, a subject letter titled "Commando Organization" was sent to major USANIF units by Hartle. This letter, which informed Hartle's command of the forthcoming organization of the First Ranger Battalion, restated and elaborated on the substance of Chaney's earlier communication. Among other things, physical and mental standards were defined more precisely. Vision had to be 20/20 without eyeglasses, hearing normal, and blood pressure within limits normal for a man of twenty-five. Men with detectable cardiac defects, slow reaction time, removable dentures, night blindness, or evidence of neuropsychiatric disorders were disqualified.[5]

Hartle's letter stressed the importance of having all USANIF units gain combat-experienced personnel by having some of their men serve in the battalion. Each major unit or command was required to furnish a specified number of men of each rank from private through captain. Divisions and separate unit commanders were directed to establish boards of officers to interview all volunteers and selected personnel to determine their suitability. Those men who were chosen would be attached to the First Ranger Battalion pending their final acceptance by Darby.

The First Ranger Battalion began to form almost immediately after USANIF units were notified of its planned organization. On 8 June, Darby began interviewing his first officer volunteers at V Corps headquarters at Lurgen and Thirty-fourth Infantry Division headquarters at Omagh. The following day orders were received from V Corps detailing the first group of officers to temporary duty with the Rangers. Additional interviews were conducted at Wilmont and, on 10 June, twenty-nine more officers were detailed to the battalion.

The officer volunteers' diverse backgrounds made a standardized examination of their professional expertise impractical. In the group of twenty-nine, for example, eleven were infantrymen; five were coastal artillerymen; four came from the field artillery; three were combat engineers; two were cavalrymen; and the Medical Corps, Signal Corps, Quartermaster Corps, and Ordnance were represented by one officer each. Darby thus interviewed his prospective officers to assess their motives and personalities rather than to measure their technical knowledge, and was more likely to ask a man why he wanted to join the Rangers than what the characteristics of various weapons were.

The selection of enlisted men began at Carrickfergus on 11 June and continued for ten days. The volunteers were interviewed by boards composed of Darby's new officers. The quality of men accepted was unusually high, but the physical standards originally established were occasionally relaxed if a man's shortcomings did not interfere with the performance of his duties. Twenty-four-year-old Cpl. Gerrit Rensinck, for example, was welcomed into the Rangers when an examining doctor satisfied himself that Rensinck's bridgework did not rattle and would not give his position away during night combat. The men who were rejected were returned to the organizations from which they had come. By 15 June, 104 of the 575 volunteers whom had thus far come to Carrickfergus were sent back to their units as unacceptable. Darby drew additional volunteers by sending six boards of officers on recruiting tours of the First Armored and Thirty-fourth Infantry Divisions.

On 19 June, the First Ranger Battalion was officially activated and three days later the 488 enlisted men who had been selected were assigned to it.[6] These men were as diverse as the officers, having come from thirty-four units ranging from infantry regiments to quartermaster detachments. The training which they would soon receive from the British would make up for the lack of combat skills among the men with technical and combat support backgrounds.

Darby's forcefulness and leadership ability were frequently mentioned in efficiency reports which were prepared while he had been in the United States. At Carrickfergus, Darby's officers and enlisted men made similar observations. Darby conveyed "the tremendous impression of being in charge" to

Captain Herman W. Dammer, whom he had chosen as battalion executive officer. Sgt. Peer Buck, who was initially the battalion mess sergeant but who would become battalion sergeant major in North Africa, sized Darby up as a man who "knew what he wanted. He was the boss; he knew it and you knew it too." When Darby said something, "you knew he meant it." This was due not only to his forcefulness, but to his ability to communicate and fix responsibility. His orders were clear and a man to whom Darby had given responsibility understood what he had to do. Buck "liked him right away."

Darby also impressed many of those around him with his adherence to traditional military values. Dammer thought him "tremendously proud" of being a West Pointer, and a believer in the values of "duty, honor, and country." Out of either a natural preference, pride, or the desire to serve as a living example of his chosen values, Darby projected an image of moderation in his personal habits. Although he swore occasionally, Buck never heard him use vulgarity, and while not a teetotaler, he did not drink to excess.

Training began while recruiting and interviewing were in their final stages. On the day the battalion was activated, seven officers and twelve NCOs were detailed to temporary duty with the Second Canadian Division at Cowes, on the Isle of Wight. They would return to the battalion on 11 July.

Until 28 June, the rest of the battalion spent most of its time drawing equipment and organizing in accordance with the TO&E and instructions which had accompanied Chaney's and Hartle's letters. The battalion was thus formed into a headquarters company and six line companies. Each line company was organized into two platoons, and each platoon was organized into two assault sections and a mortar section. When applied to the Rangers, however, the terms *battalion, company*, and *platoon* were misleading because each of these units had a stength of only about 40 percent that of its infantry counterpart. A Ranger company, for example, had only three officers and sixty-nine enlisted men while an infantry company had a total strength of about two hundred.[7]

Two notable events took place while the battalion was being organized and equipped. On 24 June, orders were published which officially appointed Darby battalion commander with an effective date of 19 June, to coincide with the Rangers' activation. On the following day, the battalion was reviewed by Brigadier R. E. Laycock, GOC (general officer commanding) Special Service Brigade; who was accompanied by a Lieutenant Colonel Glendenning, his executive; and a Captain Hunt, brigade supply officer. If the number and frequency of inspections was any indication of the interest higher headquarters had in the battalion, their interest was considerable. By 19 July, the Rangers would demonstrate for or be reviewed by three separate parties.

On 28 June, the battalions began to move from Carrickfergus to the commando depot at Achnacarry, Scotland. By 3 June the last Ranger elements had arrived at Achnacarry, and on the following day the battalion began a commando-administered training program that would last until 31 July. Col. Charles A. Vaughan, commandant of the commando depot, thus became responsible for the Rangers' training. Although some thought Vaughan a typically stuffy Britisher, the outgoing and personable Darby soon established good rapport with him and the two became fast friends.

The training which Vaughan's commandos gave was difficult but it improved the Rangers physically, conditioned them to think and act quickly, and accustomed them to face regularly the possibility of bodily injury. Speed marches, cliff climbing, obstacle courses, and tactical problems were emphasized. In the latter, commandos simulated enemy resistance by throwing grenades and firing small arms over and near the Rangers.

On 7 July, Darby and his men were visited by Lieutenant General Thorn, GOC Scottish Command, and demonstrated the tactics and techniques they had learned from the commandos. Each company was responsible for a particular demonstration and live ammunition was used. Headquarters Company demon-

The Foundation of the Rangers

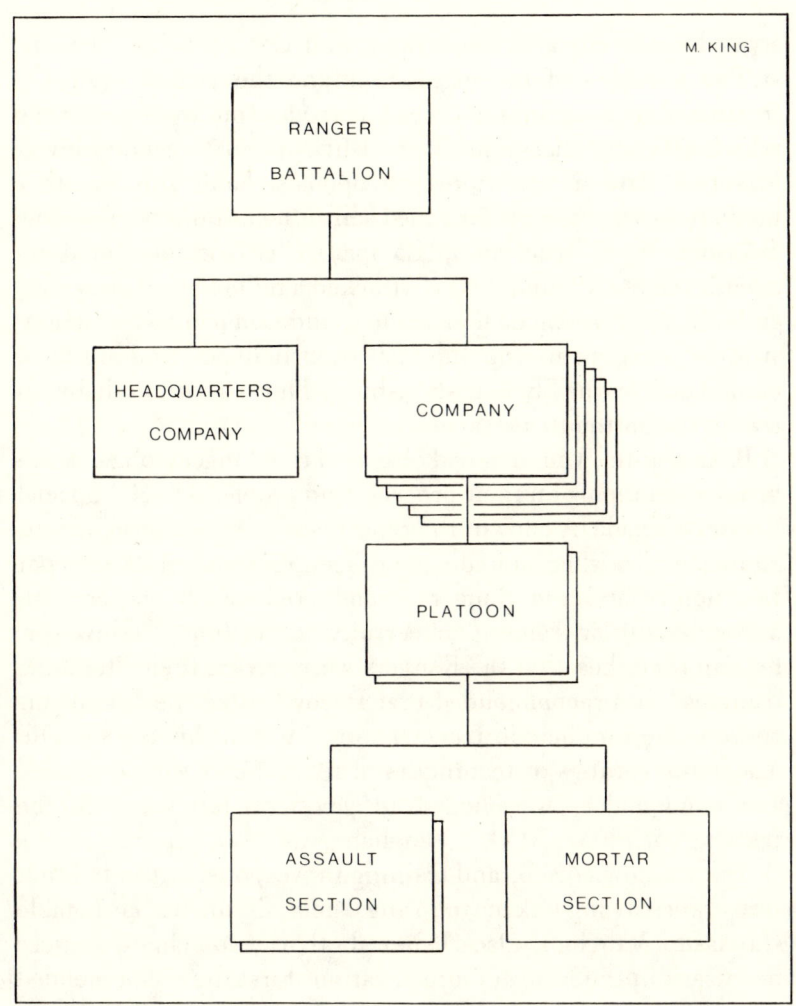

1. Organization of the First Ranger Battalion at Carrickfergus.

strated reconnaissance techniques and Company "A" demonstrated the uses of the toggle rope and the "Death Ride," a traversing technique in which a man rode a pulley down a rope which extended diagonally from a high point to ground level. Company "B" demonstrated an opposed landing in Goathly Folding Boats, which included an attack on an objective followed by a withdrawal. Company "C" demonstrated an assault course, Company "D" attacked a pillbox, Company "E" gave a rope-climbing demonstration, and Company "F" demonstrated firing from the hip, bayonet fighting, and obstacle climbing. In typically British fashion, Thorn's visit ended with tea served on the firing range.

By mid-June, Vaughan had observed the Rangers long enough to submit a report on their progress and problems to HQ Special Service Brigade. A copy of the report was given to Darby for his guidance. Vaughan noted "good feeling between the Depot Instructors and the Rangers," and credited the latter with undergoing their training "cheerfully and willingly." However, he also remarked that the Rangers were having their "teething troubles" and recommended that Darby "make the best of his time in the Commando Depot to weed out all his duds." The leadership abilities or techniques of five officers were criticized and commanders were urged to pay more attention to the training of their NCOs. Vaughan was also critical of the Rangers' knowledge of and training in weapons, but noted that steps were being taken to bring them up to an acceptable standard. Vaughan also believed that two changes were necessary in the Rangers' organization. First, he recommended that the mortars be withdrawn from the sections and placed under the control of the company commanders in their headquarters. Second, he recommended that the air-cooled .30-caliber machine guns be withdrawn from the sections and placed in a pool at battalion headquarters, and that the sections be equipped with the lighter Bren-guns or BARs (Browning automatic rifles). Both of these changes would increase the platoons' and sections' mobility by centralizing the heavier

The Foundation of the Rangers

weapons at the battalion and company headquarters, where they would be available for use on call.[8]

Darby followed Vaughan's recommendations and submitted his own progress report to Truscott on 17 July. Mortars had been centralized in company headquarters, machine guns had been replaced with BARs, and thirteen enlisted men had been returned to their units as undesirable. Like Vaughan, Darby was critical of the Rangers' performance with weapons and was confident that changes which had recently been made in their training would yield satisfactory results by the end of the month. He praised the programs in physical conditioning, small unit tactics, climbing, and boat drill. Unfortunately, the realism of the training had resulted in one Ranger drowning, two almost drowning, two receiving bullet wounds, and one being wounded by a grenade fragment. Thirty-five to forty men had also suffered sprains.

On the morning of 19 July, the Rangers were inspected by and demonstrated for Hartle. The demonstration was basically the same as that which Thorn had witnessed twelve days earlier, except that each company was responsible for a different part of the demonstration than during the previous performance. The Rangers' ability to demonstrate a variety of skills equally well attests to both the breadth and depth of their training. A less prepared unit would have had specially trained men demonstrate each skill, and its performance would have been more of a deception than a valid exhibition of abilities.

Darby and his Rangers continued to train at Achnacarry until 1 August, when most of the battalion moved by motor and rail to the vicinity of Dorlin House, Argyle, Scotland, for a month of amphibious training under the Royal Navy. The Rangers settled into their new billets on 2 August, and on the following day began a program which emphasized practice landings made from various types of boats.

Some Rangers, however, were sent into combat in fulfillment of the purpose for which their unit had originally been organized. On 1 August, four officers and forty enlisted men were attached to numbers Three and Four Commandos to prepare for a raid on Dieppe, a coastal town in German-occupied France. They were followed by an additional two officers and four enlisted men who became attached to the Second Canadian Division at Farnham on 15 August. The British did not permit key Rangers to participate in the raid due to its hazardous nature, and Darby was among those who remained behind. Had such not been the case, he would have stood a good chance of becoming a casualty. The landing, which had been planned mainly to test the German coastal defenses, was a modern charge of the Light Brigade. Some 494 officers and 3,890 enlisted men—about one-third of those who landed on 19 August—were dead, wounded, or missing by the end of that day. The Rangers lost two officers and four enlisted men killed, and four enlisted men captured.[9] Dieppe was the only operation in which the Rangers participated as students of the British commandos.

On 3 September, the Rangers moved by rail to Dundee where they were billeted with local families, and on the following day they began a new program in the vicinity of the city which lasted until 24 September. Most of the training involved attacks on pillboxes, antiaircraft sites, and coastal defenses, and emphasis was placed on planning, control, and the exercise of individual initiative. Commandos and the Home Guard played the enemy role when needed. Unfortunately, the program was not without cost. On 11 September, one Ranger was killed and another blinded by the accidental explosion of a land mine.

The battalion moved by rail to Corkerhill Camp in the vicinity of Glasgow on 24 September. There it became assigned to II U.S. Army Corps and attached to the First Infantry Division which was under the command of Lt. Gen. Terry Allen. The United States was about to play a bigger role in the European war, and Darby and his Rangers were released from their training mission with the commandos to participate in it.

III
North Africa

The Genesis of TORCH

On 24 July 1942, the British and American chiefs of staff decided to begin planning an Anglo-American invasion of French North Africa. The invading force would be commanded by an American and initially display an American character. American prominence was desirable because of the unique political situation in French North Africa, which was controlled by the Vichy government and garrisoned by French and native troops rather than by Germans and Italians. The French were expected to resist the British because of recent battles between the British and French at Oran and Dakar and in Syria. It was hoped that if the French could be led to believe that the invasion was an American venture, they might welcome it and join it against the Axis.

The plan which AFHQ (Allied Forces Headquarters) gradually developed was code-named TORCH and called for an invasion by three task forces designated Western, Central and Eastern under the command of Eisenhower, who had recently been promoted to lieutenant general. The missions and plans of the three forces had much in common. The mission of each force entailed the capture of a major city together with nearby port facilities and airfields. The plan of each force called for landings directed against the major city and flanking landings on both of its sides.

Western Task Force would be commanded by Maj. Gen. George S. Patton, Jr., and would sail directly from the United States. The main elements would land at Fedala, about ten miles northeast of Casablanca, which was Patton's principal objective. Flanking elements would land at Port Lyautey to the northeast and Safi to the southwest.

Eastern Task Force would contain a sizeable British element, but its organization and plan of action were designed to give the appearance of an all-American landing during the sensitive initial stages of the invasion. The task force would land under the command of Maj. Gen. Charles W. Ryder, CG of the Thirty-fourth Infantry Division. Ryder, however, was to command the force only until its principal objective, Algiers, had been captured. Then Lt. Gen. Sir Kenneth A.N. Anderson, GOC of the British First Army, would assume command and advance eastward to secure Tunis against Axis occupation. Flanking elements would land at Castiglione, Fort Sidi Ferrach, and Cap Caxin to the west, and at Am Taya to the east.

Center Task Force would consist of the U.S. II Corps commanded by Maj. Gen. Lloyd R. Fredendall. Its principal objective would be Oran, with flanking landings to take place at Cap Figaro and Les Andalouses to the west and Arzew to the east. Darby and his Rangers would spearhead the landing at Arzew.

Arzew

Fredendall assigned the First Infantry Division a complex mission. It was to land on designated beaches at H-hour, reduce Arzew's main coastal defenses, capture her port, and secure a beachhead for further landings. The division would also protect the left flank of Center Task Force, protect ships at anchor in

North Africa

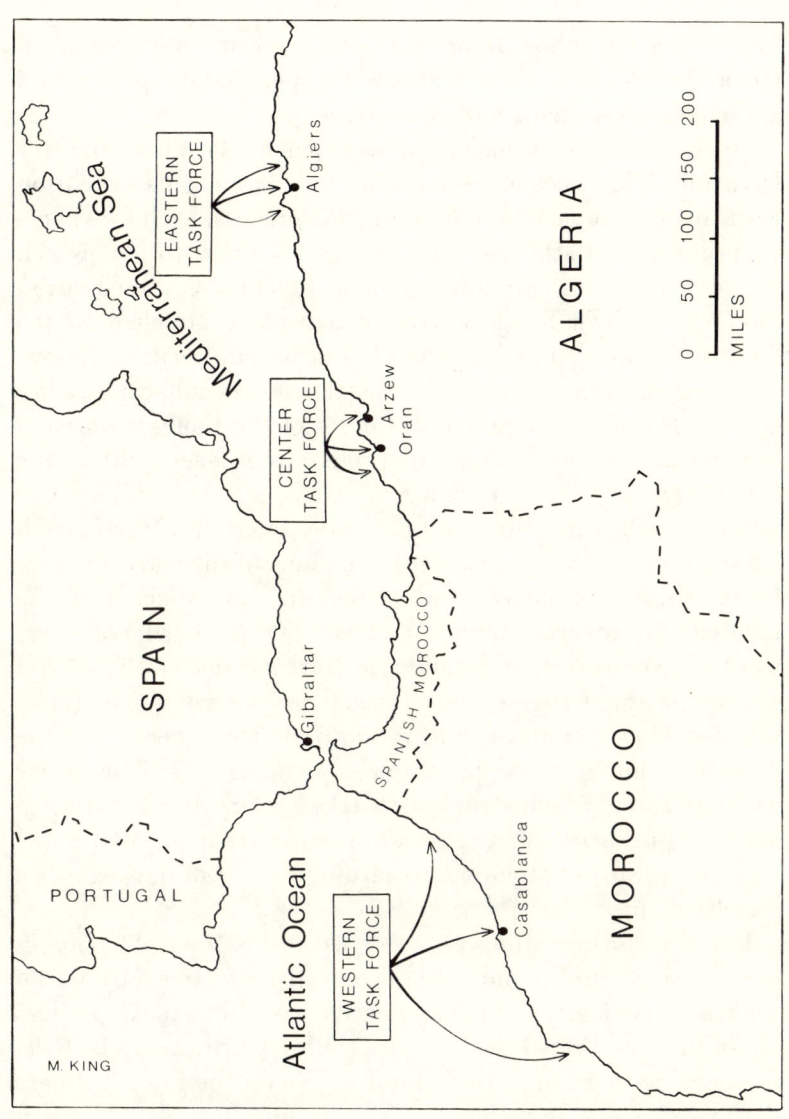

2. Allied Invasion of North Africa.

Arzew Bay from hostile artillery fire, capture the heights of Djebel Murdjadjo west of Oran, secure specified key points, and apprehend Axis agents and sympathizers.

Once this mission had been assigned to the First Infantry Division, Allen became responsible for planning its execution with the assistance of his staff. In this process, each of Allen's subordinate and attached units was given a part to play which would contribute to the accomplishment of the division mission. Darby's Rangers, who had become attached to the division on 26 September, would land in and north of Arzew, neutralize or destroy her main coastal defenses, and capture her docks.[1] The importance and difficulty of the Rangers' mission are best appreciated when that mission is seen within the context of the overall operation.

First of all, the neutralization or destruction of the French coastal defenses had to precede the landing of the main invasion force. Failure or delay would jeopardize the success of the landing. To insure success, a naval FO (forward observer) would accompany the battalion so Darby could call for naval gunfire if the Rangers were unable to silence the batteries unaided. However, naval gunfire was undesirable because of the damage it might cause to Arzew's port facilities. The entire TORCH force was instructed to take "every precaution" to avoid "unnecessary damage to ships and harbor installations," and a stringent set of policies regarding the use of naval gunfire was drawn up.

Political considerations also weighed against a naval bombardment. Naval gunfire might be tactically effective but would probably take many French and native lives, thus making it less likely that the French would rally to the Allied cause. TORCH forces were therefore ordered not to fire on the French unless the French fired first. Even then, resistance by isolated French units was not to be taken as a sign that all French troops in an area were hostile.

Military and political considerations thus favored a surprise landing carried out by stealth and causing minimum bloodshed

North Africa

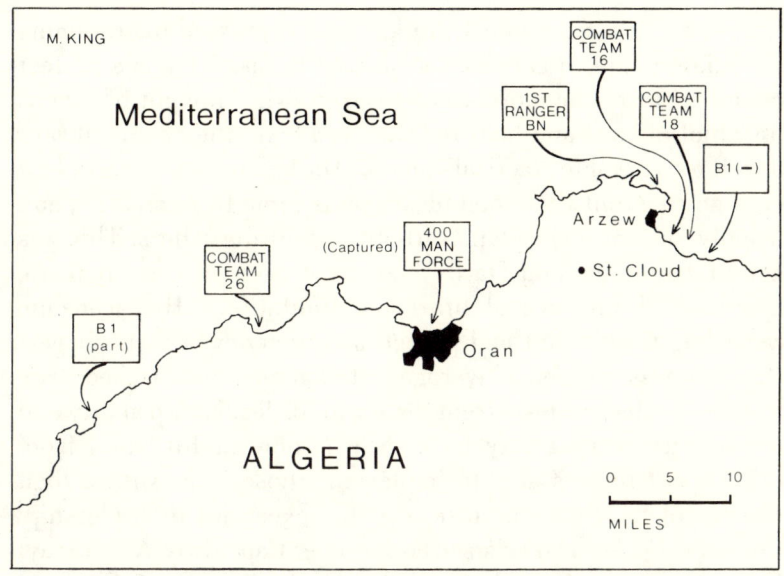

3. Center Task Force Invasion Sites showing Arzew.

and damage. It was the type of operation for which Darby and his Rangers had been well trained.

The battalion continued to train near Corkerhill Camp until 13 October, when it moved by train to Gourock. It then broke down into three groups of two companies each and boarded H.M.S. *Royal Scotsman, Royal Ulsterman,* and *Ulster Monarch.* After a few days of on-board preparation in the Clyde area, the ships left for Loch Linnhe where the Rangers participated in exercise MOSSTROOPER. MOSSTROOPER involved night landings against simulated enemy gun positions and was a rehearsal for TORCH.

While the Rangers were training near Corkerhill and in MOSSTROOPER, Darby, Dammer, and a few others made plans for the landing at Arzew. In this and subsequent operations, Darby worked very closely with Dammer. The tall, thin

Dammer was a methodical thinker who expressed his thoughts articulately and in carefully measured terms. He was a perfect complement to the more kinetic Darby, who thought of him as his chief of staff and believed that as a team they could always develop workable tactical plans. Darby was self-confident enough to admit that good ideas could come from anyone, and usually did not make plans without consulting others. This was a sound practice and Darby may have based it on a realistic appraisal of his own abilities and limitations. His academic record at West Point and peacetime efficiency reports suggest that he was of above-average intelligence, but lacked true brilliance. His greatest strengths lay in his leadership ability and personality. Darby may have drawn some of his ideas from others, but he was able to implement those ideas with a high degree of success because of his exceptional leadership. Commenting on Darby's self-assurance, Capt. Roy A. Murray, CO of Company "F," observed that Darby "was confident that he could lead anyone into combat and bring them back safely." Reminiscing about his own career thirty-one years later, Murray said that Darby was the first good commander he had had, and that he had not had a better one since.

Arzew's most dangerous coastal defenses were at Batterie Superieur and Fort de la Pointe. Batterie Superieur, situated atop high ground about fifteen hundred yards northeast of town and armed with four 105mm guns, dominated Arzew and its harbor. Fort de la Pointe was on a small hillock about thirty feet high just off the shore end of the Grand Quai, a wharf extending southward into the harbor. It was reportedly armed with two to four 75mm guns.

It was obvious to Darby and his coplanners that if the battalion maintained its unity and attempted to take the forts consecutively, the defenders of the second fort would be forewarned and have time to prepare for the Rangers' attack. Darby thus decided to split his forces and use them in a way that would allow both forts to be taken by surprise. A force composed of Companies "A" and "B" and led by Dammer

North Africa

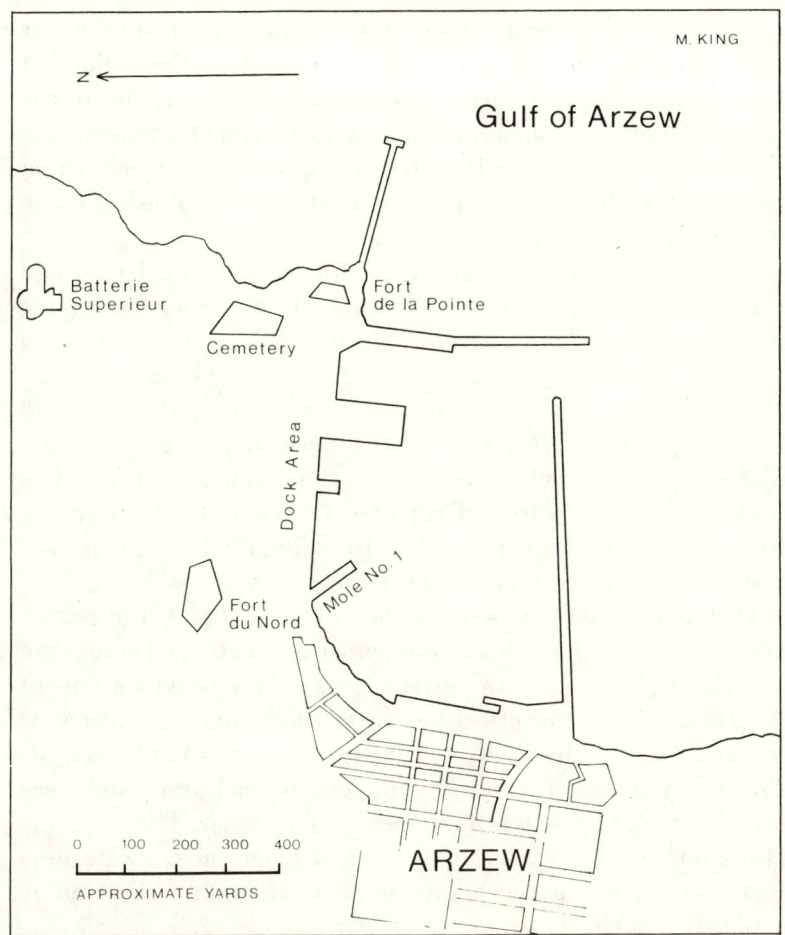

4. Port of Arzew showing Sites of Tactical Importance.

would enter Arzew harbor at night, land on mole number two, follow it to shore, and attack Fort de la Pointe. In the meantime, Darby and the remainder of the battalion would land on a small beach north of Arzew and take Batterie Superieur from the rear while its garrison was distracted by the commotion below, at Fort de la Pointe. Company "D" would set mortars up to the north of Batterie Superieur and could be called upon for fire support if the French resisted too strongly. The Rangers' 60mm mortars were replaced with 81mm mortars for this task because of the latter's greater range and effectiveness.

The plan was deceptively simple. In reality, both Darby and Dammer faced serious challenges. Darby's most pressing problem was to find his beach. It was only about a hundred yards long and thirty or forty feet deep, and was the sole suitable landing site between Arzew and Oran. Failure to find the beach immediately would make it necessary for Darby's nine LCAs to run parallel to the hostile shore until the beach was found, thus risking loss of surprise and exposure to fire. The Royal Navy captain responsible for landing Darby at the proper place was confident that he could do so.

Dammer's problems were no less challenging. Aerial photographs revealed that a boom was sometimes extended across the mouth of the harbor to restrict entry. It was impossible to determine the size or effectiveness of the boom, but skids were mounted under the LCAs to enable the craft to ride over it. These ran along both sides of the keel of each craft and were also designed to protect the propeller and rudder. The mole was also a possible hazard because its exact height above water was unknown. If it was too high, the Rangers might have trouble off-loading their LCAs.

For security reasons, those Rangers not involved in the planning were not told exactly when or where they would be going into combat. They were only told they they would make a surprise landing by night, silence two gun batteries, occupy a waterfront area, and protect subsequent landings of infantry and armor. They were also told that failure to accomplish their mission by dawn would make a naval bombardment of the objective necessary. On 20 October, the ships returned to Clyde and final preparations for TORCH began.

North Africa

The Rangers left Clyde six days later as part of the invasion fleet. On 2 November, Darby's company commanders told their men what the battalion's mission was and precisely how it would be accomplished, using several sets of aerial photographs and two highly detailed sand-table mock-ups. By D-day, 8 November, all concerned had an excellent knowledge of the entire picture, and Dammer could recommend that all future operations be planned with the same thoroughness.

Dammer and Companies "A" and "B" left H.M.S. *Royal Scotsman* aboard their LCAs at about 0015 on D-day and headed toward Arzew harbor, navigating by its entrance lights. Fortunately, the boom was not blocking the harbor and the LCAs were able to enter without difficulty. Because of errors in judging distance, and the numerous ships and small craft which were at berth in the harbor and obstructing vision, however, the LCAs overshot the mole and had to search twenty minutes to find it. "Fortunately," Dammer later said, "the Frenchmen were not alert." Unknown to the Rangers, the French were more alert at Oran, only twenty miles to the west, where they detected a two-hundred-man American force which was also making a harbor landing. Half of these men were killed and the other half, most of whom were wounded, were captured.

By about 0100 all of Dammer's LCAs had found the mole and were unloading their troops. The landing was carried out cautiously but, once again, surprise was almost lost. Small raftlike boats, used in unloading cargo, were found to have been placed alongside the mole and the Rangers had to scramble over them, making a clatter. In spite of their noise, Dammer's men were able to get on the mole, check suspected machine gun positions, and begin moving toward Fort de la Pointe without being detected. The first and second platoons of Company "B" set up their mortars at a nearby cemetery while the rest of the company isolated the fort by blocking avenues of approach which French reinforcements were likely to use. Company "A" continued on to the barbed wire embankment which surrounded the fort, established local security, and prepared to assault. Just as they began to cut the barbed wire which was strung on the forward slope of the embankment, a siren sounded in the city and soldiers began to patrol the fort and along the top of the embankment. The Rangers continued to breach the wire in silence, and when the wire was cut the assault element rushed the fort and seized the gun positions. About fifty prisoners were taken, the guns prepared for demolition, and outposts established. Only a few scattered shots had been fired during the action and there were no Ranger casualties.

Meanwhile, the operation had been going along equally well, though more hazardously, for Darby. He, along with Companies "C," 'D," "E," and "F" began to debark from H.M.S. *Royal Ulsterman* and *Ulster Monarch* at about midnight. Unfortunately, the radio which was supposed to give Darby shore-to-ship communication, and some of the pyrotechnics which were to be used for signal purposes after the landing, were lost when the forward end of one of the nine LCAs fell from its davits into the sea. No men were lost but the LCAs became misoriented while fishing them out of the water. Darby, who was in the lead LCA, asked the flotilla commander if he knew their location, but the answer was no. Fortunately, the captain of Darby's transport saw the confusion, came alongside in the larger craft, and put the LCAs on a 270° course which led the Rangers to their beach. In spite of their initial mishaps, they landed undetected at about 0130.

After crossing the beach, scaling the cliffs which overlooked the landing site, and moving toward the coast road, the Rangers were challenged by a French sentry whom they captured and took with them. Advance and flank guards were then put out and Darby's force began moving southward on the road toward Batterie Superieur. A British LCS (landing craft support), guided by a colored light which the Rangers kept pointed out to sea, ran parallel to the column ready to give fire support if needed. When the Rangers had moved far enough to the south, they struck inland toward their objective and the LCS departed. As planned, Company "D" set up its 81mm mortars in defilade about five hundred yards to the rear of the fort; in Scotland, the tubes' elevation mechanisms had been taped so the mortars would fire that distance. Approaching their objective, Companies "C" "F" and "E" came abreast of each other, crept up the back slope of Batterie Superieur's hill, and began cutting through the fort's fourteen-foot-thick belt of barbed wire. When they were halfway through the wire the French, who had either been alarmed by the sirens in the city or had otherwise detected the Rangers, began firing into the dark with rifles and machine guns. Reacting with an artilleryman's instinct, Darby had his men back off the crest of the hill and radioed the mortars for support. After fifty to sixty rounds of well-placed fire, Darby gave the Rangers the command to go in. They stormed and quickly overran the fort. About sixty prisoners were taken, including the commandant and his wife; the captured guns were prepared for demolition in case of a counterattack; and outposts were established. The attack had been almost bloodless. No Rangers were lost and only a few French were wounded.

Because of the threat posed by the French forts, the invasion fleet was to stand five miles offshore until the enemy guns had been put out of action. By about 0330, both gun positions were safely in the Rangers' hands and Darby was free to signal his success to the navy. The plan called for two signals. First, Darby was to radio the fleet; then, to authenticate the radio message, he was to fire four pairs of green flares and four pairs of white star clusters into the sky. It was this radio and the white star clusters which had been lost earlier, when an LCA had spilled its passengers into the sea. Darby decided to fire the green flares, which were the only signals he had. When Fredendall and the supporting naval commander saw them, but noted the absence of the white star clusters, they doubted the authenticity of the signal and stood fast. Darby continued to fire the green flares, but to no avail. The invasion fleet only began landing two hours later, after a small naval party had inspected the area and radioed the fleet of the Rangers' success. From this experience, Darby drew the lesson that ship-to-shore communication was "all important" and that it was impossible to spend too much time on planning for it.

With the capture of Batterie Superieur and Fort de la Pointe, the first and most delicate phase of the Rangers' mission was accomplished. The capture and protection of Arzew and its port facilities were subsequently accomplished without much difficulty. A bloodless tactical success was scored by Darby later in the morning when he parleyed with the commander of Fort du Nord, a large installation midway between Batterie Superieur and the business center of the town which was being used as a rest place by the French Foreign Legion, and persuaded him to surrender his garrison. The thought struck James Altieri of Company "F" that the Foreign Legion had not surrendered so easily in *Beau Geste*.

During the remainder of the day, a number of snipers were encountered and many more prisoners taken. At 1030, Pfc. George G. Grissamer, a rifleman in Company "B," was fatally shot in the back by a sniper while helping to clear the dock area. He was the only Ranger to die capturing Arzew.

Darby's operation was an overwhelming success in spite of the risks taken and the mishaps incurred. The French guns had been silenced, the port occupied with a minimum of bloodshed and destruction, and Center Task Force was able to come ashore without having to face serious resistance on the beaches. While moving inland, however, elements of the First Infantry Division encountered pockets of strong enemy resistance, and Darby's men were called upon to help reduce them. Ironically, the Rangers suffered heavier casualties in these actions than they had in the execution of their original mission. Although of little importance when viewed within the context of the overall invasion, this development was of considerable significance because it was the first instance of the specially trained Rangers being used in conventional ground combat. As such, it was the beginning of a trend that would become an integral part of Ranger operations, and is worth a closer look.

By midday the First Battalion, Sixteenth Infantry and

attached units encountered what they considered to be strong enemy resistance at LaMacta, but succeeded in capturing the town by 1330. By 1600, continued enemy activity on the edge of town led Allen to order Darby to send a Ranger company to Port-aux-Poules for attachment to the First Battalion, Sixteenth Infantry. Darby sent Company "E" by train from Arzew to Port-aux-Poules, where it arrived at about 0200 on 9 November. The Rangers reached American troops two hours later and established telephone contact with the CO of the First Battalion, Sixteenth Infantry by 0700. He ordered Company "E" to proceed by road to LaMacta, which was about four and one-half miles to the east. While en route, the Rangers came under harassing fire about a mile east of Port-aux-Poules, and were forced to deploy by heavy rifle and machine gun fire about a mile outside of LaMacta. They overcame the resistance, killed "a number of the enemy," and took two prisoners with the aid of two self-propelled 75mm guns from the Sixteenth Infantry. The company then entered LaMacta where it received the mission of "providing close-in protection for the town." The Rangers established and maintained a system of outposts until they were relieved at about 1400 on 10 November, and then they returned to Arzew by train.[2]

Company "E" was not the only Ranger element that Darby had to commit to a conventional role. At about 1600 on 8 November, he was ordered to furnish a company for the defense of the First Infantry Division CP (command post) at Tourville, a village on the outskirts of Arzew. Darby sent Company "C," which guarded the CP until mid-morning of the next day when it received orders to march overland to Saint Cloud. At Renan the company reported to Allen who, in turn, ordered it to report to the CO of the Eighteenth CT (combat team), which was held up on the outskirts of Saint Cloud. The Rangers arrived at 1600 and were attached to the First Battalion, Eighteenth Infantry. Both the Rangers and the infantry battalion were then ordered "to contain the enemy in the town and renew the attack on the morning of November 10." The attack on Saint Cloud was part of a division drive on Oran, an operation which Allen had declared "nothing in hell must delay or stop."[3]

After attachment to the First Battalion, Eighteenth Infantry, the CO of Company "C" was instructed to move his men out after dark in an encircling movement to the south of Saint Cloud with the mission of "blocking the exits from Saint Cloud and preventing the exit of the enemy force from the town." The company moved as ordered and established itself astride the main road leading southward out of town before dawn. At daybreak, the Rangers discovered an enemy motor column parked south of Saint Cloud and maneuvered to attack it, but were pinned down by heavy machine gun, mortar, and artillery fire when about a quarter of a mile away. Although one platoon was able to maneuver within seventy-five yards of the enemy position, heavy fire forced it to dig in and its members contented themselves with sniping at the column until about 1500 when the surrounded enemy surrendered. Its mission accomplished, Company "C" returned to the First Ranger Battalion at about 2000. Of the four Rangers who had been killed and the eleven who had been wounded during the first seventy-two hours of the invasion, three of the dead and most of the wounded resulted from the action at Saint Cloud.[4]

The use of the Rangers in conventional infantry operations a scant fourteen and one-half hours after they had set foot in North Africa bothered some of the men, including James Altieri. "What was the purpose in organizing and training Rangers for Commando-type operations," he thought, "if they are going to be frittered away in mass battles?" Dammer, however, sensed "no resentment" on Darby's part over the Saint Cloud and LaMacta battles. His attitude seemed to be that there had been a job to do and the Rangers had done it.[5] If Darby was dissatisfied with the way the Rangers were being used, there is no evidence that he ever objected to Allen or Fredendall.

The Rangers were relieved of attachment to the First Infantry Division on 10 November, and placed in II Corps reserve at Arzew. The following day, however, Allen received word from corps that the Rangers would be available to him in the event of an emergency. In Arzew, Darby was appointed town major and the Rangers went to work guarding gun positions, prisoners, and hospitals, and providing general security for the town. The Rangers also trained while in Arzew and were inspected by Fredendall on 16 December, following a tactical exercise in the vicinity of Cap Carbon.

Tactical Training and the Sened Raid

While based at Arzew, Darby made several trips to Eisenhower's headquarters at London and Algiers to discuss possible Ranger operations. He and Dammer also conducted reconnaissances along the North African coast in anticipation of such operations, but the missions were never assigned. Then, on 19 December, it seemed that things were about to change. Darby and Dammer flew from Tafaroui to Algiers where they reported to the AFHQ G-3, a Colonel Partridge, and received plans for an operation code-named PEASHOOTER. PEASHOOTER required the Rangers to make a night landing on the island of Galita, annihilate its Italian garrison except for a few prisoners to be taken for intelligence purposes, and destroy its radio and radar stations and coastal guns. The battalion would then remain on the island until the following night, when it would be evacuated by sea. Training continued through 27 December when the Rangers, minus a rear echelon, boarded H.M.S. *Princess Emma* and conducted several days of boat drill and practice landings. On 2 January 1943, while en route to Galita, Darby was notified that PEASHOOTER had been cancelled, and the Rangers returned to Arzew.[6]

Training resumed in the Arzew area on 3 January and continued until 17 January, when the battalion was assigned to Fifth Army. On the following day the Rangers became assigned to the Fifth Army ITC (invasion training center) as demonstration and experimental troops. The two months which had passed since D-day were harmful to the Rangers' morale. The war appeared to be passing them by, and many of the men began to wonder about their future. An increase in the number of men transferring out of the unit, a symptom of declining morale, led to a substantial decrease in Ranger strength. Fortunately, on 31 January, seven officers and 101 enlisted replacements reported for duty and were formed into Company "G," which Darby had established as a training detachment.

No longer having the British commandos to depend on, the Rangers had to train themselves. Quite naturally, many of the training techniques introduced by the British were kept by Darby, and speed marching, cliff climbing, rappelling, and night amphibious landings continued to be integral parts of the Rangers' regimen.

The use of the buddy system, or working in pairs, was strongly emphasized. The men would choose their buddies from within their own platoons and would then live, eat, perform KP and guard duty, and train as a team. In what was called the "Bullet and Bayonet" course, the men negotiated obstacles and reacted to surprise targets in buddy teams. Each team going through the course would advance with its men alternately moving forward over short distances or furnishing covering fire. Another course, called "Me and My Pal," was similar in concept but was presented in the form of street fighting.

As in Northern Ireland and Scotland, realism was achieved through the use of live ammunition. Captured German and Italian weapons were used by men simulating the enemy so the new Rangers could learn to distinguish between the sounds of American and enemy guns. If, for example, a training problem required the taking of a machine gun nest, a captured enemy machine gun would be set up to fire live ammunition in a fixed direction. Flares were used by the "enemy" during night problems to make them more difficult.

In fact, after initial hardening, most training was conducted at night. When operating in darkness, Darby favored moving his battalion to the objective in column formation for ease of control. Once the objective was reached and the companies went abreast in preparation for the assault, dim, shielded, colored lights were used to maintain formation. Each company used a different color light. When a company reached a predetermined location, it would signal its position to the rear. Company commanders would signal with uninterrupted beams while platoon leaders would signal with dots and dashes. Darby, who would temporarily be to the rear where he could see the lights, could then be certain that his men were where they were supposed to be when beginning the assault. Darby had some reservations about the system's value in combat, but would soon have the opportunity to try it and would find it effective.

The situation in North Africa changed considerably while the Rangers were training at Arzew. A race for Tunisia by both Allies and Germans had begun the day after D-day. On 9 November, the Germans began moving troops into Tunisia and on the following day British seaborne forces, which had formed the reserve of Eastern Task Force, were sent to Bougie as the first step in an Allied advance toward Tunisia. The Allies continued to move east and the Germans continued to move west until 17-23 November, when British advance elements and the French engaged westward-bound German columns. By 1 January 1943, a bowlike front had formed along the line Cap Serrat - Pont du Fahs - Maknassy - El Guettar, but by the end of the month the Germans had forced the Allies back from two to ten miles along most of the front from Pont du Fahs to El Guettar. It was on the southern part of this front that Darby and his Rangers went back into action.

On 7 February, the Rangers were relieved of assignment to Fifth Army and duty with the ITC, and were flown to Tebessa, Tunisia. From there they were trucked about five miles east to II Corps headquarters. Two days later the battalion reported to Gafsa where it received the mission of raiding five Italian hilltop positions protecting Sened Pass with the purpose of harassing the enemy, destroying his men and equipment, and conducting reconnaissance.[7]

At midnight on 10 February, Companies "A," "E," "F," and a headquarters element moved by truck from their bivouac area south of Gafsa to a French outpost about twelve miles from the pass. After they detrucked, Darby led them eight miles beyond friendly lines to a remote site in the mountains where they camouflaged themselves and rested until the evening of 11 February. They then moved forward to a point about three miles from their objective, from which they could watch the Italians. At about 2300, just before moonset, the Rangers began moving toward the unsuspecting Italians using the navigational and control techniques which Darby had developed at Arzew. The companies carried different colored flashlights with the company commanders following behind the platoons, watching their lights, and correcting their direction or formations when necessary. Darby, who was further to the rear and centered on the companies, observed their lights and guided them by radio.

"The Italians thought they were in an inaccessible place," Darby later remarked, "but it didn't work out that way for them." By 0100 the Rangers had crept to within two hundred yards of the enemy positions. At that point, the Italians became alerted to their presence and began to throw grenades and fire cannon, machine guns, and rifles. Pfc. Elmer W. Garrison, the only Ranger to die at Sened, had his head blown off by one of the cannon. The Italians, however, had now revealed their positions by their muzzle flashes and the Rangers, in Darby's words, "rushed them with bayonets and knives and gave them everything" they had. "We went in particularly for bayonet work, but we also caught a lot of them in their underground dugouts with our tommy guns and hand grenades."

An hour after the attack had begun, Darby ordered the Rangers to withdraw under fire of their 60mm mortars. In his estimate, the raid had been "a good example of a sustained and coordinated night attack." At the cost of one killed and twenty

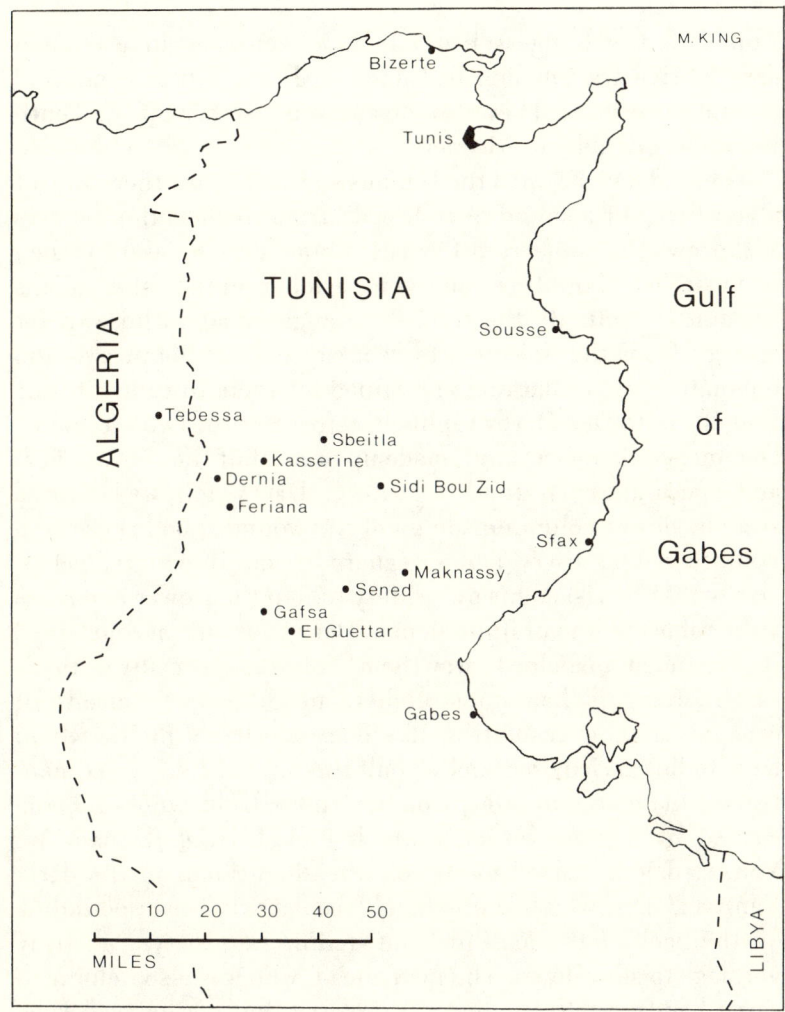

5. Ranger Battle Sites in Tunisia.

wounded, the Rangers had killed or wounded an estimated seventy-five Italians and had destroyed one antitank gun and five machine guns. They also took eleven members of the Tenth Bersaglieri Regiment prisoner.

The raid had stunned the Italians so badly that "there wasn't a gun firing or a sound to be heard" from them as the Rangers withdrew. Darby heard a few rifle shots after he and his men had marched about three miles but, aside from that, the Italians remained silent. By the time the Rangers had withdrawn far enough from the objective to reorganize, only about two and one-half hours of darkness remained for them to return to the French outpost. Darby split his force into two columns. Dammer took one column, made up of most of the unwounded, and speed-marched them to safety. Darby followed with a second, slower column made up of the wounded and those who volunteered to carry and safeguard them. It was typical of Darby that he risked his own safety to join the slower and more vulnerable column of injured men. Darby not only accompanied the wounded, he helped carry them. This was especially difficult as the Rangers had no stretchers or other easy means of evacuating their casualties. If a man was badly hit he would have to be carried on a shelter-half by shifts of four to six men. During the march to safety Cpl. Garland S. Ladd, who was being carried by a group of men which included Sgt. Donald W. VanArtsdalen, started to slip off the shelter-half in the dark. VanArtsdalen, who had one hand free, angrily began pounding on the back of the man in front, telling him in typical Army verbiage to slow down. The man ahead, who was also helping to carry Ladd, quietly replied, "I'm sorry, but we have to keep going." The voice was Darby's.

Altieri, who had just fought as a squad leader for the first time and also accompanied the wounded column, thought Darby "magnificent." He cheered the wounded up, as well as carried them, and his presence gave the column "amazing strength, both morally and physically." The return march from Sened was only one of many instances in which Darby established a reputation as a leader who always led by example, and who would not tell his men to do anything he would not do himself.

Darby's column safely reached the French outpost a few hours after dawn.

The next day, after the Rangers had returned to the Gafsa area, Fredendall decorated Darby, four other officers, and nine enlisted men with the Silver Star for their parts in the Sened raid.

Kasserine

During early February the Allies began to expect an enemy attack in central Tunisia, but did not know where its precise location would be. At that time, the extreme south wing of the Allied front extended from Gafsa southeast to El Guettar. The Allied high command did not believe that it could reinforce that area strongly enough to hold it against a determined enemy attack, so on 4 February, Fredendall informed units defending the area that American and French troops at Gafsa were to defend the town only against "attack by reasonable forces." In the event of a major attack threatening the destruction of Allied forces at Gafsa, those troops were to be withdrawn toward Feriana, fighting a delaying action on successive positions. Their final position would be on a ridge running on an east-west axis through Feriana.

The actual evacuation was triggered by an Axis attack on Sidi Bou Zid on 14 February, just two days after the Sened raid. On that day, First Army notified II Corps that the first steps to evacuate Gafsa would begin that night. In accordance with Army's decision, the Rangers received orders to withdraw from the vicinity of Gafsa, with Companies "D" and "G" serving as rear guard for Allied forces in the area.[8] It was a hazardous mission, for the withdrawal would be on foot and across an open plain. The Rangers would be armed only with rifles, machine guns, and sticky grenades, a generally ineffective antitank grenade which adhered to armor. Darby, who marched with his men, offered them characteristic words of encouragement: "If we get caught by tanks, God help the tanks." Decades later, the men who made the withdrawal would remember Darby's words more clearly than any other incident which occurred during the march. Although tanks did cross the Rangers' path once during the withdrawal, the Rangers were not seen and arrived at defensive positions on high ground east of Feriana on 15 February. On the following day, the Rangers were ordered to withdraw further to positions south of Bou Chebka astride the Feriana-Tebessa road. They remained on the defensive in this area until 1 March.[9]

During the early part of this period the Axis launched attacks against Sidi Bou Zid, Gafsa, Sbeitla, and Feriana. These were preludes to a major attack which would be made during 19-22 February and come to be known as the Battle of Kasserine Pass. All of these engagements were fought northwest of Bou Chebka and the Rangers did not, therefore, come under heavy pressure. At one point, however, it appeared as though some of them might become more deeply involved. During the early afternoon of 22 February, Allen sent a memo to Darby, to whom he felt close enough to address as "Dear Bill," in which he wrote that there was a "hell of a mess" to his front and asked for a "reinforced company with a hairy chested company commander with big nuts" for use as a reserve. An hour later, Darby notified Allen that he was sending a strengthened Company "C" which was commanded by Lt. Jim Lyle, whom he considered to be "damned capable." The company was attached to Combat Team Sixteen until 24 February when it was relieved and returned to the battalion.

When, at midnight on 27 February, Maj. Gen. Manton S. Eddy's Ninth Infantry Division relieved the First Infantry Division, Darby and his Rangers became attached to the Ninth. They remained with Eddy's division until 1 March when they moved to La Kouif and became part of II Corps's reserve.

From 16 February through 1 March, the Rangers were

involved in several minor clashes which inflicted light casualties on the enemy. They killed six Italians, captured eight Italians and eight Germans, and destroyed three wheeled vehicles and captured three. One Ranger was killed or captured while on patrol.

Gafsa and Djebel el Ank

After the Axis's February offensive came to an end, the Allies began reorganizing for the next stage of the Tunisian campaign. During the opening phases of this stage, Montgomery's Eighth Army would make the Allies' main effort. It was to attack northward along Tunisia's east coast while the British First Army and the U.S. II Corps threatened the enemy and drew his reserves further inland along a north-south line.

This change of planning was paralleled by a reorganization of the Allied command structure. On 19 February the British First Army, U.S. II Corps, and British Eighth Army were cast into Eighteen Army Group commanded by Gen. Sir Harold R. L. G. Alexander. This was initially a "paper" reorganization and Eighteen Army Group would not be operational until early March. A major personnel change also took place. Alexander had been unfavorably impressed with Fredendall's performance in the February battles—an opinion shared by Fredendall's superiors and subordinates alike—and Eisenhower decided to replace him with Patton. Patton, who had been commanding I Armored Corps in Morocco, was brought to Tunisia and took command of II Corps on 6 March. Two days later, operations in Tunisia passed under the control of Eighteen Army Group.

By the time Eighteen Army Group was a functioning headquarters, Montgomery's Eighth Army had driven the Axis forces westward until they had taken up defensive positions along the Mareth Line. The line was about twenty-five miles long, and extended northeast from the vicinity of Cheguimu in the Matmata Hills toward the Wadi Zigzauo and along the wadi to where it emptied into the Gulf of Gabes. Eighth Army was to begin its ground attack against the Mareth Line on the night of 16 March. II Corps was assigned a subsidiary role in Eighteen Army Group's operation.

Operation WOP, as II Corps's role was code-named, called for the corps to capture and hold Gafsa, which would serve as a logistical base for Eighth Army, and then conduct operations in the direction of Maknassy to threaten Rommel's lines of communication. This plan would require the Ninth and Thirty-fourth Infantry Divisions to defend the approaches to Rohia, Sbeitla, Kasserine, and Bou Chebka, while the First Infantry Division seized and secured Gafsa. The First Armored Division, reinforced, would then advance toward Maknassy.

On the evening of 13 March, Patton sent Darby a message instructing him to move the Rangers from La Kouif to a bivouac area in the vicinity of Dernaia, Tunisia, on the following day. They moved as ordered and became attached to the First Infantry Division. On 16 March, the battalion received the mission of serving as division reserve, protecting division artillery, and maintaining contact with the Sixteenth and Eighteenth Combat Teams, and was trucked to an assembly area about six miles north of Gafsa. The Sixteenth and Eighteenth Combat Teams and the Rangers attacked Gafsa at 1000 the following day, found the town lightly defended by enemy security detachments, and quickly captured it. No Rangers were killed or wounded in the attack.

The ease with which the attack on Gafsa had been carried out revealed that the Axis forces had withdrawn and broken contact. Allen decided to use the Rangers to reestablish contact. On 17 March, he sent a memo to Darby ordering him to move the Rangers toward El Guettar after dark; establish contact with enemy forces in that area; determine enemy strength, dispositions, and unit identification; and maintain himself in that locality. Allen considered the mission "vital" because the information which Darby was to collect was essential to planning an attack on El Guettar. Darby was directed to act aggressively but, because it was estimated that there were two thousand enemy troops in the area, was cautioned not to commit himself to any action from which he could not "properly extricate" his small unit.[10]

Darby received Allen's memo at 0200 the following morning and immediately began moving toward El Guettar. The Rangers found the town undefended. They occupied it, and began looking for the enemy further to the east. By means of patrols and surveillance they located an Italian force astride the Gafsa-Gabes road at Djebel el Ank pass. This was about four miles southwest of El Guettar and three miles west of Bou Hamran. It would be the site of the Rangers' first real battle since the Sened raid.

Late in the afternoon of 20 March, the First Infantry Division received a warning order to be prepared to "attack along the Gafsa-Gabes road to take the commanding ground east of El Guettar, about 18 miles southwest of Gafsa." Less than a mile east of El Guettar, the road forked into two branches. The southern branch was a continuation of the main road and led to Gabes. The northern branch, known as Gumtree Road, passed through Djebel el Ank pass and south of Bou Hamran to Mahares on the sea. The plan of attack along Gumtree Road called for a joint operation involving Darby's Rangers and the Twenty-sixth Infantry. The Rangers would infiltrate enemy lines and attack Djebel el Ank pass from the rear, while the Twenty-sixth Infantry attacked frontally. After the seizure of the pass, the Twenty-sixth Infantry would continue on to Bou Hamran.[11]

On the basis of a daylight reconnaissance which he had personally conducted, and information gained during two nights of Ranger patrols, Darby was able to map out a route which would enable his battalion to come up behind the Italians undetected. On the night of 20 March he led the Rangers six miles over a tortuous succession of hills and gorges to a rocky plateau which overlooked the Italian positions from the rear. There they awaited the dawn.

The attack began at first light with the call of a Ranger bugle. A support element brought a steady stream of machine gun and rifle fire on the enemy while other Rangers swept forward in an extended skirmish line, firing their weapons and shouting battle cries. The Italians, whose weapons had been pointed to the front, were taken completely by surprise. By about 0830 the Rangers had captured the northern wall of the pass and were guiding elements of the Twenty-sixth Infantry across a wadi which impeded entry to the pass from the front. At 1130 the division G-3 felt confident enough to instruct Darby and units of the Twenty-sixth Infantry to take the high ground beyond Bou Hamran and clean up what little enemy resistance was still being offered in the pass. Forty-five minutes later the Rangers and infantry were still advancing, but were greatly burdened by the more than one thousand prisoners which they had accumulated. By 1600 the Twenty-sixth Infantry had the situation well enough in hand to return the Rangers to the division reserve at El Guettar.

In his after-action-report Darby credited the Rangers with taking two hundred prisoners but made no estimate of Italian dead or wounded. Altieri, probably including the Italians taken by the Twenty-sixth Infantry, later wrote that fourteen hundred prisoners had been captured. He also remembered scores of enemy dead who, having been caught by surprise, were sprawled next to their unused weapons. Only one Ranger, the commander of Company "A," had been wounded. Fighting once more the kind of battle they had been trained to fight, Darby and his men had won a victory which was as absolute as those of Arzew and Sened. It is worth noting that Erwin Rommel, writing his *Infanterie greift an* as a lieutenant colonel in 1937, admitted to having failed in only one infantry attack during the entire 1914-18 war. The action, which had been fought against the Rumanians at Klautana Pass in the Carnic Alps, was very similar in concept to the attack which Darby had conducted successfully at Djebel el Ank.

El Guettar

The American attack east of El Guettar continued at a cautious pace until late on 22 March. Meanwhile, on 21 March, the Axis's Army Group Africa had released the Tenth Panzer Division to the Afrika Korps for use in a counterattack toward Gafsa. The division assembled near Djebel Ben Kheir during the night of 22 March and began moving westward along the Gabes-Gafsa road at 0300 the following morning. Its attack fell upon the First Infantry Division, and the Rangers were promptly called out of reserve and sent to strengthen the front where it was threatened.[12] As at Saint Cloud, LaMacta, and Kasserine, the Rangers were being used as conventional infantry in an emergency.

Darby's battalion first moved by foot to the left flank of the Third Battalion, Sixteenth Infantry, which had stopped a German armor and infantry attack earlier that morning. When the Rangers arrived, the Germans had temporarily withdrawn and were preparing to renew their attack, which began again at 1830 with an ineffective attack by dive bombers followed by an assault of about sixty tanks and a battalion of dismounted infantry. It was a debacle. Fifteen minutes after the attack began, Combat Team (CT) Eighteen reported to division that the Germans were "falling like flies" under American artillery fire, and that those enemy tanks still able to move were heading toward the rear. The Third Battalion and the Rangers were virtually surrounded during the high point of the attack but together they succeeded in driving the Germans off.

In spite of their initial rebuff, the Germans continued to launch local counterattacks in the areas of Gumtree and Gabes roads, and put particular pressure on Djebel Berda, an extensive hill mass south of and overlooking the Gabes road. Recognizing the Rangers' fighting ability, the division G-3 recommended that the assistant division commander, Brig. Gen. Theodore Roosevelt, send them to the area under attack, which was considered "a key point."[13] Roosevelt agreed, and Darby's

Rangers soon moved by truck and foot to the northern slope of Djebel Berda with the mission of extending the right flank of the Eighteenth Infantry, and clearing Djebel Berda of the enemy to deprive him the use of high ground. The Germans, however, continued to attack and the Rangers were withdrawn from the heights on the night of 24 March and given the assignment of extending the left flank of the Eighteenth Infantry. They accomplished this by dawn of the next day, and the First and Second Battalions, Eighteenth Infantry, withdrew through them the following night. The Rangers thus found themselves holding down the right flank of the First Infantry Division on the northern slopes of Djebel Berda, with the mission of preventing infiltration by the enemy from the south and east. They remained in these positions until 27 March when the resumption of II Corps's attack sent advancing elements of the Ninth Infantry Division through them. The Rangers were then returned to the First Infantry Division reserve in the vicinity of Gafsa. The conventional, defensive action at El Guettar had cost them three killed and eighteen wounded, heavier losses than those which they had suffered in the truly Ranger-style operations at Sened and Djebel el Ank.

The attack at Djebel el Ank and the defensive action at El Guettar earned Darby the Distinguished Service Cross, which was presented to him by Patton. The accompanying citation read in part that Darby was "always conspicuously at the head of his troops" at Djebel el Ank, and "personally led the assaults against the enemy line in the face of heavy machinegun and artillery fire." It also stated that the success of the attack "was largely due to the outstanding heroism" of Darby, "who, with complete disregard of his own safety, led and paced the entire assault." The Distinguished Service Cross was also accompanied by Patton's offer of promotion to colonel. If Darby were to accept the promotion, however, it would become necessary for him to leave the First Ranger Battalion, which only required a lieutenant colonel as commander, and assume command of an infantry regiment, which required a colonel. Rather than leave the Rangers, Darby refused the promotion.[14] If rapid advancement had been his sole interest, it would have been wise to use the Rangers as a stepping-stone and accept Patton's offer. Had he done so, he would have become a colonel at the age of thirty-two and still have the greater part of the war remaining in which to rise to general. His attachment to the Rangers, however, would not permit him to leave them so easily. His men recognized the professional sacrifice which he had made to stay with them and loved him deeply for it.

Darby showed care for his men in routine ways as well. After El Guettar, II Corps decided to use the Rangers to patrol its rear and took them from the First Infantry Division. Allen's division, which had been participating in corps' attack, attempted to get them back. On the afternoon of 28 March the division G-3 called corps, saying that the division needed the Rangers badly and would like to have them returned. Corps disapproved the request a half hour later. Similar requests and disapprovals were exchanged for two days. When, on 31 March, corps finally relented and approved the request, Darby called the corps chief of staff and said that he was "going to raise hell about it" because his men needed to be refitted and lacked shoes and other equipment. The chief of staff suggested that Darby speak to Allen and his chief of staff, who were en route to corps, and see if they could help. The records do not reflect whether the Rangers were taken care of to Darby's liking, but the fact that Darby objected to his superiors about his men being sent into further action before being properly equipped testifies to his priorities and style of leadership. Although he would ultimately have to follow orders regardless of his personal feelings, he was willing to protest if blind obedience meant exposing his troops to unnecessary danger or hardship. A more self-serving commander, overly ambitious to impress his superiors, would have had less concern for his men.

On 31 March, properly or improperly equipped, Companies "A" and "B" were trucked about twenty-five miles north to the vicinity of Madjane el Fedj with the mission of establishing an outpost, warning of any enemy threat from that direction, and delaying the enemy in the event of an attempted breakthrough. These companies were relieved on 2 April by Companies "D" and "F" which assumed their missions until 10 April, when the latter were returned to their bivouac area. None of the four companies suffered casualties during this period.

Meanwhile, elements of the battalion were committed elsewhere. II Corps was continuing its efforts eastward along Gumtree and Gabes roads when, on 4 April, German preparations for withdrawal were misinterpreted as preparations for a counterattack. On 5 April, therefore, Companies "A," "B" and "C" of the First Ranger Battalion, two companies of the 805th Tank Destroyer Battalion, and three companies of the 19th Engineer (Combat) Battalion were put under Darby's command to meet what was perceived as an enemy threat. They moved under cover of darkness from Gafsa to about four miles east of Mdilla, with the mission of delaying the enemy in the event of a breakthrough of French positions. Once in place, Darby's force established a switch line along the Keddab wadi to stop enemy attacks down the Gabes road or around the western end of Djebel Berda. Aerial reconnaissance, however, failed to reveal enemy activity in the area and on 6 April Patton's chief of staff sent Darby a memo instructing him to withdraw his force to Gafsa unless he had knowledge of a threat to his front. Darby saw no such threat, sent the antitank companies back to their original positions, released the engineer companies to the corps engineer, and returned the Rangers to corps reserve at Gafsa. Although this precautionary operation did not result in enemy contact, it was the first action in which Darby commanded a combined arms team. In spite of his being only a battalion commander, he had been given responsibilities usually entrusted to a regimental commander. It was a development which augured well for his future and the role he would play in the next campaign—the invasion of Sicily.

Although no one knew it at the time, the North African campaign was a portent of the Rangers' future. The independent or semiindependent attacks which Darby had time to plan with deliberation, and which the Rangers were able to execute with stealth, were spectacularly successful. Arzew, Sened, and Djebel el Ank, for example, were significant tactical victories yet they cost the Rangers only two lives. Real or imagined military emergencies, however, required that the Rangers be thrown into conventional actions rather than used in the types of operations for which they had been trained. The major of these actions— St. Cloud, Kasserine, and El Guettar—had cost eight Ranger lives. Although a small number, it was four times the losses suffered in the Rangers' three surprise attacks. In Sicily and Italy as well, necessity would frequently demand that the Rangers be used in conventional actions rather than in true Ranger-style operations. Their losses would mount accordingly.

IV

Sicily

The Genesis of HUSKY

Planning for the next campaign was in process while Darby and the Rangers were still fighting in North Africa. On 23 January 1943, a CCS (combined chiefs of staff) directive ordered Eisenhower to invade Sicily. CCS instructions also dictated that a separate headquarters be established to begin planning the invasion. In accordance with these instructions, during late January Eisenhower organized in Algiers the core of what would become known as Force 141. At the end of the Tunisian campaign, Headquarters, Eighteen Army Group, would be deactivated and merged into Force 141. On the day of the invasion of Sicily, Force 141 would be redesignated Fifteen Army Group.

On 14 April, Darby wrote Eisenhower a recommendation that fifty-two officer and one thousand enlisted volunteers be made available for the formation of two additional Ranger battalions for HUSKY, as the invasion had been code-named. He further recommended that the volunteers be drawn from replacement centers because the four army divisions then in II Corps—the First, Ninth and Thirty-fourth Infantry, and First Armored—were either committed or likely to be committed to combat and did not have the men to spare.

Darby's recommendations were approved and forwarded to General Marshall. On 19 April, Marshall's authorization to activate the Third and Fourth Ranger Battalions arrived at AFHQ. The authorization, however, carried the suggestion that after the need for the battalions had passed, their personnel might be returned to their former organizations. The Ranger battalions were to be provisional rather than permanent due, at least in part, to a manpower shortage which would remain critical until summer.[1] The three battalions were to be called Ranger Force.

On 22 April, the CG of the North African theater of operations authorized Darby to visit any or all replacement depots in the theater to seek volunteers for the Rangers. Darby could accept anyone he found suitable, and have the volunteers assigned to the Rangers on the condition that his battalions did not exceed their authorized strengths. Thus, on 17 May, Headquarters, Atlantic Base Section, distributed a subject letter titled "Volunteers for Ranger Battalions" which announced that enlisted volunteers were being sought, and listed desirable qualifications. Volunteers were to be white; at least five feet, six inches in height; of normal weight; in excellent physical condition; and not over thirty-five years old. They also had to have character ratings of excellent and no record of trial by court-martial. Although previous infantry training was desirable, applicants did not have to be infantrymen. Except for technicians, applicants were not to be higher in grade than private first class.[2] This last stipulation was to insure that enlisted leadership positions would be dominated by men who had trained with the original Rangers in the British Isles, and had served with them in combat.

Darby used the original First Ranger Battalion to provide a cadre for the new Third and Fourth Battalions. He made Dammer, who had since been promoted to major, CO of the Third Battalion and gave him the original "A" and "B" Companies to use as a nucleus. Captain Roy A. Murray, Jr., the former commander of Company "F," became CO of the Fourth

Sicily

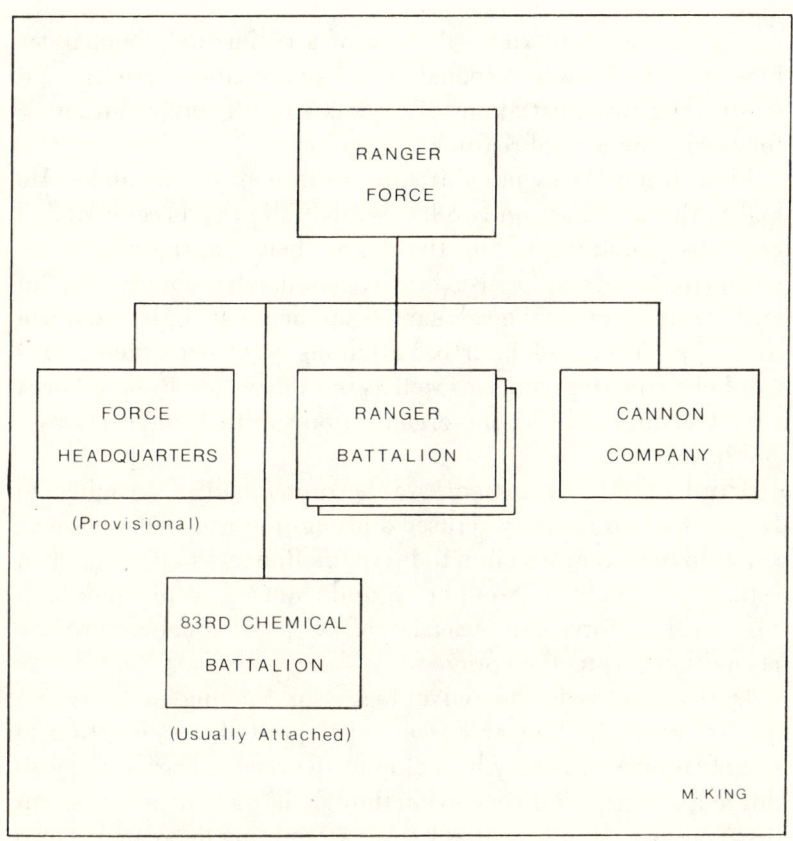

6. Organization of Ranger Force.

Battalion and was given the original "E" and "F" Companies. Darby himself retained command of the First Ranger Battalion, which had as its core the old "C" and "D" Companies.

Darby's continued command of the First Ranger Battalion was necessary because Ranger Force had not been authorized its own headquarters. Thus, Darby remained a battalion commander but his duties approximated those of a regimental commander inasmuch as he was responsible for organizing, training, and controlling three battalions. This was an unfavorable situation for Darby for several reasons.

First, it put Darby in a difficult position as a commander. He had to think and act on two levels—battalion and regimental—but was handicapped in the latter because there was no authorized staff to assist him. Second, the absence of an authorized regimental headquarters implied that Darby's control over the Third and Fourth Battalions was incomplete. This would be true in practice as well as in theory, and Ranger Force would seldom fight as one organization, unified under Darby's command.

Third, the arrangement was professionally damaging to Darby. He had recently refused a promotion to colonel because it would have required him to leave the Rangers to command an infantry regiment. Now he found himself commanding a regimentlike force but, because of its provisional nature, no promotion was forthcoming.

Darby realized the advantages of having an organic headquarters for Ranger Force and requested authorization to establish one. This may be a clue to the reason Darby clung so doggedly to the Rangers even though it was to his apparent disadvantage. It may be that he was attempting to create his own regiment—a Ranger regiment—in order to justify a promotion to colonel on his own terms. He would have thus had the best of both worlds, the Rangers and his colonelcy. If that was Darby's plan, he was badly disappointed. On 29 April, he was notified that the War Department had disapproved his request.[3]

Because of Anglo-American disagreements and the length of the struggle in Tunisia, the plan for HUSKY was not finalized until 3 May. It called for an invasion of southeastern Sicily by two armies: Montgomery's Eighth Army, which would land on the east coast from the vicinity of Syracuse south to Cap Passero; and Patton's I Armored Corps, which would lead the American forces. During HUSKY's planning, I Armored Corps

(Reinforced) was known as Force 343. On the day of the invasion it would be redesignated the Seventh U.S. Army and land along a seventy-mile stretch of coast extending from Licata to the right bank of the Irminio River. The boundary between the Seventh and British Eighth Armies was drawn approximately three miles west of Pozzallo and extended inland through Ragusa and Vizzini. These towns and the roads connecting them were to be in the British sector. As in North Africa, the American forces were intended to play a role secondary to the British. Seventh Army was to protect Eighth Army's left flank while the latter drove northward to Messina, the main strategic objective in Sicily.

Patton's immediate goals were to capture and put into operation the ports of Gela and Biscari, and Comiso. Toward these ends, Seventh Army was divided into two task forces which, exluding reserves, were organized around Maj. Gen. Omar Bradley's II Corps and Maj. Gen. Lucian K. Truscott's Third Infantry Division (Reinforced).

II Corps was to accomplish three principal missions in succession. Allen's First Infantry Division and Maj. Gen. Troy H. Middleton's Forty-fifth Infantry Division, which were Bradley's main assault elements, were to land at Gela and near Scoglitti before daylight on D-day and go on to seize the Porto Olivo airport before dawn of the following day. Corps would then move further inland and capture the Comiso and Biscari airfields by nightfall of D-day plus two. It would then extend the beachhead to the line Mazzarino-Caltagironi-Vizzini, called Line Yellow, and establish contact with the British Eighth Army at Ragusa.

The First Infantry Division was to land on beaches at and east of Gela; capture Gela and the airfield at Ponte Olivo; and occupy as rapidly as possible Line Red, the initial limit of the beachhead, for use as a base for continued operations and as a defensive perimeter if necessary. The division was also charged with maintaining contact with the Third Infantry Division on the left, and being prepared to help Middleton capture the

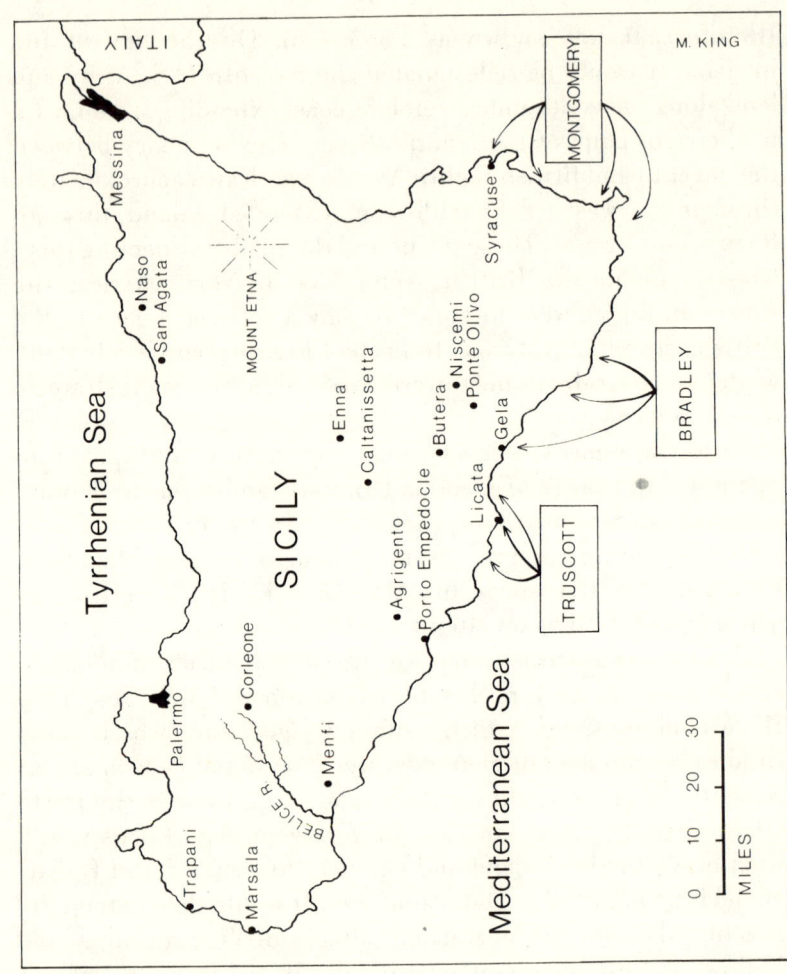

7. Sicily showing Allied Landing Sites and Principal Locations.

airfield north of Biscari. After the capture of the airfields, Allen was to extend the division beachhead to a second phase line designated Line Yellow.

Darby was selected to play a key role in the accomplishment of the First Infantry Division's mission. In preparation for this task, he assumed command of Force "X," a provisional grouping consisting of the First and Fourth Ranger Battalions; the First Battalion, 39th Combat Engineer Regiment; three companies of the Eighty-third Chemical (4.2-inch mortar) Battalion; and the First Battalion, 531st Engineer Shore Regiment. His mission was to land his force; destroy, capture, or neutralize the coastal defenses on the high ground northwest of Gela; and capture and secure Gela and its surrounding high ground. After taking Gela, Darby was to neutralize a strong point fifteen hundred yards northwest of the Gela hill mass; his First and Fourth Ranger Battalions were to police the town, with the Fourth remaining ready to assist division; and the engineer battalion would be released to division control.[4]

Darby's Gela mission had at least a surface similarity to the Arzew landing in that the silencing of the town's coastal defenses was the Rangers' most important objective. Gun batteries were known to exist on both sides of Gela, and the seizure of the town was incidental to taking out the batteries. Subsequent landings and resupply could not occur if the guns remained in Italian hands. Under no circumstances were they to be allowed to fire. If the Rangers could not silence the guns, the American cruiser *Savannah* would have to do the job.

The beach at Gela was bow shaped, with the town at its apex, and had a nine-hundred-foot jetty which extended into the sea, dividing the beach in two. It was also shallow, with a gradient of about 1:100, and had sandbars offshore. Gela, with a population of about thirty-two thousand, was on the only high ground in the immediate area, sloping upward from the beach until it reached a height of about 150 feet above sea level. Extending around the town for several miles was the treeless, grain-growing Plain of Gela. The site bothered Darby. The closeness of the town to the beach made a surprise landing difficult to achieve, and the beach's sandbars and shallow gradient might make it necessary for the Rangers to wade ashore from grounded landing craft.

Darby's general plan called for landing two battalions abreast. The Fourth Ranger Battalion would land to the right of the jetty, and the First Ranger Battalion to the left. The First Battalion, 39th Engineers Shore Regiment, would follow the Rangers ashore in that order.

The remainder of the First Infantry Division, which was organized into the Twenty-sixth and Sixteenth RCTs (Regimental Combat Teams), would land east of the Gela River along a three-mile stretch of beach which had been divided into four landing sites.

While Darby and the First and Fourth Ranger Battalions were landing with the First Infantry Division and II Corps, Dammer and the Third Ranger Battalion would land with Truscott's Third Infantry Division twenty miles to the west. The Third Infantry Division was to land in the Licata area on D-day; capture the port and nearby airfields by dark and then extend its beachhead to the line Palma di Montechiaro-Campobello-Mazzarino, called Line Yellow, and establish contact with II Corps on the right.

Truscott's plan was to secure Licata by means of a double pincer movement that would head inland from four beaches. From west to east, these beaches were designated Red, Green, Yellow, and Blue. The Seventh RCT, commanded by Col. Harry B. Sherman, would land on Red Beach and form the outside element of the left pincer. The inner element of the left pincer, which would land on Green Beach, would be a provisional composite force consisting of Dammer's Third Ranger Battalion; the Second Battalion, Fifteenth Infantry; a company of 4.2-inch mortars; a battery of 105mm howitzers; and a platoon of 75mm howitzers. It would be under the command of Lt. Col. Brookner W. Brady, executive officer of the Fifteenth Infantry. The Third Ranger Battalion's mission was to land on Green Beach, reduce all enemy installations on the beach to facilitate subsequent landings, and move to the southwest to seize and hold designated heights until relieved by units landing on Red Beach.[5] The remainder of the Fifteenth Infantry, commanded by Col. Charles R. Johnson, would land on Yellow Beach as the inner element of the right pincer. The Thirtieth RCT, led by Col. Arthur R. Rogers, would land on Blue Beach as the outer element of the right pincer. CC (combat command) "A," led by Brig. Gen. Maurice Rose of the Second Armored Division, would serve as Truscott's floating reserve and would be available either to assist the assaulting units or to be committed against Campobello, Agrigento, or Gela.

In early June, after six weeks of training in the Nemours area, Darby's three battalions joined the divisions with which they would land. The First and Fourth Ranger Battalions went to Algiers by transport and continued on foot to Zeralda, where they joined the First Infantry Division. The Third Ranger Battalion went to Bizerte by transport to join the Third Infantry Division. On 19 June, the date which marked the Rangers' first anniversary, the Third and Fourth Ranger Battalions were officially activated.[6]

Darby was concerned about the large number of relatively inexperienced and inadequately trained men he had gained during the Rangers' expansion, and sought to prepare them for the invasion in the best way possible. Together with a naval captain named Leppert, he developed a training program which was beneficial to both the Rangers and the navy. Darby's men were put on Leppert's LCIs (landing craft, infantry), which were manned by generally inexperienced sailors, and the two groups made practice landings together. By D-day, the Rangers had had about a month of training and that, Darby later reflected, "certainly paid dividends." In spite of the preinvasion training, Darby remained troubled. His finding of Gela's beach was dependent upon Force "X" meeting and being led to shore by guide boats. Darby, however, had never seen the boats, and their crews had never trained with Force "X." Although he received assurances that the boats would be in position on D-day, he remained skeptical. He was suspicious, he later recalled, because he always mistrusted plans in which the people involved did not get together to work out details and rehearse their actions. Darby's skepticism would prove justified during their landing at Gela.

It is important to note that an informal but significant change had begun to creep into the Rangers' organization. This was the attachment of the Eighty-third Chemical Battalion, an attachment which would become so routine as to be permanent.

The Rangers' association with the mortar men began in mid-May when Darby ran into Lt. Col. Kenneth A. Cunin on the streets of Oran. Cunin, a 1934 graduate of West Point and a friend of Darby's since the two had served together in the Eighty-second Field Artillery at Fort Bliss, had become CO of the Eighty-third Chemical Battalion. Cunin was accompanied by his executive officer, Maj. William S. Hutchinson, Jr. During the conversation that followed, Darby was told that several chemical battalions were scheduled to land in Sicily. Having been impressed with the 4.2-inch mortar's capabilities while stationed at Fort Hoyle with the Ninety-ninth Field Artillery, he now requested and got the Eighty-third Chemical Battalion attached to the Rangers. Cunin became executive officer of Force "X."

Darby had temporarily traded the Rangers' 60mm mortars for 81mm tubes before landing in North Africa. Now, in preparation for Sicily, he had added the even heavier 4.2-inch mortars. The artilleryman in Darby's blood was beginning to assert itself, and as it did the Rangers began to be transformed from a light, commandolike strike force into a more heavily and conventionally armed unit.

Gela and Licata

Force "X" left North Africa on transports, and was transferred to smaller landing craft off the coast of Sicily after midnight of 9 July. According to plans, the force was to land in three waves. The first wave, carried on fourteen LCAs and fourteen LCVPs (landing craft, vehicle or personnel)—half British and half American craft—would be composed of the First and Fourth Ranger Battalions. The second wave would be the engineers. The third wave, carried on three LCIs, would consist of the 4.2-inch mortars.

The success of the landing was as dependent upon the waves landing in proper sequence as upon their finding the proper beaches. For some desperate moments, it seemed that the landing might fail on both counts. Darby's earlier fears concerning the guide boats which were to lead him to shore were realized when the boats failed to arrive and the landing craft lost time waiting for them. Surprise was also lost during the confusion and hesitation, and the enemy began to probe the darkness with searchlights. Lacking guide boats, the landing craft headed toward the general area of Gela in disorder. Fortunately, Darby spotted a small craft which he though to be a guide boat, but which turned out to be Leppert bringing up the LCIs of the third wave. The mortar men were ahead of the Rangers and, had they not met, would probably have been the first to land. Leppert was certain of his location and destination, so the three waves of landing craft assembled around him and followed him toward Gela. In spite of its initial disorganization, Force "X" hit the beach on time and in proper order. "But," Darby admitted, "it was no thanks to the system or to the plan we had for getting in there, because it was just by luck that we ever ran into anybody in the middle of the ocean at night who knew where he was going."

The way in was not cheap or easy. One of Darby's landing craft ran onto a sandbar some distance from the beach and capsized, causing about twenty men to drown. Several other craft were hit by mortar fire before they could land. Darby later described the landing as "one of the wildest scenes" he had ever seen. "The place was alive with searchlights" and the Italians "had machinegun fire up and down the beach," but the men "went in like tigers."

As planned, the First Ranger Battalion landed to the left of the pier at about 0315 and began to carry out its mission of establishing an initial beachhead, reducing the coastal artillery defenses on the high ground northwest of Gela, and capturing and securing the northwestern part of Gela. The Fourth Ranger Battalion landed to the right of the pier where it went to work establishing an initial beachhead, capturing and securing the southeastern corner of Gela, and clearing the pier of all enemy installations. Lives were lost to mines and machine guns before the Rangers reached and silenced the first Italian positions. The First Battalion, 39th Engineers, landed astride the pier with the mission of clearing the beach adjacent to Gela of all mines, and capturing and securing the central section of town. When the Eighty-third Chemical Battalion, minus one company which was with the Third Infantry Division, landed astride the pier at 0500, the Italian gunners who had not yet been silenced had recovered from the initial shock of the invasion and were delivering accurate fire. Italian resistance on the beach was gradually overcome, however, and by 0830 most of Gela had been taken after heavy street fighting. During that fighting, Darby and his personal tommy gunner, Cpl. Charles Riley, met about a squad of Rangers who were engaged in a firefight with some Italians who were in a hotel. Darby and Riley personally led the Rangers in an assault on the building and about thirty prisoners were taken in the melee that followed. Meanwhile, the First Battalion, 531st Engineer Shore Regiment, had landed to organize the beaches for subsequent landings and resupply. They accomplished their task by 0700.

With Gela under control, Darby and his Rangers went after a gun battery to the west of town. Due to the invasion's loss of surprise and the delay caused by enemy resistance on the beach, the Italians had been able to put their guns into operation and were brought under fire by the *Savannah*. When Darby reached the battery he called on the *Savannah*, through the naval forward observer party which accompanied him, to lift its fire, and he and his men took the position in short order with a minimum of fighting. Those Italians not killed by the *Savannah's* fire quickly surrendered. Because of the possibility of an enemy counterattack to recapture the battery, Darby's men began to destroy the guns with explosives. This nearly led to disaster. The *Savannah*, which had the additional mission of firing at gun flashes, mistook the exploding guns for continued Italian fire and resumed firing on the battery. It ceased fire only when signalled that the flashes were caused by Force "X" destroying the guns. The episode brought home still further to Darby that ship-to-shore communications could not be left to chance or they would eventually lead to catastrophe.

By 0830 both Ranger battalions and the First Battalion, Thirty-ninth Engineers (minus one company), had accomplished their missions and gone on to establish a perimeter defense around the inland side of Gela. From left to right, the perimeter was manned by the First Ranger Battalion; First Battalion, Thirty-ninth Engineers (minus one company); and the Fourth Ranger Battalion.

The first counterattack against Force "X" took place at 1030 when nine Italian tanks attacked Gela from the east. The attack fell heaviest upon the Fourth Ranger Battalion and elements of the First Battalion, Thirty-ninth Engineers, supported by Company "C" of the Eighty-third Chemical Battalion. The tanks forced their way into town where they were met by Darby's lightly armed men. Neither tanks nor many antitank guns had landed so the Americans fought with what they had—bazookas, pole-charges, and one 37mm antitank gun. Darby led as bravely in the defense as he had in the attack. During the height of the fighting in the Fourth Battalion sector, "F" Company CO Lt. Stan Zaslaw's rocket gunner was unable to fire his bazooka at an Italian tank because Darby was riding on it and trying to open its hatch so he could grenade the crew. Later, Darby personally destroyed one of the tanks with a 37mm gun which he had brought up from the beach. By the time the attack was turned back, three of the Italian tanks had been destroyed.

Later in the day, Patton congratulated Darby for the morning's work in Gela's cathedral square. The photographic record of the event shows the helmeted, high-booted, pistol-bearing Patton shaking hands with a bareheaded, smiling Darby. Patton, who had by this time established a reputation for fining helmetless and other "improperly" uniformed soldiers, acted with greater restraint when dealing with Darby. And well he might—by the end of the day Force "X" had taken almost a thousand prisoners.

D-day was less strenous for Dammer and the Third Ranger Battalion. The Third landed on Green Beach in British LCAs at 0255, gained initial surprise, and were able to cross the beach and pass through a wide belt of barbed wire before being discovered. When the Italians revealed their positions by opening fire, the Rangers quickly overcame them. By the time the First Battalion, Fifteenth Infantry, landed, all enemy resistance on the beach had ceased and the only Italians blocking the way to Licata had been overcome by two Ranger companies on their way to high ground fifteen hundred meters to the east. This success had been achieved at slight cost. Only two Rangers were wounded, one of whom later died. The Third Ranger Battalion's experience in this regard was typical. Enemy defenses and will in the Licata area were weak and the entire Joss Force, as Truscott's reinforced division was called, suffered fewer than a hundred casualties. Later in the day, the Third Ranger Battalion was marched to an assembly area south of San Oliva, where it remained in division reserve until 14 July. By nightfall of 11 July, the Third Infantry Division had secured its objective and was established along Line Yellow.

Darby and Force "X," however, continued to come under enemy pressure. After dawn on 11 July, German and Italian units launched a general counterattack which spread across the entire front of the First Infantry Division and extended to the left flank elements of the Forty-fifth Infantry Division. This offensive was the only major enemy resistance the Allies would encounter until they reached the northeastern corner of Sicily.

A three-pronged attack against Gela was part of this enemy effort. At 0700 one estimated battalion of infantry attacked from the northwest and another from the north, and about ten tanks followed by infantry attacked from the northeast. The Americans could see the enemy advancing across the Plain of Gela and brought them under fire with naval guns, division artillery, and 4.2-inch mortars when they were about two miles from town. A combination of this heavy fire and the landing of American tanks in Gela while the attack was in progress prevented the enemy from reaching town. By 1150 the attackers were driven off with heavy losses of men and materiel, and most of the enemy who had come from the northwest were captured. At about 1300 an Italian infantry battalion resumed the attack on Gela from the northwest, but American artillery fire inflicted heavy casualties upon it and Darby went forward into the plain with a Ranger company and a few half-tracks to take the survivors prisoner.

Later in the day, Gen. Alfred Guzzoni, the Italian commander in Sicily, ordered his XVI Corps to cease offensive action in the Gela area and establish its Fourth (Livorno) Division along a defensive line extending from Mazzarino to Caltagirone, to cover the withdrawal of the German Hermann Goering Panzer Division. With Guzzoni's decision, the survival of the Gela beachhead was assured.

The Drive Inland

With the beachhead won, the drive inland got under way. As in North Africa, the drive saw the Rangers used in routine infantry operations. These began when Patton ordered Darby to attack and seize the high ground northwest of Gela on the Gela-

Butera road, and to make contact with the Third Infantry Division on the left. This was accomplished by 1400 the following afternoon.

On July 12 Darby rejected for the second time a promotion which would have required him to leave the Rangers. The 180th Infantry Regiment had captured Biscari at 2000 but only after great difficulty, and the unit's disappointing performance prompted Middleton, CG of the Forty-fifth Infantry Division, to take steps toward relieving its commander. Middleton requested a replacement from Bradley, the corps commander, who in turn asked Patton for Darby. Patton offered Darby the 180th Infantry and an immediate promotion to colonel but Darby declined. Middleton thus retained the original regimental commander but dispatched his assistant division commander to the 180th Infantry to supervise him.[7] Once again, Darby had demonstrated his loyalty to the Rangers; but he may also have been attempting to be promoted on his own terms. Darby, as strong-egoed as he was, may have thought that if he refused promotion out of the Rangers long enough, his superiors and the War Department would create a Ranger regimental headquarters within which he could be promoted, rather than see someone of his talents kept a lieutenant colonel any longer.

On 13 July the First Ranger Battalion was rejoined by companies "A," "B," and "E" which had come from Gela. Both the First and Fourth Ranger Battalions were then relieved from attachment to the First Infantry Division and attached to Maj. Gen. Hugh J. Gaffey's Second Armored Division. Darby thus found himself in command of a new regiment-sized combined arms team, and faced with another conventional mission. The new team was composed of the First and Fourth Ranger Battalions; the Eighty-third Chemical Battalion; the First Battalion, Forty-first Infantry; most of the Eighty-second Reconnaissance Battalion; and the Seventy-eighth Armored Field Artillery Battalion. At about noon, Gaffey ordered Darby to move northward under cover of darkness, and to attack and secure the town of Butera and the heights dominating it at

2230.[8] By Patton's directive, the town was to be taken by Rangers.[9] Butera was an almost inaccessible hill town which sat astride the road to Enna. Enna was at the east end of the Enna Loop, the hub of eastern Sicily's road network, and was Guzzoni's headquarters.

It is interesting to note that Butera's nearly impregnable natural position had forced many of Sicily's earlier invaders to bypass the town temporarily and return to capture it later. Indeed, when the Norman Roger Borsa made his first visit to Sicily as its duke in 1086, he found only three pockets of Saracen resistance on the island—Enna, Butera, and Noto. Until Darby was assigned the mission of taking Butera, the town formed an indentation on the left of II Corps' front and it appeared that the Americans, like the Normans, would have to bypass the town.

It was no longer the eleventh century, however, and both the technology of the attackers and the resolve of the defenders had changed. Butera fell easily. It was brought under naval gunfire from a range of twenty-two thousand yards during the afternoon of 13 July, and white flags soon appeared from the windows of some of the buildings. Scouts, however, found that the approaches to the town were still mined and covered by antitank guns and machine guns. The white flags were therefore disregarded and the attack was made as ordered. By early light of the following day, Enna had been taken and Ranger Force's initial drive inland was over. Measured in terms of enemy captured, the drive had been highly successful: from 10 through 14 July Ranger Force had taken 2,689 prisoners. After a few days of rest at Butera, the First and Fourth Ranger Battalions assembled at Campobello, about thirty miles north of Licata, with the Second Armored Division.

While Darby, the First and Fourth Ranger Battalions, and attached units had been doing well north of Gela, Dammer and the Third Ranger Battalion had been doing equally well northwest of Licata.

By nightfall of 11 July the Third Infantry Division had

established itself along Line Yellow. By early morning of 15 July the First and Forty-fifth Infantry Divisions had done likewise and Seventh Army's initial invasion objectives were met. The subsequent thrusts of Seventh Army's advances were largely determined by the subordinate role assigned to the Americans and Patton's enlargement of that role. Patton decided to capture Porto Empedocle, which would give Seventh Army a port twenty-five miles closer to the front than Licata, and would serve as a stepping-stone on the way to Palermo. Because of the restrictive secondary role which had been assigned to Patton, he could not openly launch an all-out offensive in the direction of Porto Empedocle. Instead, he did so through the subterfuge of calling his advance a "reconnaissance in force" and limiting participation in it to Truscott's command. Thanks in part to the poor fighting qualities of the Italians, the Rangers' experiences while spearheading this "reconnaissance in force" resembled a training exercise more than a combat action.

While participating in Patton's drive westward on 15 and 16 July, Dammer's Third Ranger Battalion overcame an Italian roadblock on the Favara-Agrigento road, ambushed an Italian column composed of ten motorcycles and two troop-laden trucks on the Agrigento-Raffadell road, and surprised and inflicted heavy losses on four Italian artillery batteries below Montaperto before finally taking Porto Empedocle from its Italian and German defenders. The two days netted the Rangers 91 German and about 840 Italian prisoners. Lieutenant Raymond F. Campbell, who died assaulting a machine gun nest outside Porto Empedocle, was the only Ranger killed in the operation and the first man of the Third Ranger Battalion to lose his life in combat. Fortunately for the Allies, the Rangers' lopsided success was typical of much of the initial drive inland. Weak enemy resistance encountered by the entire Third Infantry Division led Truscott's G-2 to report that the mass surrender of Italians in combat, and their voluntary surrender when not actually engaged, indicated extremely low morale and a lack of will to fight.

Sicily 91

The Drive on Palermo

On 17 July Patton conferred with Alexander in La Marsa, Tunisia, and persuaded him to consent to an American drive on Palermo. Unknown to Patton, however, the same day saw Guzzoni order his XII Corps to withdraw from western Sicily to a defensive line running from Nicosia to Cerda along Highway 120. Thus, what Patton envisioned as an impressive mechanized drive would, in fact, fall upon an area which was being evacuated by the enemy.

Reorganization for the drive on Palermo and western Sicily had begun on 15 July with the creation of a force called Provisional Corps. This was initially built on a nucleus of Joss Force, which was formally dissolved on 18 July, and was composed of the Third Infantry Division, Eighty-second Airborne Division, Thirty-ninth RCT, Fifth Armored Field Artillery, Eighty-third Chemical Battalion, Third Ranger Battalion, and miscellaneous support units. The Second Armored Division, with the First and Fourth Ranger Battalions attached, was added to Provisional Corps soon afterward and moved from Agrigento to assembly areas in the vicinity of Ribera during the afternoon and night of 20 July. The First and Fourth Ranger Battalions were relieved from attachment to the Second Armored Division and, together with the Thirty-ninth RCT and First Battalion, Seventy-seventh Artillery, formed into TF (task force) "X" under Darby's command. Darby once again found himself in charge of a unit of regimental proportions and faced with a conventional mission. Furthermore, the Third Ranger Battalion was still out of his control.

Darby was ordered to move at once by motor to the Belice River, and to attack across it without delay to seize Castelvetrano and the airfield to that town's west. He was then to continue his advance to the line Mazara-Pt. Biddusa-Salemi in order to establish a base of operations for the Second Armored Division and to protect the left and rear of Provisional Corps. TF "X" moved out of Menfi early in the morning of 21 July and by 0600 the following morning had patrols in Marsala.

With the Second Armored Division's drive under way, Keyes ordered TF "X" attached to Major General Matthew B. Ridgway's Eighty-second Airborne Division and, at about 0200 on 23 July, ordered Ridgway to reduce that portion of Sicily which lay northwest of the general line Castellamare-Marsala. Ridgway thereupon ordered Darby to take Marsala. Marsala fell by 2000 and TF "X" began moving north on Highway 115 towards Trapani. Although Trapani had been captured by the 505th RCT at about the same time Darby captured Marsala, TF "X" spent the following day reducing pockets of resistance between the two towns and occupying the high ground south of Trapani.

While the First and Fourth Ranger Battalions had been working with Darby as part of TF "X," the Third Ranger Battalion was engaged in minor outpost, reconnaissance, patrol, road guard, and POW guard duties. It served in this fashion until 23 July without suffering any losses.

On the morning of 24 July, Keyes attached the Third Ranger Battalion to TF "X." For the first time since the organization of the Third and Fourth Ranger Battalions in North Africa, all three battalions were under Darby's command. However, the Rangers were widely dispersed and assigned to guard prisoners, supplies and lines of communication, rather than to conduct combat operations.

The rest of July was a time of inactivity and uncertainty for Darby and his Rangers. Some companies relocated and there were both attachments and reliefs from attachment but, as in the aftermath of TORCH, it seemed that the war was passing the Rangers by.

Messina

Important changes in strategy and planning took place during Patton's occupation of western Sicily. During 20-23 July,

Sicily

Alexander decided to take from Eighth Army its exclusive right to Messina and make the city fair game for Seventh Army as well. A race for Messina thus began between the two armies.

Terrain dictated two unfavorable axes of advance to Seventh Army. A northern axis, which lay along the coastal road, Highway 113, was bounded by the sea to the north and the Coronie Mountains to the south. Occasional ridges which ran down to the sea from the mountains provided the Germans with a series of natural defensive barriers which could be held in succession, thus gaining time for an orderly withdrawal across the Straits of Messina. A southern axis, which lay inland along Highway 120, was dominated by mountains on both sides. Here, too, movement was canalized and opportunities for maneuver or surprise were limited.

Changes in Allied strategy were accompanied and followed by changes on the Axis side which made a difficult final struggle inevitable. On 25 July Gen. Hans-Valentine Hube assumed command over Axis ground forces in Sicily and brought more German units on line. This, together with terrain which favored the defense, would slow Seventh Army's hitherto rapid advance.

Patton gave II Corps Seventh Army's entire front and the missions of advancing eastward along the axes of Highways 113 and 120, and maintaining a sustained and relentless drive until the enemy was decisively defeated. Corps was also to make close contact with the left flank elements of Eighth Army. The attack was scheduled to be launched on 1 August from the line S. Stefano-Mistretta-Nicosia.

At the beginning of August, the First and Fourth Ranger Battalions were relieved from their assignments and moved back to Caltanissetta to receive and train replacements. Both units remained there for two weeks before moving to another training area near Corleone.

Not all of the Rangers trained, however. On 6 August, Seventh Army directed Darby to prepare either the First or Third Ranger Battalion for possible use in II Corps's attack. Darby chose the Third, and on the following day ordered the battalion from Menfi to Coronie where it became attached to the Third Infantry Division. The Rangers remained in bivouac until 9 August, when they received fifty pack animals and were ordered to the vicinity of S. Agata where they became attached to the Seventh Infantry. During the next nine days they operated in the high ground above Messina. Although Truscott was prepared for the possibility of having to take Messina by force and had already assigned the Third Ranger Battalion a role in the attack, an assault was not necessary. Those enemy soldiers capable of fighting—mainly Germans—had already been evacuated to Italy. When the Rangers sent a patrol into Messina at 0800 on 17 August, they found the city already being occupied and were able to enter peacefully. The Third Ranger Battalion was withdrawn from Messina during the morning of 18 August, and returned to Coronie where it received orders attaching it to II Corps. It remained in bivouac at Coronie until 21 August, then moved to join the First and Fourth Ranger Battalions at Corleone in receiving and training recruits. The Sicilian campaign had come to an end and preparations were being made for the invasion of Italy.

    The conquest of Sicily had been a time of transition and trial for Darby and his Rangers. While Darby had known the men of the original First Ranger Battalion intimately, having personally taken part in their day-to-day training in Scotland, the new men of the expanded Ranger Force saw little of him during training except when he led them in their daily speed marches, visited their training sites, and stood evening retreat. With a tripling of the size of his command and the lack of an authorized staff, Darby was finding it difficult to be as directly involved in the routine activities of his men as he had been in the past. Some old hands such as Eugene Kopveiler, who had been with the Rangers since their inception, missed Darby's personal touch. But to eighteen-year-old John F. Hummer, who had joined the First Ranger Battalion at Nemours while the Third and Fourth Rangers were being formed, it seemed that the original Rangers' spirit rubbed off on the newcomers until they, too, had come under the influence of Darby's personality. In later years, Hummer would recall no instance in which it ever occurred to him or the other Rangers that there was anything they could not do.

As in North Arica, Darby's exploits in combat added to his already formidable reputation. While his personal leadership during the fight for Gela is best known, he also revealed his character in minor episodes known only to those who were present. Texan Raymond Schuder, who had been with the Rangers from the start and carried so much shrapnel in his body from the Sened raid that he would "ring the bell" during electronic airport security checks later in life, remembered one night patrol in particular. Darby was leading some Rangers up a road when he suddenly brought them to a halt and told them to be silent. Something was ahead. Darby went forward into the darkness alone, only to return laughing a few minutes later. He thought he had seen a tank but it was only a haystack. It seemed to Schuder that any other lieutenant colonel would have stayed back and sent someone else forward. But, then, Darby did not think of himself as being just any lieutenant colonel.

Darby continued to show his characteristic concern for his men while in Sicily in smaller, less heroic ways as well. On one occasion he took some men to a supply depot only to be told that the items he wanted in quantity were for officers only. "All my men are officers," he snapped, and told his men to take the needed supplies. They did, and no one tried to stop them. Schuder and the others knew from this and other episodes they witnessed that Darby would do anything for them, and they reciprocated with their willingness to do anything for him.

That Darby looked out for the welfare of his men is not to say that he was soft or lenient with them. On the contrary, he was a strict disciplinarian who relied on direct, personal means of correcting his men when necessary. Drunkenness and other routine infractions of rules were sometimes punished by making the offending soldier go on a long, forced march with full field pack. Capt. Sheldon C. Sommers, First Ranger Battalion surgeon, witnessed one incident in which a medic accidentally fired a captured Italian pistol, superficially wounding a fellow Ranger. Darby punished the careless medic by making him sit shirtless in the Sicilian sun for three hours—long enough to get a sunburn he would not soon forget.

More serious and deliberate offenses were dealt with more forcefully. Sgt. Ed Mahoney recalled one such case which occurred in North Africa, when two men in his company decided to end their participation in the war by deserting into Spanish Morocco with the hope of being interned. The two were intercepted by the MPs, however, and brought before Darby. When the tougher of the pair, a former amateur boxer, talked back to Darby and threatened him, Darby removed his insignia of rank and "knocked hell out of" the man. Not surprisingly, the word among the Rangers was, "Darby don't take no shit."

Corporal punishment of enlisted men by officers is out of favor in our modern, egalitarian army, but the use of animal fear as a leadership tool has irrefutable value in combat. The Greek Xenophon, writing in his *Anabasis* nearly twenty-four hundred years earlier of the commander Clearchos, credited him with saying that "a soldier ought to fear his commander more than the enemy." In danger, Xenophon continued, "the soldiers wished absolutely to obey him and chose no other; at such times his grimness appeared brightness," and "his severity seemed strength against the enemy." And so it was with Darby. Sgt. Marcell G. Swank, who took part in the Dieppe raid and later retired from the army a lieutenant colonel, was so "scared to death" of Darby that on the way to Dieppe his main fear was that he might discredit the Rangers and have to face Darby. It never occurred to him that he might be killed by the Germans. Such is the stuff of which victories are made.

The growth of Darby's and the Rangers' reputations were, however, paralleled by the continuing erosion of the Rangers' uniqueness which had begun in North Africa. Except for the Rangers' landings at Gela and Licata, their Sicilian operations had made no use of their specialized training or capabilities and could just as well have been conducted by conventional infantry. The greatest reason for this "misuse" was the fact that the Rangers were neither given their own headquarters, nor permanently assigned to a higher headquarters which had the desire or authority to prevent their being used in routine actions. The Rangers were thus treated as small change and passed around from one headquarters to another to be used as expedience dictated.

Darby had already tried to solve this problem, but to no avail. On 10 August he tried again and wrote to Eisenhower in an attempt to obtain a permanent headquarters for the Rangers. Arguing that the Rangers' value and effectiveness had been well proven, he asked that a Force Headquarters be authorized the Rangers and that the Force be assigned to a corps, army, or higher level of command. If, on the other hand, the War Department should decide that the Rangers were not to be permanent, he requested that the three battalions be dissolved and reformed as an approved organization with an authorized TO&E. Darby further suggested that if such was to be the case, their training and experience would allow them to be transformed into a reconnaissance regiment without a great loss of time.

Two days later, when Darby's letter passed through Seventh Army Headquarters, Patton vigorously endorsed it, recommending that in view of the Rangers' performance, the battalions be formed into a Ranger regiment, allowed a suitable headquarters, and placed under Darby's command. He also asked that a suitable TO&E be drawn up for the regiment. If higher headquarters desired, Seventh Army would submit a proposed TO&E for approval. Patton liked Darby and the Rangers well enough to ask that the proposed Ranger regiment be permanently assigned to Seventh Army for use in future operations.[10]

Eisenhower did not share Patton's enthusiasm, however, and disapproved Darby's request on 3 September. Official word of Eisenhower's decision did not reach Darby until mid-October when he was in Italy. On a note accompanying the official correspondence, a sympathetic but unknown hand had written, "Back where you were Bill, a red-haired step child."[11]

V
From Salerno to the Winter Line

The Genesis of AVALANCHE

When Roosevelt and Churchill met at the third Washington conference in early May of 1943 to confirm their plans for the invasion of Sicily, they also established two general objectives in the Mediterranean. These were to knock Italy out of the war, and to tie down as many Germans as possible in the south. Decisions on how they would accomplish those objectives and where their next blow would fall were temporarily held in abeyance. Subsequent events helped them to decide.

When, by mid-May, initial Axis resistance in Sicily had proven weak, the Allied planners concluded that an invasion of the Italian mainland was feasible. Their military appraisal was soon confirmed by political developments. On 24 July, King Victor Emmanuel III removed Mussolini from power and appointed Marshal Pietro Badoglio head of a new government.

Although Badoglio announced that Italy would remain in the war despite Mussolini's dismissal, by early August his government had secretly made contact with Eisenhower and begun to negotiate for terms under which Italy might sign an armistice with the Allies. The Allied plans for the invasion of Italy were developed during, and influenced by, these events.

When completed, the plans called for three landings. The first, code-named BAYTOWN, would be made by the British Eighth Army in the vicinity of Reggio and, if successful, would open the Strait of Messina to Allied shipping. The main landing, code-named AVALANCHE, would be made in the Gulf of Salerno by Lt. Gen. Mark W. Clark's Fifth Army, then composed of the American VI Corps and British Ten Corps. The beachhead would serve as a jumping-off point for Naples, about fifty miles to the northwest. The third landing, which would become part of the Allied invasion plan in September, was code-named SLAPSTICK and would involve moving the British First Airborne Division into Taranto by ship as the Italian surrender took place and the Italian fleet became neutralized.

Darby and his Rangers would play a crucial part in the major landing, AVALANCHE.

The landing sites which the CCS (combined chiefs of staff) recommended for AVALANCHE stretched from Maiori in the north to Agropoli in the south, forming a crescent about thirty miles long. South of Salerno the beaches abutted onto a triangular plain, the longest side of which ran along the sea, and the shorter sides of which were bounded by high ground rising from two to ten miles inland. Unfortunately, much of the plain could be taken under observation and fire by an enemy holding these heights. Another disadvantage lay in the fact that lateral movement on the beachhead would be hindered by the Sele River and one of its tributaries, the Calore, which joined about five miles inland and flowed down to the sea, cutting the plain in two. In spite of these drawbacks the site was chosen over others, such as the Gulfs of Gaeta or Naples, because of its good beaches, the nearness of air support based in Sicily, and the relative absence of enemy fortifications.

While Naples was only about fifty miles northwest of the Salerno beachhead, the way to the city was made difficult by a wall of stony mountains which towered more than a thousand meters above the Gulf of Salerno in the south and the Plain of Naples in the north. These peaks, which stretched westward to become the Sorrento Peninsula, rose with picturesque abruptness to the immediate north and west of Salerno, crowding the city against the sea and limiting movement between the beachhead and Naples to several narrow passes.

The principal of these passes began at Vietri, a few miles west of Salerno, and ran about ten miles to the northwest via the La Molina defile and Cava Gap. A second major pass began at the east end of Salerno and ran due north toward Sanseverino for about eighteen miles. Each of these passes was traversed by a road and railroad. A third route began at the small coastal village of Maiori, about twenty miles west of Salerno. From there a narrow, twisting road rose gradually toward the northwest where, after twenty miles, it descended to the Plain of Naples via Chiunzi Pass. The success of either an American attack toward Naples or a German counterattack toward Salerno would depend upon control of these passes.

In planning, Clark placed Ten Corps, which had the Forty-sixth and Fifty-sixth Divisions available for landing, north of the Sele with the missions of securing the northern portion of the army beachhead and Monte Corvino airfield, and then moving through the passes leading northward out of Salerno and Vietri to seize Naples's port and Pomigliano and Capodichino airfields. Minimum forces would be left behind to maintain the security of the beachhead, and the Seventh Armoured Division would come ashore during the fifth and sixth days of the invasion.

VI Corps's Thirty-sixth Infantry Division would land south of the Sele to protect Fifth Army's right by seizing the high ground which overlooked the Salerno Plain from the east and south. The Forty-fifth Infantry Division would follow the Thirty-sixth

8. Allied Invasion of Italy.

ashore, and after Naples had been captured the First Armored and Thirty-fourth and Third Infantry Divisions would come ashore through that port.

Clark gave special attention to the three passes which led northward through the mountains to Naples. They had to be seized immediately upon landing—if the enemy got to them in strength before the Allies, their capture would be slow and costly. Clark initially intended that glider-borne troops seize the passes, but the idea was dropped on 12 August because of its impracticality. The job of taking the passes devolved upon Darby's Rangers and the First and Forty-first Royal Marine Commandos.

Fifth Army immediately requested that Darby and a small group report to Algiers to complete plans for the use of the Rangers in AVALANCHE. Darby, who had just arrived promptly in flew to Algiers with Dammer and Murray. They left behind them a Ranger Force badly debilitated by killed, wounded, and nonbattle casualties. The First and Fourth Ranger Battalions were at about 60 percent strength, the Third Ranger Battalion at about 50 percent. Sorely lacking experienced men, the Rangers assembled at Corleone to train for their next mission. Unknown to them, it lay only four weeks in the future.

The mission developed for Ranger Force during the remainder of August was based upon its seizure of Maiori and the pass to the north. More precisely, the Rangers were to land at Maiori; destroy enemy coastal defenses in the vicinity of Capo d'Orso, which was the southernmost point of land extending into the sea between Maiori and Salerno; clear the road running from Maiori to Pagani; seize the pass at Nocera; and be prepared to operate against the rear of any enemy holding up Ten Corps's advance from Vietri to Pagani.[1]

The exact nature of Ranger Force's mission and the importance of each battalion's part in it is best understood through a consideration of the terrain involved. The coast upon which the Rangers would land was rocky and mountainous with few beaches. Coastal traffic was restricted to a narrow road, which was hewn from the base of the mountains and traced a zigzag course above an unbroken succession of small promontories and inlets. Towns such as Maiori, which were at sea level and had sand beaches, could be found only at irregular intervals. Maiori's beach was at the end of a small inlet which

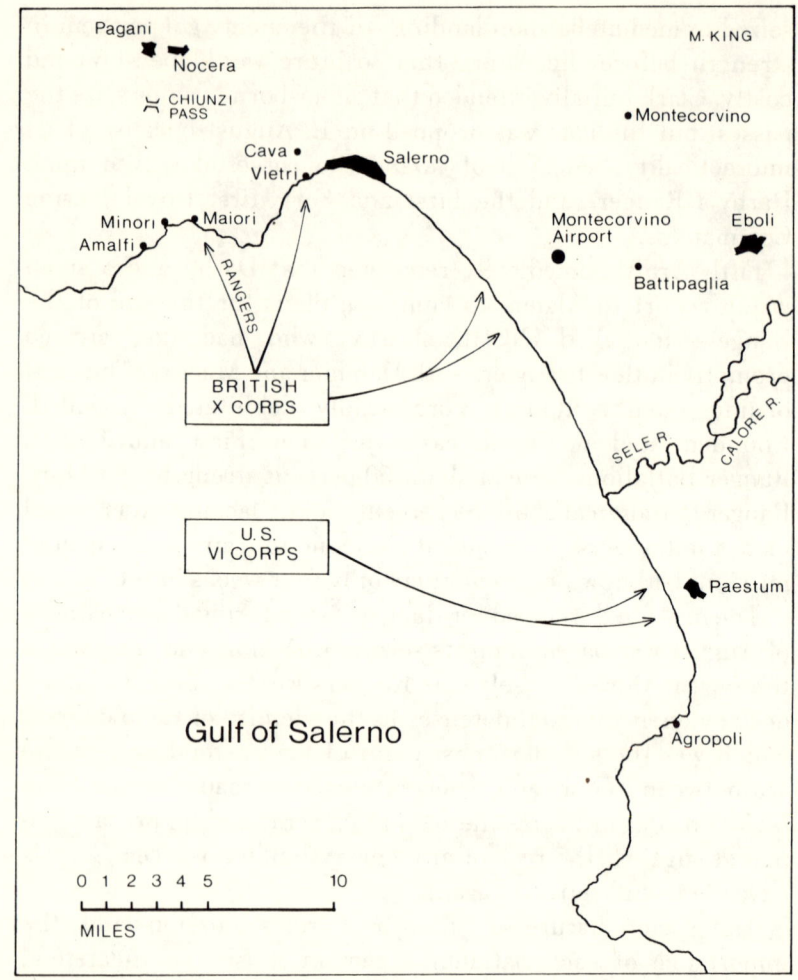

9. Salerno Landings showing Sites of Greatest Military Importance.

measured about half a mile from end to end. The town faced directly onto the beach and was separated from it only by the coastal road.

Maiori's special feature—the characteristic that gave it military value—was that it sat astride a funnellike draw which led northward into the mountains, to eventually cross them at Chiunzi Pass. Narrow, unpaved and tortuous, the only road inland from Maiori followed this draw northward along its east wall for about eighteen miles, crossed the mountains at Chiunzi at an elevation of 685 meters, and then spiralled steeply downward to Pagani and the Plain of Naples. The east wall and northern end of the draw were formed by Monte San Angelo di Cava and Monte di Chiunzi. Chiunzi Pass was the best point on the road to stop an enemy attacking southward toward Maiori, because the attackers would have to fight their way up the face of the mountains while the defenders could call and adjust artillery fire from the heights.

The tasks assigned to the battalions were planned so they would contribute to the methodical execution of the Force mission.

The Fourth Ranger Battalion was to be the first in, landing at H-hour. It would establish the beachhead, destroy coastal defenses in the Capo d'Orso area, establish a roadblock on the coastal road to the left of the landing site, and protect the left rear of Ranger Force.

The First Ranger Battalion would land at H+15; clear the Maiori-Pagani road as far as Vaccaro, which was about ten miles north of Maiori; and occupy Monte San Angelo di Cava to the northeast of Vaccaro. From the mountain they would be able to observe Route 18 between Cava and Nocera.

The Third Ranger Battalion would land at H+30, follow the First Rangers inland, occupy the high ground from the First Rangers' left to Monte di Chiunzi, and be prepared to attack Pagani.

The seizure of Monte San Angelo di Cava, Monte di Chiunzi, and the saddle between the two peaks would give the Rangers observation over most of Route 18 between Cava and Nocera, thus threatening enemy movement along the highway and aiding the British in their attack from Vietri to Nocera.

Company "B" of the Eighty-third Chemical Battalion would land with the Third Ranger Battalion at H+30, follow the Third Rangers along the road to the north, and take up a position near Monte San Angelo di Cava from which it could fire on Pagani and Nocera.

A Ranger cannon company, newly formed at Corleone and composed of four 75mm guns mounted on half-tracks under the command of Capt. Charles Shunstrom, would land at H+60 and move north to Chiunzi Pass. There, with the slopes of Monte di Chiunzi to the right, a valley to the left, and the Plain of Naples to the front, the company would protect Ranger Force and the beachhead against German armor coming out of the plain.[2]

The cannon company was an almost impromptu creation which came about when the Rangers welded some French 75mm guns to half-tracks for added firepower. The idea appears not to have originated with Darby, but there can be little doubt that he liked it. Dammer remembered Darby saying "I want cannon" after the Axis counterattack on Gela, and believed that the cannon company was formed because the fighting at Gela had impressed Darby with the Rangers' vulnerability to armor. Buck remembered Darby as having been "in favor of" the new company.

It might also be significant that Murray believed Darby never stressed the Rangers' uniqueness to its fullest extent. Murray thought that Darby chose not to emphasize the Rangers' special character out of fear that they might draw hostility from more conventional commanders and their units. If true, Darby was a more timid man than his other behavior indicates. More probably, Darby was growing to see the Rangers as less unique than many Rangers would like to believe. Dammer, who spoke of Darby as having a "fetish for firepower," was underscoring an essential element of Darby's military background—he was an artilleryman by training and previous assignments. As such, he may not have had a doctrinaire commitment to the idea that the Rangers were by definition a light, commandolike strike force. They were being used too often for conventional missions and Darby wanted them armed heavily enough to succeed in those missions. He acted pragmatically; lightness was traded in favor of greater firepower, and the Rangers grew to resemble a conventional regiment in organization as well as in function.

The Second and Forty-first Royal Marine Commandos received a mission somewhat analogous to that of the Rangers. They were to land at Vietri, about six miles to Darby's right, move inland to seize the Cava Gap, and attack Salerno from the west. Both the Rangers and the Commandos came under the command of Ten Corps, which would land on three beaches about five miles to the right of the Commandos. VI Corps would land about eleven miles to the right of Ten Corps.

Thus, Fifth Army's beaches would be spread out along an arc about thirty miles in length. They could be linked into a united beachhead more easily to the southeast of Salerno than to the west where Darby would land. To the southeast there was a virtually unbroken coastal plain and, except for the obstacle posed by the Sele and Calore Rivers, lateral communications and contact could be established with little difficulty. To the west, however, the Rangers' beach was linked to the plain by the coastal road previously described, but was otherwise isolated from it by thousand-meter-high peaks. Although the Rangers would be landing at about the same time as the main invasion force, their physical isolation would make them very vulnerable to an enemy counterattack.

The success of the landings would largely be determined by the degree to which Fifth Army could achieve surprise, and the number of German troops available to resist. Both German numbers and defensive capability grew while the Allies prepared for the invasion, for Hitler gradually increased German strength in Italy following Mussolini's arrest and replacement as premier. The senior German commander in Italy at the time was Gen. Field Marshal Albert Kesselring, commander in chief, south. Nominally subordinate to the Comando Supremo, the Italian supreme command, Kesselring was in fact accountable to the OKW (Oberkommando der Wehrmacht), the German Army's high command. On 8 August OKW created the Tenth Army of central Germany army units in southern Italy, naming Generaloberst Heinrich von Vietinghoff its commander.

German preparations were overtaken at 0430 on 3 September when Montgomery's Eighth Army crossed the Strait of Messina, launching operation BAYTOWN. Some hours later the Italian government surrendered unconditionally to the Allies, an event which remained secret until 1830 on 8 September when Eisenhower announced it over Radio Algiers. The landing at Salerno was scheduled to take place early the next morning.

Salerno and Chiunzi Pass

The amphibious movement toward Salerno got under way on 3 September, the same day BAYTOWN began, when a British convoy left Tripoli for northern Sicily. During the next three days, additional Allied convoys left Tripoli, Bizerte, Oran, and Algiers. Steaming around the west coast of Sicily, they were joined on 7 and 8 September by craft which had assembled along Sicily's northern coast. Darby and his Rangers were in this latter group, having boarded their transports in Palermo.

For the Rangers, AVALANCHE would begin more smoothly than either TORCH or HUSKY. At Arzew, a breakdown in communications had almost led to the Rangers being shelled by their own naval support. At Gela, miscoordination and the misorientation of the landing craft had resulted in a ragged landing and near disaster on the beach. In planning for AVALANCHE, Darby took steps to insure that the same mistakes would not be repeated.

Being attached to Ten Corps, the Rangers would disembark from British landing craft and be supported by gunfire from a British destroyer. Although Darby's experience with the British had always been good, he feared that differences in radio equipment and military vocabulary might make communication and coordination difficult. He discussed these potential problems with the British destroyer captain over dinner, carefully explaining that while he trusted British equipment, he would feel more at ease if he had one of his own radios and operators on the ship's bridge. The Briton, whom Darby thought "a grand person," assented; the Rangers would have good communication with their naval support during the entire landing.

The second problem, that of determining direction and finding the beachhead in darkness, was also solved. Amphibious landings conducted at night were usually scheduled to take place when the moon was new and visibility poor. This helped to conceal the invasion fleet and landing craft from enemy view, but it also hindered the invaders' view of coastal reference points. This problem was especially grave for the smaller landing craft because their compasses were confused by the helmets, weapons and other metal equipment brought on board by the troops. The solution arrived at by Darby and the British destroyer captain was to have the destroyer, with its greater stability and better compass, guide the Rangers' landing craft along an azimuth leading to the beach. When about one mile offshore, the destroyer would pull back out to sea and the landing craft would continue straight ahead to the beach. It was a simple procedure and it would work.

The Allied invasion fleet arrived off Salerno after dark on 8 September and its assault craft were lowered into the water a few minutes past midnight. At 0200 enemy batteries opened fire on the still seaborne Ten Corps. Their fire was promptly returned by Allied warships.

The beaches toward which the thirty thousand British and twenty-five thousand American troops of Fifth Army were headed were defended by the Sixteenth Panzer Division, the only fully equipped German armored division in southern Italy. The Sixteenth had seventeen thousand men, more than a hundred tanks, and thirty-six assault guns which were organized into four battalions of infantry and three of artillery. The division had recently been reconstituted following its near annihilation at Stalingrad and was at a great disadvantage: only four thousand of its troops had combat experience with the original organization, it had trained very little as a unit, was short of gasoline, and was thinly spread across a twenty-mile front.

For Darby and his Rangers, the landing went smoothly and according to plan. After the landing craft had formed up in the water, they pulled alongside the British destroyer in a column of twos with Darby and the flotilla officer in the lead boat. When the boat was opposite the destroyer's bridge, the two shouted "Let's go!" to the ship's captain and the destroyer began to guide the Rangers toward the beach. About a mile offshore, the captain shouted "Continue on your course!" to the Rangers, then left them and steamed back out to sea. The landing craft continued forward on the established azimuth and at 0310, twenty minutes before Ten Corps's main elements were scheduled to go ashore, the Rangers "hit the beach on the nose." It was "just that simple," Darby later said.

The Germans, probably discounting Maiori because of the smallness of its beach, were not defending it in strength. The Rangers encountered no organized resistance—they had achieved local surprise and began moving to their objectives. Impromptu resistance was offered by a few enemy reconnaissance parties which were surprised and quickly overcome, and two German colonels, apparently on leave, were captured while sleeping in an Amalfi hotel. By mid-morning the Rangers had occupied their objectives and were organizing on positions which enabled them to look down upon the Plain of Naples and sections of the Cava-Nocera road.

The two British Commandos landed with equal success to the Rangers' right. They hit the beach at 0330, after a German shore battery had been put out of action by naval gunfire, and by 0600 had reached the La Molina defile in the face of growing resistance. Germans firing mortars and machine guns onto the beach were forced out of Vietri after a two-hour battle, and the Commandos were soon fighting on the outskirts of Salerno.

Had the rest of the invasion force landed and moved inland as easily and successfully, the drive on Naples would have proceeded quickly and the Rangers' mission at Chiunzi Pass would have been accomplished after several days. Such, however, was not the case. Fifth Army would establish a tenuous beachhead and expand it all too slowly against increasing German numbers and resistance, leaving Darby and the Rangers to hold the pass against German counterattacks for ten days. For some, the battle would be seen as a turning point marking the end of the Rangers' use as special troops and the beginning of their regular use as conventional infantry.[3] Considering the way the Rangers would be used during most of the rest of the Italian campaign, this fear would prove to be well founded.

Unlike the Rangers, the main invasion force did not have the advantage of surprise while landing. Ten Corps encountered resistance and failed to achieve its D-day mission. When darkness fell, it had extended its beachhead no more than three miles inland. Salerno's port had not yet been taken by the Forty-sixth Division, and the Germans were successfully holding Montecorvino airport and the road and rail junction of Battipaglia against the Fifty-sixth Division.

VI Corps's landing was more successful, and by nightfall the Thirty-sixth Infantry Division was in occupation of most of the beachhead assigned as its D-day objective. Its lines ran from Paestum eastward, including Capaccio and the foothills of Monte Soprano, from which they ran parallel with the coast about three miles inland, to a point on Route 18 just short of Ponte Alla Scarfa, which remained in German hands.

D-day thus ended with Fifth Army winning the initial battle for the beaches, but it was not a secure victory. Neither Ten Corps nor VI Corps had driven more than three miles inland and a gap of five miles stood between them.

In contrast with the main invasion force, Darby and his

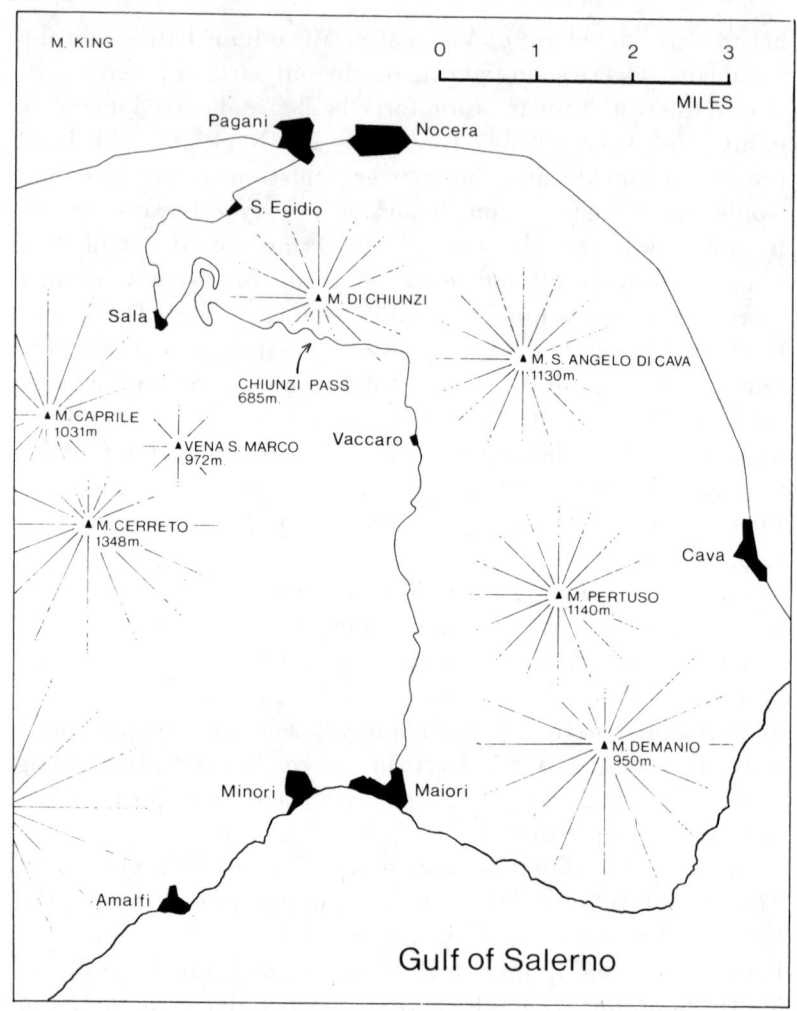

10. Maiori and Chiunzi Pass showing Most Important High Ground.

Rangers had made little enemy contact. Other than the several brief skirmishes which took place shortly after landing, their only fighting occurred when the Third Ranger Battalion sent patrols to reconnoiter routes to Pagani and Nocera and they killed all three members of a German patrol they encountered.

The day following the invasion was characterized by the building up of both Allied and German forces. Vietinghoff, faced with Allied landings at Salerno (AVALANCHE), Reggio (BAYTOWN) and Taranto (SLAPSTICK), had begun withdrawing troops from southern Italy as planned. While a rear guard continued to delay Eighth Army's advance, the Twenty-ninth Panzer Grenadier and Twenty-sixth Panzer Divisions, under LXXVI Corps headquarters, sped northward to reinforce the Sixteenth Panzer Division. Vietinghoff hoped that the advance elements of those units would arrive in the Salerno area late on 9 September.

On 10 September VI Corps attacked with some success while elements of the Forty-fifth Infantry Division, which had been acting as a floating reserve, landed to strengthen the American beachhead. The division was completely ashore by the end of the day. VI Corps's temporary advances were abruptly brought to an end on 11 September when the Twenty-ninth Panzer Grenadier and Twenty-sixth Panzer Divisions arrived from the south to strengthen the German left.

The British came under considerable pressure during 10 and 11 September. Commandos and elements of the Forty-sixth Division captured Salerno on 10 September, but when they tried to drive northward through Vietri Pass they were stopped by counterattacking units of the Third Panzer Division, which had come from Rome and which were advancing southward with leading elements of the Hermann Goering Panzer Division. The counterattacking Germans captured a total of fifteen hundred prisoners on 11 September, most of whom were British.

Enemy pressure was also brought against the Rangers. At about 1300 on 10 September, a thirty-man German patrol became engaged with the Third Ranger Battalion on Monte di

Chiunzi and was driven off with three dead after killing one Ranger. Later in the afternoon, another small German force was intercepted and twelve of its members killed in a brisk firefight. A second Ranger was killed in this encounter.

The importance of the Rangers' position and the pressure being brought against them greatly concerned Clark, who sent an observer to visit Darby's headquarters and assess the situation on the afternoon of 10 September. Upon returning to Fifth Army headquarters, the observer recommended that the Rangers be reinforced with motorized forces. Although their mobility would not be an asset in the pass, it would be valuable during the anticipated drive on Naples. Clark acted on the recommendation and the Rangers were reinforced the following day. During the late morning and early afternoon, the 1st Battalion, 143rd Infantry; Battery "A," 133rd Field Artillery Battalion; Company "B," 751st Medium Tank Battalion; Company "A," 2nd Motorized Chemical Battalion; Company "H," 36th Combat Engineers; and a company of the 601st Tank Destroyer Battalion arrived at Maiori and became attached to Ranger Force. As in Sicily, Darby was being given a regiment-sized command without benefit of a regimental commander's rank.

The Germans soon stepped up their patrolling activity in an effort to determine Darby's strength and disposition. During the early afternoon of 11 September, a small enemy patrol was discovered between the Third Ranger Battalion and the First Ranger Battalion which was to the Third's north, and driven off with mortar and cannon fire. The enemy was identified a half hour later when an officer and an enlisted man of the Hermann Goering Panzer Division were captured.

With his strength increasing, Darby was able to expand the area under his control. On 11 September three companies of the Fourth Ranger Battalion were sent southwesterly along the Sorrento Drive to a point four miles above Amalfi. From there they struck inland up the Agerola road to occupy Monte Pendolo, from which they could look down upon German troops in Gragnano. This new position was very exposed, being several miles off the Third Ranger Battalion's left flank, but it gave the Rangers control over still another secondary road leading down to the Plain of Naples. Moving further up the coastal road, patrols of the Fourth Ranger Battalion established a roadblock just outside Vico Equense on the southern rim of the Bay of Naples.

The Rangers' control of the heights overlooking the Plain of Naples gave them the observation needed to call accurate artillery fire on the enemy below. Darby's thoughts and actions were appropriate to his artilleryman's background and love of firepower. "If ever there was an artilleryman's dream," Darby later recalled, "here it was." He was fortunate to have two naval forward observer parties with him, and was able to call on fire support from the battleship H.M.S. *Howe* and several cruisers for the duration of the Rangers' stay at Chiunzi. The enemy on the plain "was the most beautiful target I believe I have ever seen," Darby added. The effectiveness of the shelling showed "what you can do if you have the communications and are prepared." Additional support was given by the half-tracks of Shunstrom's cannon company, which would quietly creep downhill toward the Germans in neutral gear at night, fire a few quick shots in the early morning twilight, and then scoot back up the road before the Germans could react.

For the Allies, the most desperate phase of the battle began on 12 September. By that time Kesselring had gathered a substantial part of the combat elements of six divisions, including six hundred tanks and mobile guns, to oppose Fifth Army. He planned to bring continued pressure against Ten Corps from the north while sending most of the reinforcing units into the Eboli-Battapaglia area. From there they were to attack westward along Route 19 to trap Ten Corps between themselves and the German forces to the north. They were also to attack to the southwest astride the Sele River in an effort to reach the sea and divide Ten and VI Corps. The British and Americans could then be defeated separately.

The German plan almost succeeded. During 12 and 13 September the British suffered heavy casualties around Battapaglia and the Montecorvino airfield, but were able to hold their ground because they were backed up by overwhelming naval gunfire and air support. The same day saw the Thirty-sixth Infantry Division forced from Altavilla and Point 424 in VI Corps's sector. During the afternoon of the following day, a German combined-arms team of tanks, self-propelled guns, and infantry forced its way through the Forty-fifth Infantry Division on the Sele, coming within two miles of the beach. Virtually every available man was used in a desperate effort to save the beachhead. At one point, when Clark asked which unit was holding a nearby hill, his intelligence officer replied that it was not defended because every unit except a band was committed. Clark thereupon directed that the musicians be sent to defend the height and dubbed it "Piccolo Peak." The Germans were finally stopped by two field artillery battalions which fired over open sights while cooks, clerks and drivers organized in the rear to form a final line of defense. The severity of the German attacks forced Clark to make contingency plans for withdrawal at the same time he was accelerating the buildup in the beachhead.

The German attacks of 12 and 13 September brought relatively light pressure to bear on the Rangers. At about 0600 on 12 September, a three-man enemy patrol was intercepted on the ridge south of Chiunzi Pass, and one of its members was killed. It was the preliminary to an abortive German attack. Four hours later a sizeable German force was seen moving into positions opposite the Third Ranger Battalion and taken under fire by six 60mm mortars. The enemy quickly withdrew. A wounded prisoner later revealed that the German force had been composed of two hundred men of the Hermann Goering Panzer Division and had suffered "many" casualties during the mortar bombardment. A Ranger reconnaissance patrol which was later sent to the area found only seven dead, but bloodstains and scattered bandages evidenced further losses. The Third Ranger

Battalion continued to occupy its positions until relieved by the Fourth Ranger Battalion on 17 September. There were no major attacks mounted against the battalion during that period, but it came under mortar and artillery fire of varying intensity.

Before relieving the Third, the Fourth Ranger Battalion had been busy probing the enemy. On 12 September the battalion occupied several heights overlooking Castellammare, and one of its companies sent a patrol into the town to determine the enemy's strength. The patrol ran into heavy resistance and withdrew, leaving three men behind who mapped the German defenses and returned to friendly lines that night. The day's experience, coupled with surveillance, convinced the Rangers that Castellammare was too strongly defended to be easily taken. On the same day, two companies of the Fourth Ranger Battalion which were on Monte Pendolo mounted an attack on Gregnano with the aid of a company of paratroopers. The Rangers and airborne were taken under heavy fire as they were deploying to attack and were forced to pull back. Gregnano was also held too strongly to be taken.

In spite of its failure to take Castellammare and Gregnano, the Fourth Ranger Battalion played an important role during the German attack. On September 13 troops of the Hermann Goering Panzer Division infiltrated Vietri as far as the coastal road, and threatened to isolate the Rangers from the main body of Ten Corps. McCreery lacked the reserves to counterattack and asked Darby if he could spare a battalion of Rangers for that purpose. Darby responded to the request affirmatively, relieved the Fourth Rangers from their defensive responsibilities, and temporarily put them under the command of the Forty-sixth Division. The battalion drove the Germans out of Vietri and was promptly returned to Ranger Force.

During the fighting at Chiunzi, Darby established his forward headquarters at a shell-pocked stone house at the mouth of the pass. It was called "Fort Schuster" after Captain Emil Schuster, the Third Ranger Battalion's medical officer who maintained his aid station there. Darby's rear headquarters was at Maiori.

Ironically, it was at the rear headquarters that Darby gave one of his most notable demonstrations of direct and forceful leadership. During some of the battle's more difficult fighting, Maiori was brought under enemy fire and Darby's supporting artillery began to pull out without his approval. Darby left a staff meeting he had been conducting, found the colonel commanding the artillery and, in the words of Peer Buck, "chewed" the artilleryman's "ass out." Though still only a lieutenant colonel himself, Darby told the colonel, "I'll give the order to withdraw if there's going to be a withdrawal." There was no withdrawal and there would be none.

How Darby could reprimand an officer one grade higher than himself and get away with it is explained by a now obscure letter which McCreery had sent to Clark on 12 September. By that time, Darby had gained numerous attachments and reinforcements. As his composite force grew, and the number of officers in it who outranked him also grew, it became increasingly likely that the command of the force might pass to one of them. While McCreery wanted Ranger Force to grow, he did not want Darby replaced as the American commander at Chiunzi and took steps to insure that he would not be. "I am very glad that you have reinforced Colonel Darby," he wrote to Clark. "This additional support will enable him to play a prominent part in helping 46th Division break out into the Naples Plain. I am very keen that Colonel Darby shall remain in command of this force. A naval signal yesterday ... stated that those reinforcing units would be under Brigadier-General Hilbur of the VI Corps. Please confirm that Colonel Darby remains in command with Brigadier-General Hilbur under him."[4]

If Darby was to be given command over a general, his reprimand of an errant artillery colonel was relatively minor fare. There is no record indicating that Clark objected to McCreery's request. Clark was forming his own favorable opinion of Darby, who would remain in command through the end of the battle.

On 14 September the last German reinforcements arrived—elements of the Twenty-sixth Panzer Grenadier Division from the south, and of the Third Panzer Grenadier Division from the north. The Germans continued to attack south and west of Persano throughout the day and were able to break through Ten Corps's line in places. Unfortunately for the Germans, there was massive Allied naval and air support during 14-16 September.

The direction the fighting was taking was apparent to Vietinghoff, who sent a message to Kesselring late on 16 September asking permission to break off the battle. The German attacks, he wrote, were unable to reach their objectives due to fire from naval guns and low-flying aircraft, as well as the approach of Eighth Army from the south. On that day, patrols of Montgomery's Eighth Army had established contact with VI Corps near Vallo. The next day Kesselring approved Vietinghoff's request on condition that the Volturno Line, upon which Tenth Army was to fall, would not be abandoned before 15 October. That would give Kesselring's chief engineer, Generalmajor Hans Bessel, time to fortify the Gustav Line further to the north. The German withdrawal northward began on that day.

Clark's confidence waxed as the Germans' waned. On 16 September he radioed to Eisenhower, "We are in good shape now. We are here to stay." Clark thought Darby's contribution to the army's effort especially worthy of note and added, "Darby has done his usual grand job and I recommend that he be promoted to the grade of colonel...." A typed version of the same message carried more commentary on Darby. "Do not know how long he has been a Lieutenant-Colonel," Clark continued, "but feel that he has done a superior job here and has several thousand men under his command and should be given the increased promotion."[5] Regardless of Clark's interest and Darby's ability, however, Darby was still only the commander of the First Ranger Battalion. He would have to wait longer for his promotion.

Late in the afternoon of 17 September, Allied reconnaissance pilots saw heavy German traffic moving to the north. The German withdrawal encouraged the Allies to advance to objectives they had previously been unable to take. On 18 September infantrymen of the Seventh Armored Division entered Battipaglia without meeting resistance, and units of VI Corps drove beyond Altavilla and Persano. With the beachhead secure, additional troops began to land. The Third Infantry Division came ashore and moved into an assembly area north of the Sele, and the Eighty-second Airborne Division headquarters air-landed at Paestum.

This buildup was only part of Fifth Army's preparation for the coming advance. McCreery readied for the drive on Naples and the Volturno by moving the Forty-sixth Division to Vietri and the Fifty-sixth Division to Salerno, thus relinquishing the Eboli-Battipaglia area to VI Corps. While massing most of his forces south of the Vietri-Nocera and Salerno-Sanseverino passes, he also planned a breakthrough via Chiunzi Pass.

To help assure the success of the breakthrough, McCreery reinforced Darby on 19 September and charged him with seizing the high ground east of Pagani. These reinforcements were from the Twenty-third Armoured Brigade, to which were attached an artillery battery, an antitank battery, an engineer company, a reconnaissance squadron, and an antiaircraft troop. On the following day, Fifth Army ordered still more reinforcements for Darby: the 325th Glider Infantry Regiment minus its 2nd Battalion, which had become attached to the 1st Ranger Battalion four days earlier; and the 3rd Battalion of the 504th Parachute Infantry Regiment minus its howitzer company, which had also become attached to the Rangers earlier. These latest arrivals reached Maiori at 1830 on 21 September and moved up on line. The 319th Glider Field Artillery Battalion also became attached to the Rangers.[6] By the end of the buildup, Darby was in command of about five thousand men.

The parts played by Darby and the Rangers at Salerno enhanced their already formidable reputations. Darby clearly demonstrated his ability to command a large body of men in a prolonged engagement with a hard-fighting enemy. Although he had led a regiment-sized combined-arms team in western Sicily, Italian resistance had by then all but collapsed and he gained little serious combat experience. Thus, Salerno clearly marked a new stage in Darby's growth as a commander. The British showed their appreciation of his performance by recommending that he be created an Honorary Companion of the Distinguished Service Order.

The Rangers also gained recognition. Both the First and Third Ranger Battalions were awarded Distinguished Unit Citations for their performance. It was the First's second such award—the first had been won at El Guettar—and the Third's first. The cost, however, had been high. The First had lost thirteen men killed, and twenty-one wounded seriously enough to be evacuated. About ten more men were slightly wounded. The Third had lost seven killed, one missing, and fourteen wounded. The Fourth Ranger Battalion had lost eight killed, eight missing, and twenty-one wounded. All but a few of these casualties had been suffered during the conventional fighting that followed the seizure of Chiunzi Pass. In other words, the losses had occurred in the type of action which most Rangers did not believe they had been organized to fight, a battle of materiel and attrition. The commitment of the Rangers to such a battle had not been premeditated; rather, Fifth Army's slowness to expand its beachhead had necessitated the Rangers' holding the pass longer than had been planned. Explanation aside, the fact remained that the Rangers had once again been used largely as conventional infantry. The practice would become more common as the drive northward continued.

The Drive on Naples

After the landings at Salerno, Kesselring planned to delay the Allies in southern Italy long enough to enable the Germans to build a strong defensive line in the northern Apennines. Toward this end, he planned a series of defensive lines across the peninsula. Each of these was to be defended long enough to slow and disrupt the Allied advance before being evacuated in favor of the next line.

The southernmost line would be based on the Volturno River about eighteen miles north of Naples, and extend eastward to the Adriatic port of Termoli. Another line, known to the Germans as the Reinhard or Bernhard Line and soon to become known to the Allies as the Winter Line, was planned about fifty miles north of Naples and ninety miles south of Rome. About twelve miles further north, the terrain around Monte Cassino was incorporated into plans for still another line—the Gustav Line.

Vietinghoff applied the same principle on a smaller scale south of the Volturno, where he established temporary defensive lines between the river and Naples, and specified dates through which they were to be held by a delaying rear guard. To guarantee that the Allies would advance slowly at best, all lines of communication and transportation leading to the river were to be destroyed. This policy of destruction was defined in detail by Kesselring. Tenth Army was to evacuate all cars, busses, trucks, and railroad rolling stock; to dismantle and evacuate militarily valuable industries; and to destroy all communications and transportation installations, food, and water they could not take with them. Roads and bridges were to be mined.

Fifth and Eighth Armies were to advance against the delaying Germans abreast. They would be controlled by the Fifteenth Army Group and their respective objectives were to be Naples and the airfields in the vicinity of Foggia. On 18 September Clark conferred with his major commanders and key staff regarding the coming operations, and it was decided that Ten Corps would fight its way through the passes leading to the Plain of Naples. Once in the open, McCreery could deploy his armor to take Naples and drive north to the Volturno. VI Corps would make a flanking movement through the mountains to the east; take a line running along Route 7 through Avellino,

Montemarano, and Teora; and maintain contact with Eighth Army on the right.

In developing his part of the general plan, McCreery decided that each of three task forces would clear a pass leading north from the beachhead onto the Plain of Naples. The Fifty-sixth Division would clear the pass running north out of Salerno and turn west at Sanseverino and Castel San Giorgio. The Forty-sixth Division would clear the pass running north out of Vietri. Darby and his composite force would assist the Forty-sixth's advance by breaking out of Chiunzi Pass and seizing the Pagani defile, which formed the north end of the Vietri-Pagani Pass. In so doing, the Rangers would also secure a bridgehead on the Maiori-Pagani road at the north gate of Chiunzi Pass. The Twenty-third Armoured Brigade and its reinforcements were then to debouch through the bridgehead and onto the plain, to capture the defile with the Rangers' aid. As planning progressed, however, more emphasis was placed on the Forty-sixth Division's role and less on that of the Rangers. Once the Forty-sixth had secured the Vietri Pass as far as Nocera, the Seventh Armoured Division was to pass through it and take the high ground above Pagani, previously a Ranger objective. Most of Ten Corps's artillery would support the Forty-sixth Division.

Ten Corps's attack began at 0330 on 23 September. Although there were only a few miles between the line of departure and the Plain of Naples, progress was slow. Many of Ten Corps's problems were caused by the terrain—the passes were narrow, steeply walled, and densely settled, thus favoring the defenders by canalizing the attackers and restricting their mobility. During the first day, the Fifty-sixth Division gained little ground and the Forty-sixth Division was only able to reach the outskirts of Cava, about one mile north of Vietri. Even the Rangers failed to make gains.

Very little progress was made during the next several days. The Rangers made no gains on 24 September and were stopped again the following day by a well-dug-in enemy on Monte San Angelo di Cava, the major hill mass between the northern

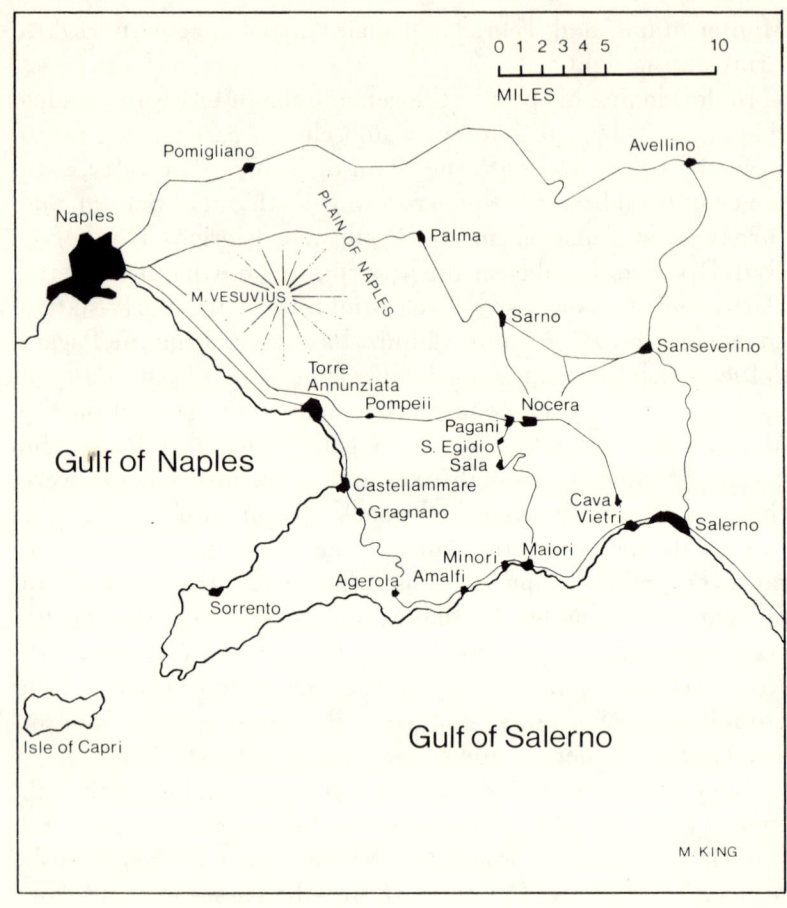

11. Sites of Importance in the Drive on Naples.

reaches of the Chiunzi and Vietri-Nocera passes.

Ten Corps's slow progress led Clark to reinforce it and make some changes. At 0810 on 26 September he spoke to Maj. Gen. Matthew B. Ridgway by telephone, gave him command over

Ranger Force, and released to him all those units of the Eighty-second Airborne Division which he could transport to the battle site. This should not be seen as reflecting adversely upon Darby. Inasmuch as the bulk of the Eighty-second was being shifted to the area held by Ranger Force, it was proper that the division's commander take over in the sector.

Ridgway designated his command the Eighty-second Airborne Division, Reinforced, and divided it into eastern and western sectors. Darby would be in command of the eastern sector and would retain Ranger Force less the Twenty-third Armoured Brigade; the 504th Parachute Infantry; and the 80th Antiaircraft Battalion minus Batteries "A," "B" and "C." In the western sector, Col. James M. Gavin would command the 505th Parachute Infantry, 376th Field Artillery Battalion, 320th Field Artillery Battalion, Company "H" of the 504th Parachute Infantry, Batteries "B" and "C" of the 80th Antiaircraft Battalion, and a small number of divisional troops. The Twenty-third Armoured Brigade and troops not assigned to either sector would form the division reserve.

A great deal of patrolling took place on 26 September, and Ranger night patrols reported the enemy in occupation of Sala and Egidio but few enemy in Pagani and Nocera. Thus armed with knowledge of the German dispositions, the Eighty-second Airborne Division began its general advance on the night of 27 September with the main attack taking place in Chiunzi Pass and a secondary attack along the Agerola-Gragnano road. The advance met only light opposition and the Twenty-third Armoured Brigade was able to debouch onto the Plain of Naples on 28 September. After passing through Sala, it turned west and reached Castellammare that evening after taking Angri and San Antonio. By the following evening it had patrols in Torre Annunziata. The progress of Ridgway's troops helped the Forty-sixth Division to advance three miles. Although the Forty-sixth was still several miles short of Nocera, McCreery sent the Seventh Armoured Division forward through it. In the face of this pressure and the threat posed by VI Corps, which was approaching Avellino, the Germans withdrew from Sanseverino and the Fifty-sixth Division was able to advance to the north.

With the plain open to the Allied advance, Ridgway briefly cast the Rangers in a less active role. At 0600 on 29 September all three Ranger battalions, two companies of the Eighty-third Chemical Battalion minus one section, and Company "H" of the Thirty-sixth Engineers were temporarily placed in the Eighty-second Airborne Division reserve under Darby's command. They followed the main drive into Naples, entering that city on 2 October.

Their immediate combat roles over, the Eighty-second Airborne Division and Ranger Force, together with their attached units, were relieved from attachment to Ten Corps on 3 October and brought under the control of Fifth Army. Later that day, all three Ranger battalions went to Castellammare. On 8 October the Rangers were detached from the Eighty-second Airborne Division and assigned to Fifth Army's reserve. Three days later, Darby received a letter from Fifth Army informing him that while no specific mission was being planned for the Rangers, several were being considered. In view of this, Darby was directed to have two of his battalions ready for combat by 20 October and the third ready by 27 October.

The Winter Line

Eisenhower's planners had overoptimistically expected the Germans to withdraw north to a line anchored on Pisa and Rimini soon after the establishment of the Allied beachhead in the Salerno area. Kesselring, however, was equally optimistic and believed that he could hold the Bernhard Line for six to nine months. Meanwhile, the Germans continued to delay northward as scheduled. As the autumn rains began to fall, the Germans replaced their mobile troops with infantry better suited to mountain fighting. By the time Fifth Army approached the Winter Line at the end of October, its six divisions were opposed by five German divisions, one of which was in reserve. Although the Allies enjoyed numerical superiority, they lacked the overwhelming advantage which is usually necessary to conduct a successful frontal attack on prepared positions. Nonetheless, they still planned to try.

The Mignano Gap, which was the southern entrance to the Liri Valley, the gateway to Rome, was Fifth Army's immediate objective on the Winter Line. The gap was what its name implies—a break in the mountains upon which the Winter Line was based—and as such it was dominated by high ground to its right and left. Differences in elevation between the valleys and the surrounding heights were no less extreme than those which the Rangers had seen at Chiunzi Pass. The nearby Volturno River stood at 130 meters above sea level and the valley through which it flowed was relatively flat, seldom rising as much as 40 meters higher than the river. The valley which formed the Mignano Gap ran northwesterly from the generally north-south Volturno Valley, and was level with it. The high ground which formed the walls of the valleys occasionally rose 1,000 meters above sea level, or nearly 900 meters above the valley floors. To the right, or northeast of the Mignano Gap and extending about ten miles from southeast to northwest, was a chain of mountains formed by the high ground above Presenzano, and Monte Cesina, Cannavinelle hill, Monte Rotondo, Monte Lungo, and Monte Sammucro. To the left, or southwest of the Mignano Gap, were Monte Camino, Monte la Difensa, and Monte Maggiore. These stony peaks, from which the earth had been washed by millennia of erosion, rose in gray contrast above the fertile, relatively well vegetated and populated lowlands, giving the men who held the heights clear views and fields of fire over the Volturno Valley, Highway 6, and the Mignano Gap. If the road to Rome was to be opened, the high ground which controlled it would have to be taken.

Responsibility for securing the gap was divided between Ten Corps, which was to take the high ground to the left of the gap, and VI Corps, which was to take the high ground to the right.

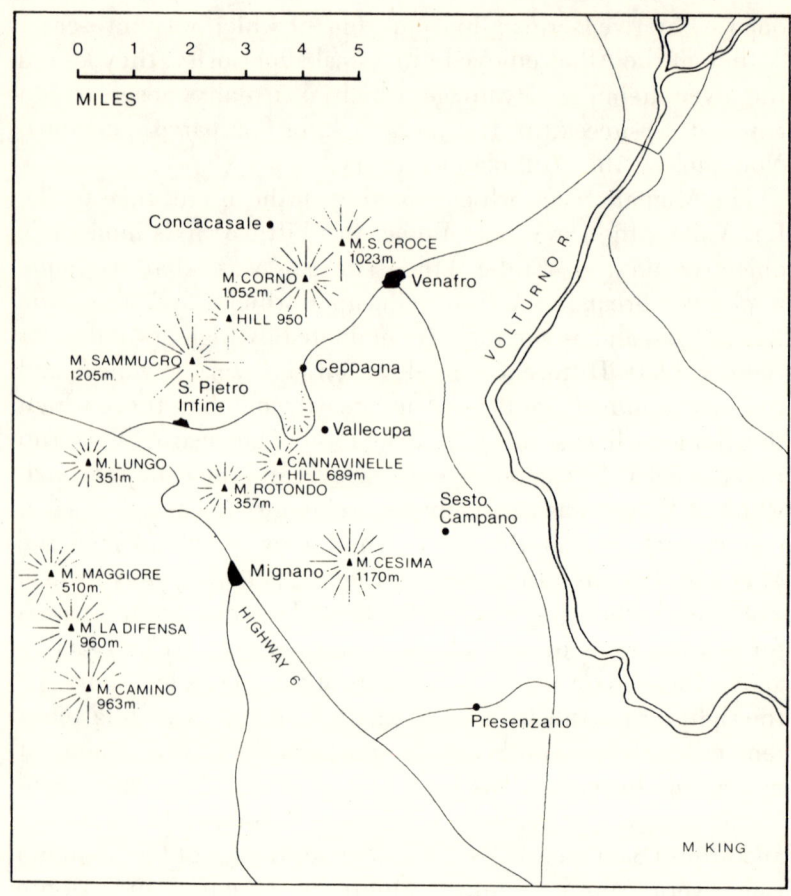

12. Ranger Battle Sites on the Winter Line showing High Ground Important to Ranger Operations.

The Third, Forty-fifth and Thirty-fourth Infantry Divisions would attack in VI Corps's sector, with the First and Fourth Ranger Battalions accompanying the Forty-fifth Infantry Division.

The task of assaulting the Winter Line was complicated by geography. The Volturno River flowed southwesterly across the right half of VI Corps's front and then veered south to split the corps in two. The Third Infantry Division, to the left and outside the Volturno's loop, would be able to advance without having to cross the river.The Forty-fifth and Thirty-fourth Infantry Divisions, caught inside the loop, would have to make a river crossing to reach the Winter Line.

At 0100 on 1 November, Murray's Fourth Ranger Battalion was removed from Darby's control and attached to VI Corps in anticipation of the attack. Shortly after noon on the following day, VI Corps issued orders outlining how it would cross the Volturno and seize a line based upon Isernia, Monte Tassero, Cervaro, and Mignano while maintaining contact with Eighth Army on its right. The Forty-fifth Infantry Division was to cross the Volturno after 1900 on 3 November, seize the high ground in the vicinity of Ceppagna and north of Venafro, continue its advance to the north, and take the high ground west of Acquafondaia and to the south and east of Cardito. The Fourth Ranger Battalion would cross the Volturno at about 1730 on 3 November, seize the high ground near Vallecupa, and block Highway 6 southwest of Monte Rotondo.[7] This would open a way to the Mignano Gap which would bypass the hill mass stretching from Presanzano to Monte Lungo, and would cut the principal route of withdrawal for those Germans defending the gap to the south.

On the day the Rangers were to go into combat, there was concern at Fifth Army over the attrition they had suffered and their need for replacements. Although replacements were arriving at army, they were not filtering down to the Rangers. By 3 November the Thirty-fourth, Thirty-sixth and Forty-fifth Infantry Divisions were overstrength and replacements were available for the Third Infantry Division, although it had not yet received them. Lt. Col. Robert J. Wood, of Fifth Army G-3, pointed out to Fifth Army's chief of staff that the problem of Ranger replacements had "not been solved too well in the past," and proposed that a number of men in the Twenty-ninth Replacement Battalion be earmarked for the Rangers. These men, he continued, could be selected and trained by a Ranger cadre of three officers and nine NCOs. Brig. Gen. Donald W. Brann, Fifth Army G-3, wanted the cadre drawn from a single Ranger battalion which would be held in reserve. Darby, on the other hand, wanted the cadre drawn from all three battalions. In that way, no one battalion would be so weakened that it would have to be taken off the line, and all three battalions could be committed as a single unit if they were needed. Indeed, if one battalion was regularly held in Fifth Army reserve, that fact would weaken any argument that the three Ranger battalions were one unit and should have their own permanent headquarters. In the end, an unsatisfactory compromise was reached. No battalion was put into permanent reserve for training purposes, but the three battalions were not used as one. The detachment of the Fourth Ranger Battalion for use in the opening battle on the Winter Line was a case in point.

The Fourth Ranger Battalion crossed the Volturno uneventfully at 1800 on 3 November, and by 0800 the following morning was engaged in combat with the Germans. By 0400 on 6 November the Fourth Rangers had lost seven dead, nine missing, and twenty-one wounded. They had not been resupplied with rations or ammunition for over eighty hours. Under these circumstances, Murray asked corps to relieve his battalion. His request was granted later in the day and the Rangers were able to withdraw to Sesto Campana at 1500 after being relieved by units of the Thirtieth Infantry Regiment.

Early in the afternoon of 8 November Brann asked Darby to alert the First Ranger Battalion and its attached units to report to Lucas, and several hours later the First Rangers became attached to the Forty-fifth Infantry Division. The following morning the Forty-fifth's G-3 asked Murray to report to him, and told Darby that the Fourth Ranger Battalion was being detached from Ranger Force by corps order. Darby, apprehensive that the depleted battalion would be sent back into combat, warned Martin that it was short of many weapons and "not in good shape." However, the decision to use both the First and Fourth Ranger Battalions in the attack had already been reached at corps and Darby's admonition had no effect.[8]

On the same day, corps ordered the 45th Infantry Division to seize and hold a two-mile-long ridge which ran on a north-south axis to the immediate west of Ceppagna. In fact, part of the ridge was already occupied; the northern half was held by the 1st Battalion of the 180th Infantry, which would be relieved by the 1st Ranger Battalion. The southern half was unoccupied and would be taken by the 4th Ranger Battalion. At 1400 that afternoon, Murray's battalion moved out with one company of the 83rd Chemical Battalion and a mine-sweeping squad from the 120th Engineer Battalion to take the southern stretch of the ridge. They met no Germans, occupied their objective during the night, and began sending patrols to the north and west in the direction of Monte Sammucro. By 0925 the next morning, the battalion established a roadblock where the Ceppagna-San Pietro Infine road skirted the southern tip of the ridge they occupied. Thus far, all had gone smoothly. As in the crossing of the Volturno, however, the battalion's easy start would prove to be the prelude to tough fighting.

Darby's First Ranger Battalion arrived near Sesto Campana during the night of 8 November and began to relieve the First Battalion, 180th Infantry, on the afternoon of the following day. When the relief was completed, the First and Fourth Ranger Battalions were roughly abreast, although thinly spread out. Darby's battalion had had as easy a time as Murray's. During the night of 9 November the First Rangers saw little activity beyond the firing of the Eighty-third Chemical Battalion's mortars and the surrender of one German.

The Rangers spent the first few days consolidating their positions and receiving reinforcements. On the afternoon of 10 November, corps attached the 509th Parachute Infantry

Battalion to the Forty-fifth Infantry Division, which in turn transferred the men to Darby's command. Darby put them on line the next morning.

For the next several days the First and Fourth Rangers were under heavy German counterattack. Darby, whose battalion had had an easier time than Murray's, wanted the Fourth Rangers to have as much rest as possible on 14 November, and arranged to have the First Ranger Battalion take over patrolling their sector to prevent the Germans from infiltrating. Early on the morning of the 14th, Darby had Murray's battalion pulled off the line completely. It was relieved by the Third Battalion, 180th Infantry, that night and became attached to the First Ranger Battalion.

The Rangers were not alone in having had a difficult time. On 13 November Clark told Alexander that continued frontal attacks would exhaust Fifth Army and, with Alexander's approval, he halted offensive operations two days later. A two-week period of reorganization and reinforcement followed. On 16 November the Thirty-sixth Infantry Division began to reinforce the Third Infantry Division, which was temporarily taken off the line to receive new men and equipment, and on the following day it was made responsible for the Mignano area. On 18 November Maj. Gen. Geoffrey T. Keyes's II Corps headquarters arrived in the Mignano area and took control of both the Thirty-sixth and Third Infantry Divisions. Fifth Army thus formed a three-corps front, and II Corps's front was narrowed. In VI Corps, Middleton was replaced as Forty-fifth Infantry Division commander by Maj. Gen. William W. Eagles, and returned to the United States. The First Armored Division, which had no opportunity to exercise its mobility on the Winter Line, would remain in army reserve until open terrain and a more fluid situation permitted its use. Sorely needed reinforcements also arrived in November and December.

On 16 November units of Fifth Army were notified that army would hold its positions, regroup its forces, and prepare to launch an attack on or about 30 November. While preparing, army would aggressively probe the Germans' defenses to prevent them from resting.

With Fifth Army's offensive temporarily at a halt, Darby attempted to have the depleted Fourth Ranger Battalion replaced by the Third Ranger Battalion. His request was approved by the Forty-fifth Infantry Division and VI Corps but was rejected by Fifth Army, which had other plans for the Third Rangers. This demonstrates how little control Darby had over the three Ranger battalions. For the time being, the Fourth Ranger Battalion would remain attached to and continue to reinforce the First Rangers.

The First Ranger Battalion had little contact with the enemy during the first days of Fifth Army's rest and reorganization. By 20 November, however, enemy activity and infiltration began to increase and Darby thought the Germans might be growing more aggressive. The Rangers fought to dislodge those Germans who were dug in dangerously close, but had only mixed success.

By 22 November the Fourth Ranger Battalion was back in action. The battalion's Companies "A" and "C" were moved up to protect the First Ranger Battalion's left flank while the First Rangers continued to clear the Germans off Monte Corno. Company "A" performed especially valuable service during the operation by driving the enemy off the American side of the hill with mortar fire and sniping. Companies "B" and "C" contributed to the effort by establishing an outpost line on the southern slope of Monte Corno. Although the Fourth Ranger Battalion was able to assist Darby considerably, it had not yet recovered from its opening battle on the Winter Line. Lt. Walter F. Nye, who prepared the daily G-3 periodic report, noted that the battalion's morale was good but its combat efficiency poor due to recent losses.

The Winter Line was taking its toll of the First Ranger Battalion as well; 21 and 22 November had cost the battalion nine killed and nineteen wounded. Nor did it appear that the casualties would stop.

Seven days of almost incessant German counterattacks on the

Rangers' positions came to an end on 27 November. Official records, which are incomplete, show that the Rangers lost more than seventy killed and wounded during the week-long battle. Ironically, the official history prepared by Martin Blumenson ignores the fighting and refers to the second two weeks of November as "The Lull."

Respite came the following day. At 1203 on 28 November the Fourth Ranger Battalion was relieved by the Third Battalion, 180th Infantry, and moved to Caiazzo, about twenty-seven miles to the south. Upon arrival, the battalion was detached from the 45th Infantry Division and VI Corps and came under control of Fifth Army. For the First Ranger Battalion, which remained on line, a true lull finally began.

An episode that took place during the battle which had just ended is noteworthy because of the insight it provides into Darby's views on leadership and human nature. One day while Maj. William S. Hutchinson, the executive officer of the Eighty-third Chemical Battalion, was lying prone on the ground adjusting artillery fire on the Germans, Darby walked up next to him and carried on a conversation standing in full view of the enemy. It was one of about a dozen occasions in which Darby needlessly and casually exposed himself to the enemy in Hutchinson's presence. Why did he do it? Hutchinson thought that "Darby was deathly afraid that his troops would show fear," and encourage the enemy. This could be fatal in the case of the Rangers because of their small numbers and light weapons. As their leader, Darby had to show courage in front of his men as a way of inspiring them to act bravely. Darby thus seems to have possessed certain attributes of the "military mind" as described by Samuel P. Huntington. According to the latter, "the military view of man is ... decidedly pessimistic," and maintains that "man's weakness makes successful conflict dependent upon organization, discipline, and leadership." By his actions, Darby continually acknowledged the importance of all three of these elements.

With the Fourth Ranger Battalion resting, Murray prepared a

letter outlining problems which the Rangers had encountered since their inception and submitted it to the War Department "for the betterment of Ranger activities." He began by pointing out that the Rangers did not have "a clear cut directive" defining their purpose and were thus "hampered in long-range planning." One such directive had been issued on 1 June 1942, but it had said that they were to be organized as a "commando unit for training and demonstration purposes."[9] Their introduction into combat as a unit during TORCH had marked a departure from this original purpose and no consistent written or unwritten policy ever replaced it. Several problems resulted.

The first and "most pressing problem" was the replacement of casualties. After losing well-trained men in combat, the battalions had to remain out of action for a month or more to receive replacements and train them to Ranger standards. Murray saw hope in the fact that the Second and Fifth Ranger Battalions had been activated on 1 April and 1 August, respectively, at Camp Forrest, Tennessee. If some of their trainees could be diverted to the First, Third and Fourth Rangers, Darby's battalions could continue as "an effective fighting force without interruption."

The second problem, closely related to the first, concerned the advancement of junior Ranger officers and the retention and use of experienced Ranger officers who were unfit for further combat because of wounds and other physical disabilities. Murray recommended that the former be given command of new Ranger battalions and that the latter be sent to Camp Forrest to train replacements. These measures would allow the younger men to advance but would not force the more experienced men out of the Rangers.

A third problem was the absence of a Ranger Force headquarters "to handle the administrative problems, intelligence, long-range planning, the allocation of assignments to the various battalions, and, most important, to decide if the assignment is a proper one for the Rangers." The need for such a headquarters had become more urgent since the formation of the Second and Fifth Ranger Battalions. Murray recommended that the headquarters be given to Darby, "the senior Battalion Commander of Rangers," and "the best suited man for such a position" he knew. The fact that Murray described Darby as the Rangers' senior battalion commander rather than as Ranger Force commander suggests the flimsiness of Darby's control over the battalions which he had organized.

No documents are present in the Rangers' files to indicate that the War Department ever responded to Murray's letter.

While the First and Fourth Ranger Battalions were under Darby's command and repelling German counterattacks, the Third Ranger Battalion was preparing to take part in separate operations under Dammer's command. Between 29 November and 13 December the battalion conducted two reconnaissances in force against San Pietro Infine, and an attack and a defense near Monte Sammucro. On the night of 13 December the Third Rangers were taken off the line and sent into bivouac near Venafro.

While the Third Ranger Battalion was conducting operations in the San Pietro Infine area, the First Ranger Battalion was on the defense. The First Rangers' front had become relatively quiet, and their journal reflects little combat activity from 29 November through 14 December beyond the loss of two dead and three wounded from artillery fire, and the slaying of six Germans who ventured too close to the battalion's positions. Most of the other journal entries are minutiae. We read, for example, that Darby had diarrhea on 30 November and sent his medical officer to inspect the mess's sanitation. On 4 December he put two men to work on the production of a Ranger Christmas card. The next day he sent an officer to "eat the ass out of the cooks" and teach them the right way to prepare ham. A class on ham cooking began the next morning. Although the period was quiet, it was punctuated by an event of great importance for Darby; on 11 December he was finally promoted to colonel.

On the morning of 13 December the Third Battalion, 180th

Infantry began to relieve the First Ranger Battalion, and at 0600 the following morning the Rangers were relieved from attachment to VI Corps and reverted to the control of Fifth Army. By 15 December all three Ranger battalions had assembled at Lucrino. It was the first time they had been together at one place and were all under Darby's command since the landing at Salerno. Their purpose in gathering was to prepare for the landing at Anzio. Unknown to any of them, it would be their last landing and the prelude to their last battle, Cisterna di Littoria.

The way in which Darby and his Rangers were used from the time they landed at Salerno until they were pulled out of the Winter Line to prepare for Anzio was of great significance. Although their initial landing and the seizure of Chiunzi Pass were missions appropriate to their training and self-concept as American commandos, the missions they subsequently performed inland were suitable for any conventional infantry unit of the same size.

Why this apparent misuse of a specialized unit? Clark answered this question when I posed it to him during an interview by saying that "the overwhelming need" at the time "was to fill gaps in the line," and that holding special troops in reserve until special missions presented themselves was an unaffordable luxury. Clark's answer was an expression of a general truth that was being brought home to the Rangers with ever greater frequency. While the increasing complexity of modern warfare was leading to a growing number of specialized individuals and units, necessity often dictated that those same individuals and units perform duties which differed from the tasks they were originally created to perform. Clark's use of musicians as infantry on Piccolo Hill was only one of the most extreme illustrations of this development.

While the fighting on the Winter Line had been professionally frustrating for Darby, his reputation continued to grow among those with whom he served. Clark greatly admired Darby's fighting abilities and later identified him in lectures as being one of the three top combat leaders he had known, along with Col. Reuben Tucker of the 504th Parachute Infantry and Col. William Yarbrough of the 509th Parachute Infantry. None of the three were "intellectual giants or Phi Betta Kappas," Clark observed , but lofty mental ability was never a guarantee of success in combat.

As in earlier campaigns, Darby continued to endear himself to his men. While not above stowing an occasional steak away for his personal enjoyment, he avoided the more brazen displays of privilege which too often breed resentment within the enlisted ranks. Melvin Dodge, who was first scout for Company "C" of the Third Ranger Battalion, witnessed a minor drama in which Darby impressed his philosophy of leadership upon a captain who had joined the Rangers when they came out of the Venafro sector. The captain, who firmly believed upon his arrival that rank had its privileges, was seen by Darby moving ahead those of lower rank to the front of the chow line. Darby promptly told him that in the Rangers no man was better than any other and sent him to the back of the line.

Thomas Prudhomme of the Third Ranger Battalion's Company "D" saw a similar incident. On an especially cold, damp Italian winter day, when there was supposedly no milk or cream to be had at the mess tent, Darby saw a number of officers drinking suspiciously lightened coffee. When Darby asked them what was "wrong" with their coffee and they seemed puzzled, he scolded them, saying, "I don't see how in the hell you can drink that coffee without it being black. Everyone else has black coffee." Shamefacedly, the offending officers spilled their creamed coffee out and replaced it with black. "And that's the way Colonel Darby was," Prudhomme mused thirty-five years later. "How can you keep from loving a man like that?"

VI

Anzio and Cisterna di Littoria

The Genesis of SHINGLE

On 8 November 1943, when the Rangers were just beginning their struggle on the Winter Line, Eisenhower authorized Alexander to begin planning an amphibious landing in the Rome area. Alexander relayed his own instructions to Fifth Army the same day. In them, he designated Anzio as the landing site. Situated about thirty miles south of Rome, Anzio possessed good beaches and a sheltered port, and was situated on a coastal plain which would facilitate maneuver inland. Furthermore, good roads linked Anzio to the Alban Hills, about twenty miles inland. The Alban Hills stood between Highways 6 and 7, the two major roads to Rome from the south, and formed the last natural barrier which the Germans could use to defend Rome against the northward moving Allies. Alexander believed that a landing at Anzio followed by a drive on the Alban Hills would cause German resistance in the south to collapse, leaving Rome open to Fifth Army. Furthermore, inasmuch as the fighting to the south was becoming stalemated, it was hoped that the capture of Rome would be a psychological tonic to the Allies and a blow to German confidence. Clark, as Fifth Army commander, was given primary responsibility for planning the operation, which was code-named SHINGLE.

The landing force would be headed by the United States VI

Corps Headquarters under Maj. Gen. John P. Lucas. The American units originally scheduled to land were the 3rd Infantry Division, 504th Parachute Infantry, and Ranger Force. Ranger Force, consisting of the three Ranger battalions and their organic and attached units, was redesignated the 6615th Ranger Force (Provisional) for SHINGLE. The British units scheduled to land were the 1st Division and two Commandos formed into a special service brigade. Clark would add part of the 1st Armored Division and a regiment of the 45th Infantry Division in follow-up roles when additional transports and landing craft became available. The rest of the 1st Armored and 45th Infantry Divisions would form a reserve to be used only if needed to help establish or hold the beachhead.

On 15 January IV Corps published Field Order Nineteen, which laid down the plan for SHINGLE. The British First Division would land on Peter Beach, a 1½-mile-long stretch about five miles northwest of Anzio. The Third Infantry Division would land at X-ray Beach, a two-mile-long stretch less than three miles east of Anzio and about two miles east of Nettuno. Nettuno was to become the site of VI Corps's headquarters.

Ranger Force—which consisted of a force headquarters; the 1st, 3rd and 4th Ranger Battalions; 509th Parachute Infantry Battalion; 83rd Chemical Battalion, minus Companies "C" and "D"; Company "H" of the Thirty-sixth Engineer Combat Regiment; a twenty-seven man detachment of the 57th Signal Battalion; and a three-man detachment of the 163rd Signal Photography Company—would land directly in Anzio at 0200 on D-day. The beach the Rangers were to land on was code-named Yellow Beach. It was a typical sand bathing beach about half a mile long, occupying most of Anzio's frontage on the Tyrrhenian Sea. In order of priority, Ranger Force would seize the port facilities at Anzio and protect them from sabotage; destroy enemy gun batteries in the vicinity of Anzio; clear the beach area between Anzio and Nettuno; secure and establish a beachhead; and contact the British First Division on the left and

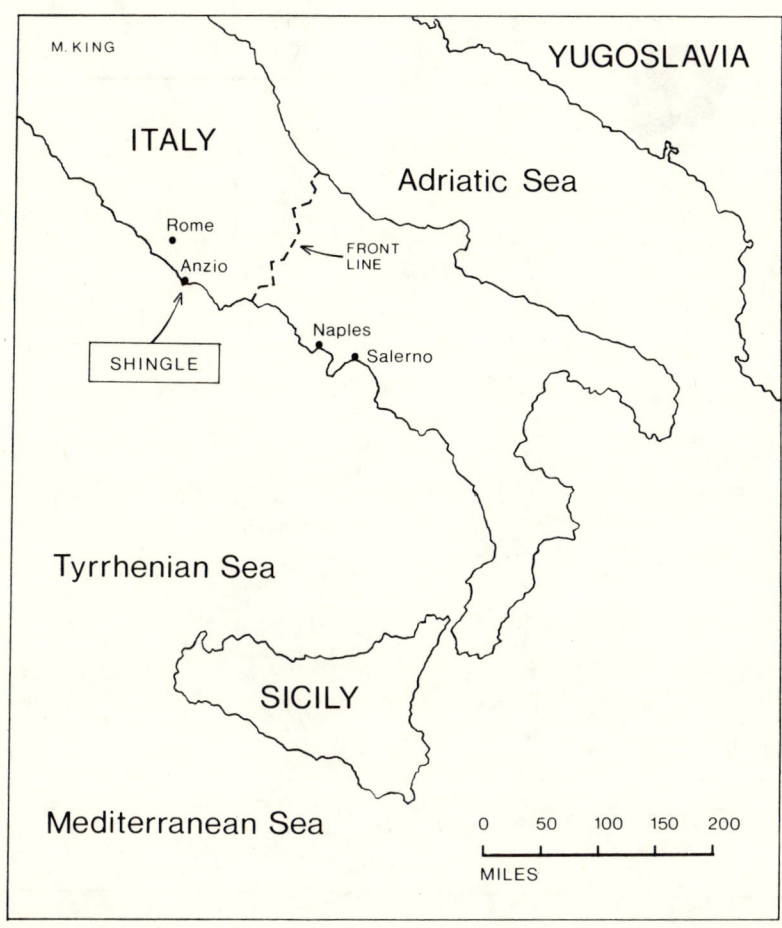

13. Military Situation in Italy at the Time of the Landing at Anzio.

the Third Infantry Division on the right. Upon contacting the Third, Ranger Force would become attached to it.[1]

In detail, the First Ranger Battalion would land on the right

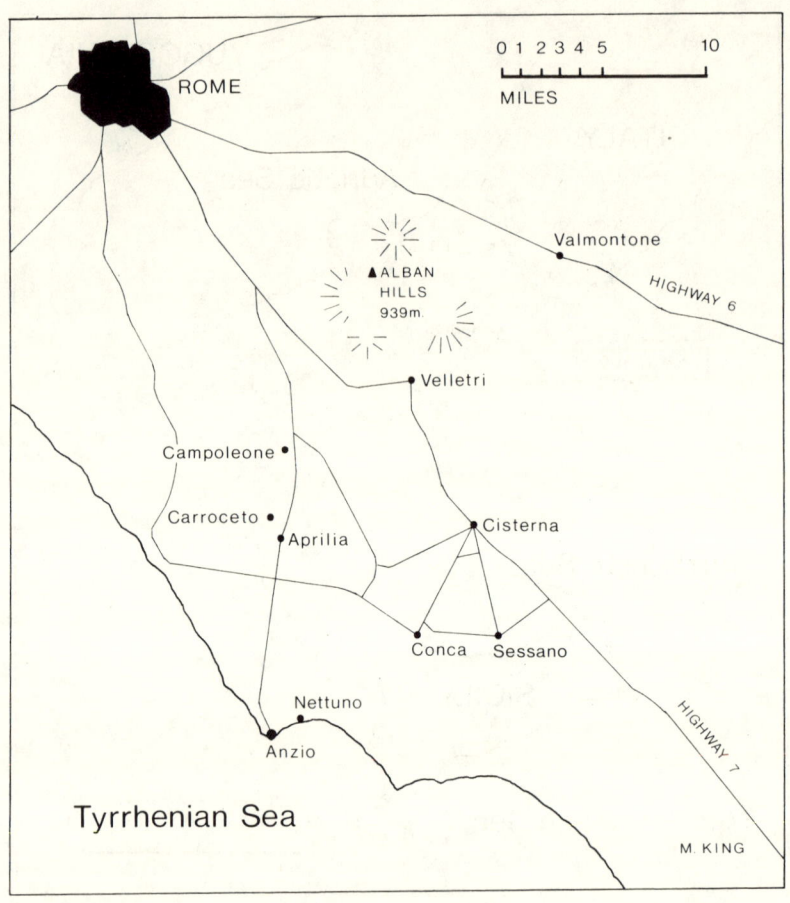

14. Anzio and Sites of Greatest Military Importance.

half of Yellow Beach at H-hour, destroy coastal defenses and other installations within its sector, and establish a beachhead. The Fourth Ranger Battalion had an identical mission on the left half of Yellow Beach.

Companies "A" and "B" of the Eighty-third Chemical Battalion would land on Yellow Beach one hour later and take up firing positions.

The Third Ranger Battalion would land on Yellow Beach two hours after the First and Fourth Ranger Battalions, pass through the Fourth Rangers, clear the town of Anzio of the enemy, and destroy coastal defenses and other enemy installations in its sector.

The 509th Parachute Infantry would land on Yellow Beach at the same time as the Third Ranger Battalion, assemble for possible use as Ranger Force's reserve, and be prepared to clear the beach area between Anzio and Nettuno and to attack Nettuno on force order.

Company "H" of the Thirty-sixth Engineer Combat Regiment would clear the beach of mines, wire and obstacles; prepare exits from the beach; establish roadblocks; and supervise the subsequent debarkation of men and material.[2]

Yellow Beach was about forty yards deep, covered by rough sand, and backed by a sea wall which varied in height from three to six feet. It was flanked by a jetty to the west and a stone pier to the east. Due to the beach's slight gradient, the landing would involve about 150 yards of wading. Fortunately, there seemed to be no fixed defenses on the beach, although a dual purpose battery and a suspected coastal defense battery in the British sector and two light coastal guns in the Third Infantry Division sector were probably capable of firing on Yellow Beach and its approaches. Reports indicated that the beach was seeded with Teller mines, but the mine fields were not large and there seemed to be gaps between them.

Remembering the landing at Gela, where guide boats which were to have led the Rangers to the beach failed to be in position, Darby insisted that the planning for Anzio be accompanied by close army-navy coordination. Fortunately, a Captain Lewis, the naval officer in charge of the Anzio planning staff at Caserta, agreed and cooperated wholeheartedly. "This time you are going to have the guide boats there," he promised

Darby. "I will have a man sitting off the end of that dock waving you in."

To insure that Lewis's promises would be fulfilled, the Rangers conducted a practice landing with their naval support on the night of 17 January at Pozzuoli Bay to the immediate west of Naples. The landing was part of a Third Infantry Division exercise intended as a rehearsal for Anzio. Illustrating the closeness of army-navy coordination, Darby later said that the navy "ate in my mess and we got to know each other by the first name and had dinner together and a drink or so. And then we felt we would see those people there...."

Darby was very specific about where he wanted the Rangers landed on D-day. "I kept telling Captain Lewis," he later recalled, "that when I ran out of the landing craft, I didn't want to look to the right or left ... I'll be going so fast that I want to make sure that when I hit the beach and start running, that I will run right through the front door" of a large, white casino that dominated the beach. The casino Darby was speaking about was still the most prominent building on the beach when I visited Anzio thirty-three years later. It had been transformed into an Italian navy headquarters.

Although the exercise at Pozzuoli Bay was a fine example of planning and coordination on Darby's part, it revealed a serious deterioration of the fighting skills of the Ranger battalions. Lt. Col. Roy W. Kenny, a Forty-fifth Infantry Division artillery officer who acted as chief umpire for the exercise, thought the operation was generally successful and "was much impressed by the enthusiasm and spirit displayed by everyone." However, he noted numerous violations of tactical principles and sound combat techniques. For example, the First Ranger Battalion became congested shortly after landing; several of its companies made excessive noise when they were to have been practicing stealth; one-third of its men moved when flares were fired, an action that would have made them more visible to the enemy in the dark; it established itself in an indefensible position; and it failed to send local security forward after moving inland. The

Third Ranger Battalion performed much better and was criticized only for having its landing craft too close together and moving in flarelight. The Fourth Ranger Battalion combined several potentially fatal errors. In addition to moving in flarelight, it travelled up a road in column without sending an advance guard forward, and went through a defile seventy-five yards long without first reconnoitering it. Either one of the latter two practices could have led the battalion into an ambush. Furthermore, the battalion failed to establish communications with Force Headquarters.

The number and gravity of the Rangers' errors demonstrated the decline in quality which had taken place since their formation and early training in Northern Ireland and Scotland. The conventional fighting to which the Rangers had too often been committed had cost them dearly in the lives of trained and experienced men. The vacancies were filled by replacements who were highly motivated, but who received nothing equal to the time and training that had been lavished on their predecessors.

The formation of the 6615th Ranger Force (Provisional) finally gave Darby his coveted separate headquarters, but it also caused a change of leadership within Ranger Force just before a major landing—a condition which further weakened the Rangers' fighting ability. When Darby left the First Ranger Battalion to become force commander and Dammer left the Third Ranger Battalion to become force executive officer, their battalions were taken over by Majors Jack Dobson and Alvah Miller, respectively. Murray remained in command of the Fourth Ranger Battalion.

Miller had served as Dammer's executive officer and fit in easily as the Third Rangers' commander. Dobson's appointment, however, caused some resentment. A West Pointer, he had made the mistake of joining the Tank Destroyer Corps when that branch was touted as being the nemesis of German armor. But as the war progressed the army discovered that the best antitank weapon was another tank, and the Tank Destroyer

Corps's importance and attractiveness to career officers waned. Dobson, who was thus caught in a dying branch when the army as a whole was expanding, was "looking for a place to go" at Fifth Army Headquarters when Darby invited him to join Ranger Force. Until then, the noncommissioned and officer leadership of the Rangers had generally been promoted from within the force, and Dobson's academy background gave rise to suspicions that Darby was helping a fellow West Pointer to the detriment of his Ranger officers' careers.

Their suspicions may have been justified. Darby's selection of Dobson as a battalion commander may well have been an instance of the West Point "mutual protective association" at work, it being generally understood that academy graduates often further each other's careers in much the same way that the alumni of Harvard Business School or any other civilian university might assist each other professionally.

In view of the Rangers' difficulties with ill-trained and inexperienced replacements, changes in leadership, and possible morale problems due to Dobson's assignment, it was fortunate that their landing was not expected. On 15 January Generalmajor Siegfried Westphal, Kesselring's chief of staff, told the commanders of the Tenth and Fourteenth Armies that he considered "a large-scale (Allied) landing operation as being out of the question for the next four to six weeks." The SHINGLE invasion force departed from Naples six days later and arrived off Anzio a few minutes after midnight of 21 January.

Anzio

The first assault waves headed for the beaches shortly before 0200 on the morning of 22 January. To Darby, it was the most perfect landing the Rangers had ever made. The guide boats were there and a man was at the pier to wave the Rangers in, as Lewis had promised. Darby's landing craft missed the casino by no more than ten or twenty yards and he was able to run through the building's door as he had half-jokingly told Lewis he intended to do. Two Germans met Ranger Force during the landing—one died by the knife and the other was nearly dissolved by machine gun fire—but real resistance was nil. In fact, the Germans were taken completely unawares and the landing was virtually unopposed. The only enemy fire came from a few coastal artillery and antiaircraft batteries. By 0450 Lucas felt secure enough to praise the invasion force for their "splendid landing" and encourage them to "continue the drive to make" 1944 "the year of victory."

The establishment of the initial beachhead was no more difficult than the landing, for there were only two German coast-watching battalions inland to resist the twenty-seven-battalion Allied force. The two battalions were undermanned and had come from the Gustav Line for rest and rehabilitation. They were quickly overrun.

Darby's portion of the beachhead was easily established. All Rangers were ashore by 0645 and Company "H" of the Thirty-sixth Engineer Combat Regiment was clearing the beach for subsequent landings of men and materiel by 0730. Nine enemy vehicles and four soldiers were captured, and about eight enemy killed during these early hours. At 1015 the 509th Parachute Infantry Battalion captured and occupied Nettuno, thus securing Ranger Force's right flank. The only other recorded combat activities of Ranger Force on D-day involved the seeking out and neutralizing of isolated enemy gun positions.

The other two portions of the beachhead were established with equal ease. The Third Infantry Division, landing to the south of Anzio, drove three miles inland and brought all its armor and artillery ashore by mid-morning. Taking measures to safeguard the beachhead's right flank, the division destroyed four bridges which crossed the Mussolini Canal and dug in. The British First Division, landing to the north of Anzio, was two miles inland by mid-day, and commandos cut the road leading to Albano, thus establishing a roadblock to the immediate north of the beachhead. By midnight, VI Corps had landed about 36,000 men and 3,200 vehicles, and taken 227 prisoners at a cost of 13 killed, 97 wounded, and 44 missing. The landing was an unqualified success.

Kesselring became aware of the landing an hour after it began, and concluded that it was a full-scale operation three hours later. He correctly estimated VI Corps's mission and at 0500 ordered the Fourth Parachute Division, which was being activated north of Rome, and several replacement units of the Hermann Goering Panzer Division to block the roads leading from Anzio to the Alban Hills. Additional units were summoned from the Gustav Line, northern Italy, France, Germany, and Yugoslavia. At 1700 the I Parachute Corps Headquarters arrived near Anzio and took temporary command of all German units in the area. By nightfall they succeeded in establishing a thin defensive line around the beachhead.

On 23 January Company "H" of the Thirty-sixth Engineer Combat Regiment was relieved from attachment to Ranger Force, and the Rangers, who had become attached to the Third Infantry Division on mid-morning of the previous day, were put on line to perform what had sadly become a routine task for them—serving as conventional infantry.[3] They were put on the division's extreme left flank, where they were to the immediate right of the British First Division.

During the next few days VI Corps cautiously expanded its beachhead, which had grown to be seven miles deep and sixteen miles long by 24 January. Unfortunately, Lucas hesitated to make a decisive thrust inland and gave the Germans time to gather strength. Thus, when Fourteenth Army commander Generaloberst Eberhard von Mackensen took command of the beachhead defenses from I Parachute Corps on 25 January, he had elements of eight divisions deployed and elements of five more on the way. Furthermore, Mackensen's mission was not defensive; he was to counterattack as soon as possible and to eliminate the Allied beachhead so his troops could return to the Gustav Line and to France, where an Allied cross-Channel attack was expected in the spring. The counterattack was scheduled for 2 February.

Darby was impatient with the slow progress of VI Corps's advance and correctly believed that "if everyone had moved forward from their existing positions instead of taking time to regroup," a drive inland would have been successful. Darby was not alone in his feeling; Clark had begun to register dissatisfaction with Lucas's timidity in his diary as early as 23 January.

Meanwhile, the Rangers participated in VI Corps's slow advance. By 0910 on 25 January Ranger Force reached the stream running northeast from Padiglione Woods, about nine miles inland from Anzio, and at about noon of the following day drove back a local counterattack directed against Carocetto in the British sector, taking six prisoners. By 0900 on 27 January the Rangers had advanced two and a half miles further to the north.

Cisterna di Littoria

On 28 January Clark urged Lucas to take more aggressive action, and on the following day VI Corps Headquarters published a field order outlining a major attack. According to the plan, the British First Division would make the main attack toward Albano, and the First Armored Division, minus Combat Command "B," would exploit British gains in the direction of Rome. The Third Infantry Division, with Ranger Force and the 504th Parachute Infantry Battalion attached, was to seize Cisterna di Littoria, or Cisterna, thereby cutting Highway 7, and be prepared to attack toward Valmontone.

The Third Infantry Division, which was still commanded by Maj. Gen. Lucian K. Truscott, Jr., issued its own field order on 28 January in anticipation of VI Corps's order. According to the division order, Ranger Force would cross the line of departure at 0100 on 30 January, move rapidly by infiltration to Cisterna, and seize and hold the town until relieved. The Seventh Infantry would operate on the left of Ranger Force, and the Fifteenth Infantry would operate on the right.[4]

The mission was acceptable to Darby, who did not believe that an attack the size of that about to be mounted could fail.[5] The Rangers were thus relieved from their positions on line by the British during the morning of 29 January, and the battalion commanders met with Darby at 1800 that evening to discuss Ranger Force's field order.

The force order, which was signed by Dammer and issued at Darby's command, was simple and reasonable. The First Ranger Battalion would cross the line of departure, which was a road running generally parallel to and about three and a half miles south of Highway 7, at the designated time and infiltrate to Cisterna by way of previously reconnoitered routes under cover of darkness. The terrain between the line of departure and Cisterna was flat farmland with little cover other than drainage ditches and scattered farm buildings. Because the Rangers would be vulnerable in the open country, they were to use the drainage ditches for concealment when possible, and avoid enemy contact before reaching their objective. Upon its arrival at Cisterna, the battalion was to enter the town, destroy the enemy therein, occupy the ground to the immediate northwest, and prepare to repel enemy counterattacks. At daylight it was to send a patrol to the northwest to contact the Seventh Infantry.

The Third Ranger Battalion would cross the line of departure fifteen minutes after the First Ranger Battalion cleared it, and follow the First Rangers to Cisterna. If the enemy interfered with the First Ranger Battalion, the Third Rangers were to engage them, thus freeing the First Rangers to continue their attack on Cisterna. The Third Ranger Battalion would assist in the capture of Cisterna if necessary, occupy the ground immediately northeast of town, and prepare to repel enemy counterattacks. At daylight it was to send a patrol to the northeast to contact the Fifteenth Infantry.

The Fourth Ranger Battalion, with an eight-man minesweeping party attached, would cross the line of departure at 0200 and advance on Cisterna astride the Conca-Isola Bella-Cisterna road, clearing the road of mines and enemy. Upon arriving at Cisterna, they would become part of Ranger Force's reserve.

The cannon company and a platoon of the 601st Tank Destroyer Battalion would be prepared to move on Cisterna by way of the Conca-Isola Bella-Cisterna road, and furnish antitank protection for Ranger Force once in Cisterna.

The Eighty-third Chemical Battalion would assemble on the Conca-Isola Bella-Cisterna road and be prepared to move forward to positions from which it could give fire support to the advanced units on Darby's order.[6]

Although a notation in Ranger Force's daily journal indicates that it was believed at Darby's headquarters that enemy opposition in Cisterna might be "considerable," an estimate of enemy capabilities prepared by the Third Infantry Division G-2 was optimistic and suggested that Ranger Force could accomplish its mission without undue hazard. While there was still a healthy respect for the ability of the higher German commanders and the quality of training and discipline found at battalion and company levels, it was noted that the enemy had not recently shown the same tenacity or elan which he had in the past. This was evidenced by the frequent surrender of small enemy groups and the enemy's lack of aggressive patrolling, and was believed to be due in part to the integration of Poles and other non-Germans into German units. As early as October of 1943, a VI Corps G-2 report had claimed that "the increasing number of" Wehrmacht "deserters appears to be in proportion to the increasing percentage of foreign elements arriving as replacements." VI Corps records also indicate that by the end of November 1943 a German-Polish buddy system had been put into effect in some Wehrmacht units, with Germans and Poles occupying alternate foxholes in defensive positions.

A further reason for believing the attack would be successful was the fact that the Germans facing division and to the immediate rear of Cisterna were on generally flat ground, which was not well suited for defense. However, the lower slopes of the Alban Hills, which gave good observation and could easily be defended, rose from the coastal plain a few miles to the rear of Cisterna. It was there, in the estimate of division intelligence, that the enemy would establish his main line of resistance.

In all of this analysis, one fact was ignored. Members of the Hermann Goering Panzer Division had been taken prisoner in the Cisterna area.[7] The presence of this division had usually been thought to indicate that the Germans were reinforcing their troops or preparing to mount a counterattack. Why its presence was not so interpreted this time has never been satisfactorily explained.

At 2315 Ranger Force began to move its CP forward from a location well behind the lines, and by 0125 the next morning it had reached its new site, an isolated house near the line of departure and just to the right of the Conca-Isola Bella-Cisterna road. Darby would supervise the attack from this house and, as the battle progressed, from positions forward.

The First and Third Ranger Battalions passed through the line of departure in a single file as scheduled, and began to move toward Cisterna in a ditch that offered a measure of cover and concealment. At 0248 the first of several events took place that did not augur well for the success of the mission. Four radio operators who were to have accompanied the Third Ranger Battalion reported lost to the force CP. Darby, who was all too aware of the importance of good communications, thought the loss of the radiomen "the god-damndest thing" he had "ever heard of."

A second problem developed when the Third Ranger Battalion lost contact with the First Rangers about halfway to the objective. Then, half a mile ahead, the First Rangers became split with three companies continuing to advance and three remaining in place. The dangers of conducting a night infiltration with too many relatively untrained and inexperienced men were becoming apparent.

Capt. Charles Shunstrom took command of the First Rangers' three rear companies and sent a runner back to locate the Third Ranger Battalion. The runner returned with word that Maj. Alvah Miller, the Third Rangers' commander, had been killed by a round from a German tank, and that the battalion was moving forward to reestablish contact with the First Rangers. Although the Third Rangers had been fired on and Miller killed, there had been no concerted attempt to stop the battalion and no reason to believe that the enemy was alerted to the operation. On the contrary, the First Ranger Battalion seemed to be very successful in spearheading the infiltration with stealth. Although German patrols crossed in front and on both sides of the battalion, they did not appear to be aware of the Rangers' presence. Two groups of German sentries encountered by the point were killed with knives. Lt. James G. Fowler, who led the point, slew two of the enemy personally. At about 0545, with the first light of day, the First Rangers passed close enough to an enemy artillery battery to hear the gunners' voices. They did not fire on the Germans but tried to radio Darby, failed to make contact, and continued to creep forward through some unoccupied trenches until they reached a flat field on the southern edge of Cisterna.

The field was roughly triangular in shape, being about a thousand yards long on each side, and was both surrounded and subdivided by roads and drainage ditches. The Rangers began running toward the town in the hope of reaching it before the sun rose. About six hundred yards outside Cisterna, they passed through what appeared to be a German bivouac area and killed a large number of the surprised enemy with bayonets and knives before moving on. The Rangers ran four hundred yards further when they were stopped by violent fire just outside town, and returned the German fire as well as they could from a position astride a road that paralleled a canal. The position did not provide much cover, but it was the best that was available.

The Third Ranger Battalion and the three companies of the First Ranger Battalion which had been separated were able to approach to within three hundred yards of the three lead companies before encountering any enemy. After Ranger bazooka men destroyed two German tanks which had been blocking the way, Shunstrom went forward with a runner and two other men and made contact with Dobson, who briefed him on the situation.

The Fourth Ranger Battalion began its attack up the Conca-Isola Bella-Cisterna road as scheduled, but was stopped short of Isola Bella by fire from German tanks, self-propelled guns, automatic weapons, and small arms. Cisterna was more strongly held than had been thought, and a platoon of the Third Reconnaissance Troop attempting to approach the town from the northwest later in the morning was ambushed and all but one man were lost. Darby, concerned about the virtually nonexistent communications with his two forward battalions and the "hell of a time" Murray's battalion was having, recognized the need to break through the German roadblock. Indeed, the fate of the First and Third Ranger Battalions depended on his doing so.

Although it was not fully realized at the time, the circumstances in which Darby found himself were the results of conscientious planning by the Germans and poor intelligence by the Americans. Kesselring had accurately judged Lucas to be too cautious to move directly on the Alban Hills and, instead of falling back to the high ground as the Americans had expected, he had concentrated considerable strength in Cisterna in preparation for the counterattack which had been scheduled for 2 February. The counterattack was also unexpected by American intelligence, which had interpreted German intentions in the area to be "purely defensive."[8]

Kesselring, however, foresaw the likelihood of an American attack on Cisterna and took steps to blunt it. A German officer, who participated in the battle and was later captured, stated in his interrogation that Cisterna had been reinforced on the night of 29 January in anticipation of the attack.[9] Ironically, a young Pole named Stempkofski who was serving in the Wehrmacht

Anzio and Cisterna di Littoria 155

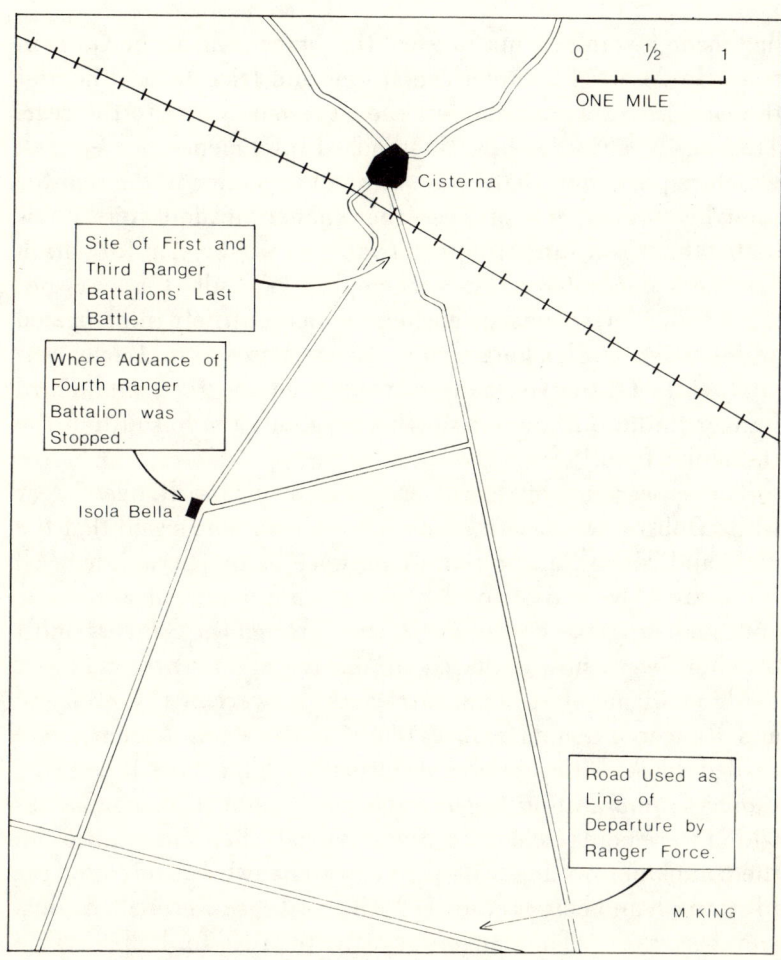

15. Sites of Importance in the Rangers' Battle for Cisterna. Minor Roads are not shown.

had made a vain attempt to warn the Americans of the German trap. He deserted to American troops and tried to tell them of the German preparations, but they evacuated him to the rear. This was in accordance with standard intelligence procedures, which require immediate evacuation of prisoners to the rear for interrogation on the premise that higher headquarters know better than front-line troops the value of whatever information prisoners might have. Thus, Stempkofski's full story was not known until after the battle when he was routinely interrogated at Fifth Army Headquarters.[10] Also unknown to Darby was another fact—the Germans had detected the First and Third Ranger Battalions moving northward about a mile south of the triangular field.[11]

The appearance of three German tanks in the Rangers' rear while Dobson was briefing Shunstrom as much as said that the First and Third Ranger Battalions were being surrounded. All three tanks were destroyed by rocket gunners, but automatic and small arms fire continued to lace through the Rangers, most of whom were now gathered in an area about three hundred yards in diameter. German attempts to overrun the Rangers, and Ranger attempts to break out of the encirclement, were turned back with reciprocal ferocity. After two hours the Rangers' ammunition began to run short and three companies which were being held in reserve gave half their ammunition to the companies on line. The Germans, meanwhile, were growing in strength and being reinforced with tanks, self-propelled guns, and flak wagons. The Rangers repeatedly called for help by radio during the battle, but it was to no avail since Darby and the rest of Ranger Force had been fought to a standstill south of Isola Bella. Isola Bella was also known as Femina Morta, the place of the dead woman.

Shortly after noon, enemy foot soldiers supported by armored personnel carriers began marching about a dozen captured Rangers toward the center of the First and Third Rangers' position in an attempt to force an American surrender. When Ranger marksmen picked off two German guards, the latter retaliated by bayonetting two of the prisoners and continued to march the rest forward. The same sequence was repeated a second time—two Germans were shot and two prisoners bayonetted. This time more Rangers surrendered. The Germans continued to march their captives, now numbering about eighty, toward the center of the Rangers' position shouting that they would shoot the prisoners if the remaining Rangers did not surrender. For a third time the surrounded Americans opened fire. When three or four prisoners were accidentally killed along with one or two Germans, "a few" men "who were evidently new to combat got hysterical and started to leave their positions and surrender." They were ordered not to give up, but continued to do so. "Even an attempt to stop them by shooting them failed." Once began, the piecemeal surrender continued.

Some cooler heads had time to disassemble their weapons and bury or scatter vital parts before the Germans overran the area. Others destroyed radios after telling Darby what was happening. Robert Ehalt, sergeant major of the First Ranger Battalion, was the last man to speak to Darby from Cisterna. He told Darby by radio that the commander of the First Rangers was wounded, the executive officer of the Third Rangers dead, that he himself had only five men left, and that German tanks were closing in. "So long, Colonel," he finally said, "maybe when it's all over I'll see you again."

Darby told Ehalt that he would never forget the surrounded men and would be with them till the end. Ehalt then destroyed the radio and continued the fight with the few men he had left. Darby, realizing that the First and Third Rangers' plight was hopeless, put his head down on his arm and broke into tears. To Sgt. Carlo Contrera, who had been Darby's jeep driver since the Rangers were first organized, it seemed that Darby "had always put the safety of his men first, and he couldn't stand the thought of what was happening to them." Cry he might—only 6 of the 767 men who infiltrated to Cisterna made their ways back from the battle. The rest were killed or captured.

The loss of the First and Third Ranger Battalions was a

traumatic experience for Darby. He blamed himself for the disaster, wrongly believing that the outcome of the operation would have been different had he been with the forward battalions.[12] He became "despondent" and "didn't want to see anyone." Some men felt the events at Cisterna had aged him.

While Darby was recovering from the experience of losing most of his command, others began to avoid responsibility for the debacle. Clark had it entered in his diary that he was "distressed to find that the 3rd (Infantry) Division had led with the Ranger force in its attack on Cisterna. This was a definite error in judgment, for the Rangers do not have the support weapons to overcome the resistance indicated."[13] Clark, who was responsible for the overall operations of Fifth Army, was not involved in the detailed planning of the attack on Cisterna and did not know that the Rangers had been chosen to lead the way.[14] Indeed, he would have been violating his own chain of command and improperly interfering had he bypassed VI Corps Headquarters to tell a division commander how to plan an attack. Giving proof to the proverb which asserts that success has many fathers while failure is an orphan, a report prepared by VI Corps's G-1 stated that had the attack on Cisterna succeeded, "it would have been a brilliant tactical move with far reaching effects.... Its failure was an incident of campaign contributed to by so many factors that it can be ascribed only to chance." The G-1 would have been more accurate if he had placed the blame on poor intelligence and Lucas's timidity.

The Rangers' fate at Cisterna illustrates the difficulties inherent in working within the army or any organization characterized by a high degree of interdependence. No matter how much effort the capable put into the performance of their duties, success depends on the wisdom and effectiveness of individuals and institutions far more influential than they. When those individuals and institutions go awry, the capable person's ability, preparation and effort count as naught. So it was at Cisterna. Uninspired generalship and poor intelligence on the American side all but guaranteed that the attack on Cisterna would fail. The new Rangers' relatively poor state of training did not cause the disaster, nor could Darby's presence with the lead battalions have prevented it. Ranger Force's failure was a consequence of failure by division and corps. While none of Darby's superiors assumed responsibility for the disaster, none of them thought to blame Darby.

VI Corps's attack came to an end on 1 February. None of the Allied commanders realized at the time that although the attack had failed, it had caused fifty-five hundred German casualties, forced the Germans to commit all their reserves, and come close to succeeding. It also pushed German plans to counterattack back two days, giving the Americans and British more time to prepare the beachhead's defenses. During VI Corps's defensive preparations, the Fourth Ranger Battalion guarded lines of communication. Ranger Force Headquarters continued to maintain an uncertain existence until the Rangers' future was decided.

The German Fourteenth Army launched a preliminary counterattack early in the morning of 4 February. It succeeded in taking a series of limited objectives and pressed on toward the sea with renewed impetus on 7 and 10 February. On the latter date the Fourth Ranger Battalion, which had been placed in division reserve, became attached to the 504th Parachute Infantry and was put on line. Fourteenth Army's major counterattack was scheduled to take place on 16 February.

The 179th Infantry

The Fourteenth Army, which by this time had 125,000 men in the Anzio area to oppose the 100,000 men of VI Corps, launched its counterattack as scheduled. The 179th Infantry Regiment of the Forty-fifth Infantry Division, which was north of Padiglione Woods, was one of the units most hard hit. On 17 February it was forced back to the final beachhead line, a last-ditch defensive perimeter that generally corresponded with the limits of the original beachhead, with heavy losses.

Darby, who had been slightly wounded by a bomb fragment on the night of 15 February, was relieved as commander of Ranger Force on 17 February and assigned to the Third Infantry Division. On the following day he was reassigned to the Forty-fifth Infantry Division and given command of the badly battered 179th Infantry Regiment.

When Darby arrived at regimental headquarters, he found one battalion seriously understrength, a second at less than half strength, and the third practically destroyed. To all appearances, Darby had rebounded from Cisterna and "his contagious confidence, energy, and enthusiasm invigorated the headquarters."[15] He was, however, unable to alter the unbattleworthy condition of the regiment and it almost disintegrated later in the day when the Germans stepped up their counterattack. Darby called division at 1748 to describe his plight and declare his intention to withdraw: "We are getting attacked all along the front. We will have to get out of here. We can't keep this CP here any longer and still function.... These people are pretty shaken. There's men streaming back from all directions and it's going to be a job to get them organized."[16] But Maj. Gen. William W. Eagles, commanding general of the Forty-fifth Infantry Division, would not permit Darby to pull the regiment back; he had to stand fast on the final beachhead line.

Had the Germans continued their pressure on the 179th Infantry, Darby would most likely have witnessed the destruction of his second command in three weeks. Luckily, the Germans did not realize how close they were to breaking through the unit and redirected their attack against a neighboring regiment. On 20 February the five-day counterattack came to an end.

Darby continued to serve as CO of the 179th Infantry at Anzio for about two months. During that time he demonstrated the appreciation of firepower that had characterized him in the past. Apparently his quickness to use artillery had become part of his reputation. During the German counterattack that was in progress when he assumed command of the regiment, he made lavish use of artillery support, prompting a division staff officer who knew him to remark, "that's like Darby." He also continued to be parsimonious with his men's lives and willing to experiment with means that might save them. Once, when Murray visited Darby, he found him testing a grenade-throwing slingshot made from the crotch of a tree and inner tubes. Darby's reason for experimenting with the device was typical— he had "more grenades than men."

The same innovativeness that had led to his slingshot experiment made him open-minded enough to compare his experiences with the Rangers and the 179th Infantry, with surprising results. Although his name was firmly linked with the Rangers, he now questioned their practicality. This is not to say that he changed his opinion regarding the soundness of Ranger-type operations. On the contrary, he continued to believe in their value. However, his recent experiences as the commander of a true regiment had impressed him with the might that could be brought against the enemy by a unit that was several times larger than Ranger Force. With such an infantry unit trained in Ranger-type operations, Darby believed that he could do what he had done with the Rangers, but on a larger scale.[17]

As for the Rangers, those who had survived Cisterna were attached to the Canadian-American First Special Service Force on 19 February, and assigned to conduct a scouting and patrolling school for Fifth Army at Civitavecchia, near Naples, in the spring. The men who were Rangers of very long standing were sent to Camp Butner, North Carolina, on 6 May. They remained there until 26 October when the First, Third and Fourth Ranger Battalions were inactivated. The men who had joined the Rangers more recently were absorbed into the First Special Service Force and not returned to the United States.

To Darby's dissatisfaction, unfolding events did not allow him the opportunity to provide Ranger training to a unit of regimental strength. Gen. Mark W. Clark, who had personally decorated about twenty men with the Medal of Honor, believed that they and others who had formidable combat records were too often used recklessly because of their reputations. Fearing that their lives might be lost unnecessarily, he wrote a letter to Army Chief of Staff George C. Marshall asking that Medal of Honor winners and certain other exemplary combat soldiers be returned to the United States and sent on tour for "inspirational" purposes. Darby was among those recommended for rotation by Clark, and in early April was assigned to the Operations Division of the War Department General Staff in Washington, D. C.[18]

VII

The War Department and the Tenth Mountain Division

The War Department

In early April of 1944, Darby joined the Operations Division of the War Department General Staff (OPD WDGS) in Washington, D.C. OPD WDGS occupied a lofty and central place in the chain of command, being in direct line under the president and the chief of staff of the army. The president, as commander in chief, was responsible for plans relating to strategy, tactics and operations; the chief of staff was the president's executive for issuing or changing orders relating to strategy, tactics or operations; and OPD WDGS was considered the chief of staff's CP and the agency through which orders relating to strategy, tactics and operations were issued. In brief, the division was the army's Washington command post.

OPD WDGS was divided into a Strategy and Policy Group, Theater Group, Executive Group, and Logistics Group. Theater Group was the staff agency for exercising the chief of staff's command function in each operational theater and was organized into sections which corresponded to those theaters. Because of Darby's combat experience, he began his assignment serving as a member of the North African and Mediterranean Sections.

Before beginning work in earnest, however, Darby returned

home to Fort Smith to visit family and friends for the first time in four years. If the promise to become great which he had made in his high school annual fifteen years earlier remained in his memory, he could take special satisfaction in the parade which his hometown had arranged in his honor. It was, in the words of the *Southwest American* newspaper, intended to accord him "the greatest ovation for a military hero in Fort Smith since General Zachary Taylor rode away to the Mexican war."

Garrison Avenue, Fort Smith's main business artery and the street down which the parade would march, began in front of the red brick, neo-Gothic Immaculate Conception Catholic Church and ran down a gentle slope for half a mile to the Arkansas River, where it crossed a bridge and headed westward to Oklahoma as an interstate highway. The parade started at the church, the town's most prominent building, at four o'clock on the afternoon of Tuesday, 25 April, and marched down a flag- and bunting-draped Garrison Avenue. A police detail led the parade, with the color guard, Darby, and a contingent of National Guardsmen right behind. Further along in the column was the Fort Smith High School Band and cars carrying Darby's family; local, state and federal officials; and representatives of the American Legion. When the parade reached Sixth Street, near the bridge, it wheeled left and continued marching for a block to pass the statue honoring the area's Confederate dead and halt at the Sebastian County courthouse lawn. There, on the west steps of the courthouse which were bedecked with red and white flowers, Darby was introduced to over twenty-five hundred Fort Smithians by Mayor Chester Holland.

Holland, describing Darby as "Fort Smith's foremost citizen and soldier," presented him with a parchment scroll bearing greetings from the townspeople. Savoring the moment, Darby recalled how he used to be shooed off the mayor's front porch when he was just one of the neighborhood kids, and quipped that he was happy the mayor was allowing him to stand on the courthouse steps that day. Such were the sweet ironies of being a local boy made good. His parents and sister, Doris Nell, were also singled out for recognition, introduced to the crowd and presented with baskets of flowers. Following a speech in which he spoke glowingly of his family and hometown, a band from nearby Camp Chaffee played the "Star Spangled Banner" and Darby settled down to a siege by hundreds of friends, admirers and autograph seekers in the courthouse foyer.

While Darby may have enjoyed the adulation heaped upon him by the people of Fort Smith, he also bore with him the memories of war. In conversation with his parents, he spoke of the thirst he had known in the North African desert. Later, as a symbolic gesture, Percy Darby and his family had a drinking fountain installed in the First Methodist Church in honor of their son. Visitors to the church may still refresh themselves with a drink from the fountain and read the commemorative plaque which hangs on the wall behind it. Heavier than the memories of unquenched thirst were the memories of dead and missing Rangers. Darby spent much of the time he had at home contacting the families of those who had been left behind.

Refreshing though it was, Darby's visit to Fort Smith was brief and he was back at work at the War Department in late April. Since the success of combat operations was influenced by the quality of the troops furnished from the United States, it was important that OPD WDGS monitor training. Thus, training inspections took Darby to Fort Meade, Maryland, at the end of April, and to Camp Butner, North Carolina; Camp Croft, South Carolina; Fort McClellan, Alabama; and Fort Benning and Camp Wheeler, Georgia, in late May.

When Darby returned to Washington he prepared a report in which he evaluated the training he had observed according to its realism and usefulness. He was well pleased with the emphases being placed on patrolling and camouflage techniques at Fort Benning's Infantry Replacement Training Center (IRTC) but, possibly remembering Cisterna, remarked that a training exercise involving an attack on a town was unrealistic because the town was in a thick forest rather than in the open, and gave the attacking trainees more concealment than they would have in actual combat. He was also critical of the procedure being taught in which buildings that had been cleared of the enemy were marked "cleared" but left unoccupied by advancing troops. Not only were such buildings open to reoccupation by the enemy, but the enemy had pointed out to them the buildings from which they might fire with greatest surprise.

Darby also demonstrated concern with general training problems which were the inevitable by-products of military expansion during wartime. At Fort McClellan, for example, he rated most of the training "excellent" and thought the trainees enthusiastic, but believed that the quality of instruction was suffering because of the large number of inexperienced officers among the cadre. Deficiencies which he observed included lapses in military courtesy by instructors and the failure of the cadre to correct mistakes which they saw trainees committing. Darby believed that the deficiencies resulted from a central problem which would grow more acute with the passage of time: trained and experienced infantry instructors were being sent into combat and replaced with men who were neither experienced nor properly trained.

Darby ended his report with several recommendations. He had seen large dumps of captured German Teller and S-mines in North Africa, Sicily and Italy, and thought that some of them should be sent to the United States for instructional purposes. In the same vein, instruction could be made more realistic if German uniforms, weapons and equipment were used by the mock enemy against which recruits usually trained. Finally, recalling a Ranger technique, Darby recommended that a buddy system be used in all training to engender teamwork and an attitude of interdependence.

Darby's visit to Fort Benning was especially appreciated. Brig. Gen. George H. Weems, assistant commandant of the Infantry School, had received many favorable remarks about a talk which he had heard Darby give, and personally believed that it was "one of the finest" given by an officer returning from combat. Weems was particularly interested in Darby's use of flashlights

The War Department 167

to control a battalion's movement at night and asked him for a detailed explanation of the procedure so it could be taught at Fort Benning. Darby explained how the Rangers had used the technique on the Sened raid.

The Fort Benning visit also gave Darby the opportunity to renew some old ties, for five of his former Ranger officers were on duty as instructors at the Infantry School. Darby also took part in an NBC broadcast of "The Army Hour" while at Fort Benning. Speaking about the Rangers, he said that they were not supermen, "just Infantry foot soldiers, well trained, eager and willing to fight." They had also been "willing to go through the toughest kind of training to insure the success of their mission."

Darby spent very little time in Washington before going on another inspection trip. In early June he visited Camp Robinson, Arkansas, and Camps Fannin, Wolters, and Hood, all of which were in Texas.

On 13 June Darby prepared his report. At Camp Robinson he was most favorably impressed with the physical training program. At Camp Fannin he thought the platoon attack exercise well thought out, the battalion attack exercise the best such problem he had seen, and the night patrol training particularly outstanding. He was especially happy with a class on the calling and adjustment of artillery fire in which the instructor demonstrated with live artillery. At Camp Wolters he thought the patrolling instruction excellent, the village combat exercise the best of its type he had seen, and the RTC as a whole "superior." At Camp Hood, however, he saw another example of the growing pains which accompanied the rapid expansion of the army; the construction of training facilities had not kept pace with the need for them and a shortage had developed.

As in his previous report, Darby concluded with some general comments, recommending very strongly that all radio operators be taught basic radio repair. In a closing statement, Darby expressed surprise at the realism of the training he had observed, writing that the American IRTCs were "on a much higher plane and far more developed" that the British commando depot he had known at Achnacarry. The army had come a long way since the Louisiana maneuvers of 1940.

Darby travelled intermittently during the later part of the year, occasionally mixing pleasure with business. On 19 June he was at Camp Butner, where those Rangers who had returned stateside after Cisterna were temporarily garrisoned, to visit the men and celebrate with them the second anniversary of their activation. In mid-November he took a ten-day leave to visit family and friends in Fort Smith once again. In mid-December, his leave over, he visited Camp Ritchie, Maryland, for the War Department.

In the meantime, Darby rose within the Operations Division. Having begun as a member of the North African and Mediterranean Theater Sections, he became executive of Theater Group by the end of the year. His annual efficiency report indicates that during this time he continued to display the character and personality traits which had typified him in the past. His rater, Brig. Gen. J. DeF. Barker, acting chief of Theater Group, described him as "an extremely energetic and forceful officer with a wide and varied knowledge of combat," and possessing "a very agreeable personality which complements his energy and force." While advancing in his assignment, Darby received orders awarding him decorations for which he had previously been recommended. Among these were the Legion of Merit, French Croix de Guerre, Soviet Order of Kutuzov Third Class, and Oak Leaf Cluster to the Purple Heart. The Order of Kutuzov had not been awarded directly to Darby by the Russians; the Soviet government had authorized Fifth Army to award a dozen medals to men of the latter's choice in Italy, and Darby was among those selected.

In spite of Darby's advancement and honors, he was unhappy with staff work and often wrote to ask Mark Clark, who was still Fifth Army commander, if he could use his influence to get Darby back to Italy. To Darby's dissatisfaction, Clark was unable to help.[1] Frustrated, Darby lamented his apparent fate in conversations with old friends and acquaintances. Former West Point classmates Edward T. Ashworth, Morris O. Edwards, Guy C. Lothrop, Edward D. Marshall, and Jack W. Rudolph were all assigned to staff positions in Washington while Darby was there, and all were struck by his unhappiness at not being in combat. In talking to others, he speculated about new possibilities. In a conversation with former classmate Lawrence J. Lincoln, who was also assigned to OPD WDGS, Darby spoke of the success he believed his Ranger techniques might achieve against the Japanese. Darby also visited Dammer, who had been assigned to The Adjutant General's Office, and Dammer's wife Elizabeth. He spoke to them about his distaste for staff work and, despairing of ever again seeing combat, conjectured about the possibility of organizing a peacetime unit along the Rangers' lines which could demonstrate proper combat techniques.

For a brief instant the Darby-Dammer team was resurrected when Darby, with Dammer's assistance, addressed the faculty and students of the Army and Navy Staff College in Washington on the history of the Rangers and lessons learned from their operations. While speaking, Darby accidentally caught and split a finger in a sliding map board. Darby being Darby, the incident was not totally without humor; he claimed that the accident had caused him to lose the most blood he had lost since the war began.

The chief of staff kept informed of conditions in the various theaters of operation through the continual dispatch of OPD WDGS officers to the field. In keeping with this practice, orders were published on 29 March 1945 sending Darby on a ninety-day tour of the European Theater for the main purpose of evaluating aerial support of ground combat. The orders were amended on the following day to allow him to visit other theaters if he thought it necessary. Of course, ninety days of temporary duty was not what Darby wanted—it was only a step toward a more substantive goal. According to the practice of the time, an officer visiting a major command might be transferred to it if the commanding general requested that he stay. Thus, if once in Europe Darby could persuade a division commander or higher to ask OPD WDGS for him and CPD WDGS assented, Darby would be transferred to the requesting general's unit.

Darby laid the groundwork for such a transfer well in advance. Before leaving for Europe, he intimated to Dammer that he was going to Italy to join the Tenth Mountain Division, which had been organized and trained especially for mountain warfare and which appealed to him because of its uniqueness. Darby, who had developed an almost superstitious faith in the unbeatability of the Darby-Dammer team while commanding the Rangers, explained that once established in Italy he would use his influence to have Dammer transferred there too.

Darby's accomplice in the plan was the commander of the Tenth Mountain Division, Maj. Gen. George P. Hays. Hays had commanded the Ninety-ninth Field Artillery Battalion (Pack) as a lieutenant colonel in 1940 and 1941, when Darby commanded that battalion's Battery "A." Hays had been favorably impressed by Darby at that time, describing him in an efficiency report as "an officer of splendid temperament and exceptional ability, qualified for selection for important assignments involving heavy responsibilities," and predicted that "superior results" would be forthcoming from Darby in his future assignments. Hays would be happy to have Darby under his command again.

The Tenth Mountain Division

Darby left Washington for Europe on 31 March 1945, and soon made his way to Italy where he visited the Tenth Mountain Division and sought to become assigned to it. Coincidentally, a vacancy was created shortly after Darby's arrival when the assistant division commander, Brig. Gen. Robinson E. Duff, was wounded and evacuated. Hays asked Clark if Darby might be assigned as assistant division commander and Clark, aware that the war in Europe was drawing to a close and that assignment to a position normally held by a brigadier general would mean a promotion for Darby, consented and obtained orders from Washington authorizing the transfer.[2] It was one of Clark's last official acts as Fifth Army commander; on 14 April he turned the army over to Maj. Gen. Lucian K. Truscott, Jr., and became Army Group commander.

Darby no doubt thought himself fortunate to have gotten back into the war in Europe before it ended. In the west, the Allies had encircled the Ruhr and were advancing to the Elbe; in the east, the Russians had taken Vienna. In Italy, the Germans were being pursued northwest of the Senio River by McCreery's Eighth Army and north of the Via Emilia by Fifth Army in the final stages of an Anglo-American offensive that had begun on 9 April.

By 24 April the Tenth Mountain Division had advanced to the Po River and established a bridgehead across it. At that point, Darby was made assistant division commander and given a task force with the mission of taking Verona. Task Force Darby, as the provisional grouping was called, was composed of the 13th Tank Battalion, engineers with bridging equipment, the Eighty-sixth Mountain Infantry Regiment, Company "B" of the 701st Tank Destroyer Battalion, the 1125th Field Artillery Battalion, elements of the 126th Engineers, and the 10th Medical Battalion, in order of march. The division CP would follow the Eighty-sixth Mountain Infantry, and the Eighty-seventh and Eighty-fifth Mountain Infantry Regiments would follow the task force to mop up bypassed enemy and collect prisoners. Symptomatic of the division's optimism, prisoner collection points were to be established every ten miles in the wake of the planned advance.

With substantial elements of the division already north of the Po, the advance on Verona was able to proceed smoothly, as a continuation of the drive in progress. The division continued to expand its bridgehead during the morning of 24 April, encountering only light enemy delaying action, and by night all three regiments were north of the river. They then patrolled to the west, north and east, but saw little enemy activity.

16. Northeastern Italy showing Principal Cities and Sites of Importance during Darby's Assignment to the 10th Mountain Division.

On the morning of 25 April the Eighty-fifth Infantry advanced to the Villafranca airfield, a gain of forty miles, without encountering enemy resistance until the airfield itself was reached. The enemy troops protecting it were overcome. Task Force Darby was late crossing the Po due to a delay in setting up the bridging equipment needed for its armor, and was unable to advance until noon. It reached the Villafranca airfield by nightfall; resumed its advance until 2000; and arrived at Verona, which was already controlled by anti-Fascist partisans, at 0745 the following morning. With Verona in friendly hands, Task Force Darby was dissolved. No serious resistance had been encountered and it was becoming apparent that the Germans were withdrawing northward to the Adige River.

On the night of 26 April, Hays held a special conference of unit commanders at the Villafranca airfield to bring them up to date. He pointed out that the enemy had begun to use routes along both sides of the Adige and on the west side of Lake Garda in a withdrawal from Trento and the Brenner Pass. Tenth Mountain Division would attempt to outrun and head off the retreating Germans by pushing up the east side of Lake Garda and capturing Trento, where all three routes being taken by the Germans converged. Each of the division's three mountain infantry regiments would take turns leading the advance for eight hours and resting for sixteen. By rotating the lead position in this fashion, comparatively fresh troops would always be in front and the momentum of the attack maintained. The Germans, however, had geography in their favor. The road running up the east side of the lake was bounded by water on one side and high ground on the other, and toward the northern end of the lake it passed through six tunnels. The Germans could thus delay the advancing Americans at any number of natural bottlenecks. Hays planned to overcome enemy efforts at obstruction by using DUKWs (2½-ton amphibious trucks with six-wheel drive) to bypass and encircle enemy delaying elements.

The division remained in the Villafranca-Verona-Bussolengo area through the night of 27 April and began its leapfrogging attack up the east side of Lake Garda at 0700 the following morning. The advance proceeded with a minimum of difficulty, and by noon of the 29th the town of Torbole at the northeast corner of the lake was entered by elements of the Third Battalion, Eighty-sixth Mountain Infantry. It was there that the division encountered its heaviest resistance. German armor, artillery, machine gun, and small arms fire kept the battalion from entering Torbole in strength until 2214 when the town was taken by close combat in the wake of a heavy artillery bombardment. A concurrent attack upon the neighboring town of Nago by the First Battalion, Eighty-sixth Mountain Infantry, had been less successful and was unable to advance beyond the town's outskirts.

A little before 0100 on the morning of 30 April the Germans launched a counterattack against Torbole and Nago with armor and infantry. After a half hour the American position had become so tenuous that Hays authorized the Eighty-sixth Mountain Infantry's commander, Lt. Col. Robert L. Cook, to withdraw if necessary. Although the troops at Nago were forced to pull back about fifteen hundred yards, those defending Torbole held their ground and by 0230 the German counterattack was broken.

Darby's Death

With enemy pressure off, Cook's CP moved into Torbole and occupied a hotel toward the north end of town. Darby, carrying out his duties as assistant division commander, visited the CP to assess the local situation for Hays. Cook briefed Darby, who was ready to leave by 1745. Before returning to division, however, Darby and Brig. Gen. David Ruffner, who commanded division artillery, planned to visit one of the tunnels along the east side of the lake where an especially serious engagement had taken place earlier in the day. M. Sgt. John T. Evans, the regimental sergeant major, volunteered to take them in Cook's jeep which was quickly brought to the CP by Lt. James H. McLellan of the regimental staff.

McLellan parked directly in front of the hotel where Darby, Cook, Evans, and a few other men were standing. There had been no enemy shelling of the CP or its immediate area since the regiment's arrival, and no one in the group recognized that they might be taking an unnecessary risk by standing in the open. Then, suddenly and without warning, one round from a German 88mm gun hit about thirty feet from the group at the edge of a small stone wharf which extended into the lake from where the men were standing. Evans, almost decapitated by a large shard of shrapnel, died instantly. Cook was hit in the left hip by a small shell fragment and McLellan fell with severe thigh and ankle wounds. Darby received a shell fragment in the chest and was escorted back into the CP by Cook, who was so dazed by the blast's concussion that he had not yet become aware of his own wound. Stunned and silent, Darby was lain on a cot under the care of two medics who had been in a neighboring building. Two minutes later, without having spoken or regained full consciousness, he died.[3]

The timing of Darby's death was tragically ironic. The day before Darby was killed, Mussolini had been slain by Italian partisans in Milan and Vietinghoff had agreed to surrender unconditionally all German forces in Italy effective at noon on 2 May. With further irony, on the day of Darby's death his name appeared on a list of nominees for promotion to the rank of brigadier general being submitted to President Truman. On 2 May Secretary of War Henry L. Stimson recommended to the president that, in view of Darby's outstanding combat record, his name remain on the list and that he be promoted posthumously. Truman agreed and on 15 May 1945, just over three months after his thirty-fourth birthday, Darby was promoted to the rank of brigadier general.[4] He was the only army officer to be posthumously promoted to star rank during the war.

VIII

Epilogue

Darby's success in the army and his rise to the rank of brigadier general at the age of thirty-four were due to a variety of factors, among which were his personal qualities, luck, the willingness to use old friendships to advantage, and an ability to turn peculiar characteristics of the army's bureaucracy toward his own ends.

The personal characteristics which Darby found to be assets as an adult were evident during his childhood when he showed the self-assurance that would contribute to his later success. His positive outlook was accompanied by an active mind, although he lacked true brilliance and did not distinguish himself against the strong competition he encountered at West Point. Typically of Darby, however, his strong personality and leadership ability compensated for his unextraordinary scholarship and he rose to the rank of cadet captain.

The qualities which Darby displayed in his youth continued to characterize him during the early years of his army career. His peacetime efficiency reports spoke most highly of his aggressive leadership and pleasing personality and least highly, though by no means poorly, of his intelligence. True to his kinetic temperament, Darby become bored with military routine and sought variety and adventure through unsuccessful attempts to transfer to the Army Air Corps, or to Hawaii or the Philippines.

While it may appear as though the individual soldier is helplessly at the mercy of the army's bureaucracy, such is not always the case. On the contrary, an ambitious officer who has a practical understanding of the army's bureaucracy can use it to his advantage. Darby's career is proof of this truth. His promotions were swiftest and most predictable when he made use of certain peculiarities of the army's bureaucracy, but were frustrated when he misperceived or disregarded those peculiarities.

Ordinarily, an officer is assigned to perform duties which are a function of his rank. Under certain circumstances, however, the opposite is true; an officer may be promoted as a means of bringing his rank in line with his duties. Darby's recognition and use of this fact explains in part how he was able to advance to the rank of brigadier general at the age of thirty-four. The fact that an officer is eligible for promotion because of seniority, or time in grade, does not mean that he will automatically be promoted. His selection is contingent upon many things. Among these are his efficiency reports, civilian and military schooling, and the army's need for officers of the next higher grade. This last point is important. One of the ways an otherwise eligible officer can enjoy an increased chance of being promoted is by holding an assignment which calls for someone of higher rank. For example, if a captain eligible for promotion is already serving in the capacity of a major, he will usually be recommended for promotion ahead of other equally qualified captains who are performing captains' duties. Darby was promoted to both lieutenant colonel and brigadier general under such circumstances.

Darby was a captain of twenty months when he was promoted to major on 1 June 1942. This was not too short a time in grade for Darby considering his West Point background, favorable efficiency reports, seven years of active duty, and the fact that a war was in progress and officers of all grades needed. That Darby received his majority almost three weeks before the First Ranger Battalion was formally activated suggests that the

Epilogue

promotion was probably routine and unconnected with his new assignment.

In contrast, Darby's promotion to lieutenant colonel was clearly an instance in which he used certain characteristics of the army's bureaucracy advantageously. He could thank fortune for having been made Hartle's aide and been given the opportunity to lay claim to the Rangers. That he actually did so is a tribute to his shrewdness; not only was he thus able to escape from an assignment he disliked but, because a battalion is commanded by a lieutenant colonel, he put himself in line for a promotion. Indeed, Darby was made a lieutenant colonel eighteen days after his official appointment as battalion commander and only sixty-seven days after his appointment to major. By being promoted as a consequence of his assignment, he had advanced from captain to lieutenant colonel in less than ten weeks.

In view of Darby's apparent ambition and willingness to avail himself of opportunity, it might seem strange that, while in command of the Rangers, he rejected two offers of promotion to colonel. An examination of the conditions under which the promotions were offered suggests an explanation. In each case promotion was contingent upon Darby leaving the Rangers and assuming command of an infantry regiment. Transfer was necessary because, while an officer might be assigned to duties customarily performed by one of higher rank, he cannot ordinarily be assigned to duties performed by one of lesser rank. Thus, in accepting a promotion to colonel, Darby would be accepting a promotion out of his assignment as battalion commander. His first opportunity for such a promotion came in late March of 1943, less than eight months after he had become a lieutenant colonel. His second opportunity came in mid-July of the same year. In both cases, Darby stated that he chose to pass up promotion because he would rather remain with the Rangers.

There is no reason to believe that loyalty to the Rangers was not a factor in Darby's rejection of promotion. To believe that it was the only factor, however, would be to underestimate his ego and ambition. Although Darby twice turned his back on promotion, he labored to expand the Rangers and transform them into a regiment, a unit requiring a colonel as its commander. Instead of simply accepting a promotion to command a conventional infantry regiment, he was probably striving to make his Rangers—Darby's Rangers—into a regiment in order that he might be promoted as its commander.

Darby's expansion of the Rangers began when he requested the formation of two additional Ranger battalions on 14 April 1943. Marshall gave his approval five days later and the Third and Fourth Ranger Battalions were activated on 19 June. However, Darby was not provided with a headquarters to control the three battalions, and remained commanding officer of the First Ranger Battalion with the Third and Fourth Ranger Battalions attached. Disregarding this organizational handicap, Darby continued to expand his command by gaining the virtually permanent attachment of the Eighty-third Chemical Battalion prior to the invasion of Sicily. On 10 August, one month after the invasion began, Darby sought to obtain a regimental headquarters for his command. Patton enthusiastically endorsed Darby's request but Eisenhower denied it. Undaunted, Darby persisted in expanding his command by forming a Ranger cannon company in preparation for the landing at Maiori.

Ironically, Darby probably owed his promotion to colonel less to the Rangers than to the temporary command which he frequently exercised over other, attached units. While in North Africa, Darby commanded only one Ranger battalion of slightly more than five hundred men. Landing in Sicily, he commanded Force "X," a provisional grouping of two Ranger battalions, two engineer battalions, and three companies of the Eighty-third Chemical Battalion. During the subsequent drive on Palermo he commanded a second provisional grouping called Task Force "X," composed of two Ranger battalions, a regimental combat team, and an artillery battalion.

Epilogue

Darby thus fought the most important actions of the Sicilian campaign in command of regiment-sized provisional groupings although, as a lieutenant colonel, his rank was similar to that held by a battalion commander. During the opening phases of the landing at Salerno, Darby commanded what had come to be known as Ranger Force: the First, Third and Fourth Ranger Battalions; the Eighty-third Chemical Battalion; and the new Ranger cannon company. As the Germans were reinforced and the struggle to expand the beachhead became more difficult, additional units were attached to Darby until he commanded about five thousand men. Indicative of the high regard in which Darby was held by his superiors, a brigadier general was temporarily placed under his direction during the battle—a situation which is contrary to any standard procedures governing the chain of command. Noting the large number of men Darby was commanding and the level of his performance, Clark asked Eisenhower to promote him. Darby was promoted to full colonel almost ninety days later, on 11 December 1943.

While the delay between Clark's recommendation and Darby's promotion suggests that the former did not lead directly to the latter, it remains true that Darby's promotion was probably due more to his performance as commander of regiment-sized provisional units than as commander of the Rangers. There are two arguments to sustain this view. The first is based upon the fact that although Darby's name is inextricably linked with that of the Rangers, he seldom commanded the three Ranger battalions as a cohesive unit. The Rangers never fought united under Darby's command in Sicily and, during the early stages of the campaign, were together only at Salerno. Thus, in spite of Darby's identification with the Rangers, his most substantive contributions to the war effort through the early phases of the Italian campaign took place when he led regiment-sized provisional groupings of which Rangers were only a part.

The second argument is based on the fact that promotions are intended to be awarded on the basis of an officer's potential value to the army, not as a reward for past service. Darby would not have been promoted to colonel if his superiors had intended him to remain a battalion commander. He was proving his ability to lead larger groupings and his superiors were preparing to make him a true regimental commander. Thus, although Darby was awarded his colonelcy, he did not receive it on his own terms and never saw the establishment of a permanent regimental headquarters for Ranger Force. If he thought the army would modify its organization to suit him or his Rangers—and he apparently did—he was mistaken.

Soon after the disaster at Cisterna, Darby was transferred to command the 179th Infantry Regiment. In April 1944, as a result of Clark's bidding, he was further transferred to the Operations Division of the War Department General Staff in Washington, D.C. The circumstances under which Darby was given the latter assignment make it an excellent example of how decisions made by an officer's superior can radically alter his career. In Darby's case, the alteration was short-lived. He was unhappy in the War Department General Staff and conspired to escape from it and return to combat.

The means which Darby used to achieve that end show him once again to have been adept at using the army's bureaucracy to his professional advantage. Darby availed himself of his friendship with Maj. Gen. George P. Hays, commander of the Tenth Mountain Division, to be assigned to that unit. Coincidentally, the wounding of Hays's assistant division commander created a vacancy which Hays then appointed Darby to fill.To Darby's good fortune, the position of assistant division commander called for a brigadier general and he was recommended for promotion to that rank about one month after assuming his duties. Once again, in this instance for the final time, Darby was promoted as a consequence of his position. He had advanced from captain to brigadier general in twenty-three months.

Although it is true that top posts in the military tend to be reserved for graduates of the service academies, and that

Epilogue

Darby's attendance at West Point could hardly have hampered his career, there is no evidence to indicate that any of his promotions were the direct results of his academy background.

It would be unfair to credit Darby's rapid advancement solely to his understanding of the army's bureaucracy. All such knowledge would have been to no avail had it not been for Darby's exceptional leadership ability. The strong qualities which were apparent during his youth and in peacetime efficiency reports were especially evident in combat. He played a direct and prominent role in all of the Rangers' more important North African operations, and disregarded his own safety to accompany the wounded back to friendly lines following the Sened raid. During the landing at Gela he participated in the storming of an Italian-held hotel, rode on the top of an Italian tank while attempting to destroy it, and personally put an enemy tank out of action with a 37mm gun. He continued to take direct part in combat actions and to expose himself to enemy fire during the Italian campaign.

A controversial theme which parallels and is frequently interwoven with Darby's wartime career concerns the utilization of the Rangers. *FM 21-50: Ranger Training and Ranger Operations* defines Ranger operations as "overt operations by highly trained infantry units to any depth into enemy-held areas for the purpose of reconnaissance, raids, and general disruption of enemy operations."[1] This biography, however, reveals that Darby's Rangers seldom took part in this type of operation.

The First Ranger Battalion, which was in North Africa from 8 November 1942 through 10 July 1943, spent only 8 days conducting true Ranger-type operations, but spent 30 days in conventional infantry combat and 212 days in reserve and training duties. During the Sicilian campaign, which lasted from 10 July through 17 August, only the initial amphibious landings were appropriate to the Rangers' training and stated specialties. As in North Africa, they spent most of the campaign performing functions which could have been done by conventional infantry units. In the fighting which took place from Salerno to the

Winter Line, the Rangers fought almost exclusively as conventional infantry, the only exceptions being their initial landing and a reconnaissance conducted by the Third Ranger Battalion at San Pietro Infine. The Rangers' participation in the fighting at Anzio was too brief to establish a new trend or continue the old. After the initial landing on 22 January 1944, the Rangers spent a week in conventional infantry combat before beginning their ill-fated attack on Cisterna on 30 January. In the twenty-one months which led to Cisterna, the Rangers spent only about two weeks conducting true Ranger-type operations.

Although it is impossible to determine with certainty the precise reason for each and every instance in which the Rangers were cast in a conventional role, it is not too difficult to appreciate the circumstances which weighed against their being used exclusively for special missions. In each of the four instances in which the Rangers spearheaded an invasion, their landing was immediately followed by a conventional role being thrust upon them by tactical necessity. Arzew led to LaMacta and Saint Cloud, the landing at Gela to the repelling of a counterattack by Axis armor, Salerno to the unexpectedly long defense of Chiunzi Pass, and Anzio to the defense of the beachhead prior to the attack on Cisterna. In view of the emergencies which followed the landings, it would have been wasteful of manpower for the commanders responsible to have held the Rangers in reserve.

The fighting which took place inland after the winning of each beachhead differed greatly in character and also influenced the way in which the Rangers were used. The fighting in North Africa was generally characterized by great movement but, at Sened and Djebel el Ank, provided the Rangers with opportunities to engage in the type of fighting for which they had been trained. The Sicilian campaign was marked by rapid movement and did not afford the Rangers much occasion to operate against stationary defensive positions. The fighting on

Epilogue

the Winter Line, however, was quite different. When it developed into a stalemate, it could have provided the Rangers with conditions and objectives ideally suited to their training, but they were used for conventional operations instead.

When asked in an interview why the Rangers were not given the opportunity to exercise their special skills against the Winter Line, Gen. Mark W. Clark maintained that, while he believed in the Ranger concept, he was chronically short of manpower and could not take them off the line for special missions.[2] It is difficult to believe, however, that the Rangers' participation in conventional combat was so important to the outcome of the fighting on the Winter Line that they could not be used in a role which was commensurate with their skills. It may have been that Clark, his staff and subordinate commanders lacked the time or imagination to develop missions appropriate for the Rangers. Ironically, it was at Cisterna, where the Rangers were conducting the type of operation at which they were supposed to excel, that they met disaster. Under examination, however, catastrophe was virtually inevitable given the faulty intelligence developed by the Third Infantry Division, and should be blamed neither upon Darby nor the Ranger concept.

Surprisingly, Darby himself might have contributed in no small measure to the Rangers' increasing use as conventional infantry. It must be remembered that the Rangers were not Darby's idea. He was an artillery officer who, through good fortune and ambition, gained the opportunity to organize and lead the First Ranger Battalion. While he might thus be expected to take a personal interest in the Rangers, there is no reason to believe that he had any strong convictions regarding their proper or improper use. Although his conversations with Dammer and others while assigned to the War Department General Staff show that he appreciated the value of Ranger-type operations, his actual handling of the Rangers shows that he subordinated that appreciation to other considerations. Indeed, under Darby's leadership the Rangers grew from a lightly armed battalion to three battalions with a cannon company and heavy mortars permanently attached.

There were two reasons for this growth and metamorphosis. The first of these has already been examined: Darby apparently wanted to be promoted to colonel as the commander of a Ranger regiment, and labored toward that end even though it involved altering the Rangers' very nature. The second reason concerns Darby's professional background. As an artillery officer he had a great love of firepower. Indeed, all of the important organizational changes which Darby led the Rangers through resulted in increased firepower. If the Rangers were going to be used in conventional combat, Darby probably reasoned, they might as well be armed heavily enough to do the job effectively. On the other hand, as they came more and more to resemble conventional infantry, it became increasingly likely that they would be used as such.

The end of World War II saw the deactivation of the Ranger battalions and a temporary break in the modern Ranger tradition begun by Darby. Following the outbreak of war in Korea, Ranger units were once again called into being. On 25 August 1950 the 8213th Army Unit was organized at Camp Drake, Japan, from volunteers in the Far East. This unit was informally known as the Eighth Army Ranger Company and was attached to the Twenty-fifth Infantry Division. The 8213th took part in the drive to the Yalu before being deactivated in March 1951. Between September 1950 and September 1951, fourteen airborne Ranger companies were organized and trained by the newly formed Ranger Training Command at Fort Benning, Georgia. Six of these companies were assigned to divisions in Eighth Army and used as line infantry in Korea. These units were deactivated in September 1951 and their men disseminated throughout the Army.

In October 1951 the army Chief of Staff, Gen. J. Lawton Collins, directed that Ranger training be spread to all Army combat units. Toward the end, the Commandant of The

Infantry School was directed to establish a Ranger Department for the purpose of conducting a Ranger course. The goal of this program was to place one Ranger-qualified officer in each rifle company and one Ranger-qualified NCO in each rifle platoon. In July 1954 it became mandatory for all newly commissioned regular army officers in the Infantry, Armor, Artillery, Corps of Engineers, and Signal Corps to attend Ranger or airborne school. The following year this requirement was extended to include newly commissioned regular army officers in the military police corps.

The policy of training individual Rangers rather than maintaining Ranger units was departed from during the war in Vietnam, when Ranger companies were assigned to divisions and separate brigades. These companies were given a distinct identity by being designated member companies of the Seventy-fifth Infantry Regiment but, inasmuch as the army is not organized along regimental lines and there is no regimental headquarters, the designation was only a formality. The companies belonged to the divisions or brigades to which they were assigned rather than to any central Ranger command.

Following the war in Vietnam, the Ranger companies were replaced by two newly formed Ranger battalions. These are the First Battalion, Seventy-fifth Infantry (Ranger), stationed at Fort Stewart, Georgia; and the Second Battalion, Seventy-fifth Infantry (Ranger), stationed at Fort Lewis, Washington.

While the modern Ranger tradition begun by Darby continues, the struggle which he waged has yet to be won. The First and Second Battalions, Seventy-fifth Infantry (Ranger), like the Ranger battalions and companies which came before them, are without their own Ranger headquarters.

Abbreviations

Clark   Mark Clark Archives, The Citadel, Charleston, South Carolina.

McNair   U. S. Army Center of Military History, Fort Lesley Mc Nair, Washington, D. C.

SF   Suitland Files. The number following "SF" is the file number under which the records are stored at the Washington National Records Center, Suitland, Maryland.

TAGO 201   The Adjutant General's Office Personnel File, National Personnel Records Center, St. Louis, Missouri.

Notes

Notes to Chapter I

[1] Interview with Doris Nell Watkins, Cleveland, Mississippi, 23 April 1973; Edwin P. Hicks, "Story of Bill Darby—A Fort Smith Boy Who Has Gained National Fame As Outstanding Soldier in World War 2," *The Fort Smithian*, 11 November 1943, pp. 1-2.
[2] Interview with Bill and Ruby Hogan, Fort Smith, Arkansas, 11 August 1973; War Department Adjutant General's Office form 0104-1, 4 December 1928, TAGO 201.
[3] "Report of Physical Examination of Candidate for Admission to the United States Military Academy, West Point, N.Y. for William O. Darby," 5 March 1929, TAGO 201.
[4] First and second endorsements to "Report of Physical Examination of Candidate for Admission to the United States Military Academy, West Point, N.Y. for William O. Darby," TAGO 201.
[5] Interview with Col. William S. Hutchinson, Jr., USA (Ret.), Jacksonville, Florida, 14 June 1973.
[6] War Department Special Order (SO) No. 265, 13 November 1941, TAGO 201; subject letter "Orders," 5 January 1942, to Darby, TAGO 201; HQ Thirty-fourth Infantry Division SO No. 6, 6 January 1942, TAGO 201.

Notes to Chapter II

[1] Lt. Gen. Lucian King Truscott, Jr., *Command Missions: A Personal Story* (New York: E. P. Dutton and Company, 1954), pp. 16-23.

[2] Technically, the word *Commando* denotes a battalion-sized unit of "commandos." The word was commonly used in referring to the individual soldier who was a member of a Commando. I use the word in both senses and, to avoid confusion, capitalize its first letter when referring to the unit.

[3] Subject letter "Commando Organization," 1 June 1942, by command of Maj. Gen. James W. Chaney to CG USANIF, SF-INBN 72-37 R1 F4-6.

[4] Maj. Gen. Edmond H. Leavey, USA (Ret.), to James J. Altieri, 3 August 1965, James J. Altieri.

[5] Subject letter "Commando Organization," 7 June 1942, by command of Maj. Gen. Russell P. Hartle to Distribution, SF-INBN 72-37 R1 F7-10.

[6] HQ USANIF and V Army Corps (Reinf.) General Order (GO) No. 7, 19 June 1942, SF-INBN 72-37 R8 F83. The TO&E authorized the battalion 441 enlisted men. The figure 488 includes a 10 percent overstrength in each grade to offset 10 percent attrition anticipated during training.

[7] Subject letter "Commando Organization."

[8] "Progress Report on U.S.A. Rangers," Col. Charles A. Vaughan to HQ Special Service Brigade, SF-INBN 72-37 R8 F84-85.

[9] "First Ranger Battalion Diary," SF-INBN 72-37 R1 F93-101; interview with Col. Herman W. Dammer, USA (Ret.), McLean, Virginia, 15 July 1972; R. W. Thompson, "Massacre at Dieppe," *History of the Second World War*, 37 (1973); 1017.

Notes to Chapter III

[1] First Infantry Division Field Order (FO) No. 1, 1200 10 October 1942, Report of Operations Eighteenth CT (8-10 October 1942), SF-201-Inf (18)-0.3.

[2] After Action Report (AAR) Torch Operation (8-12 November 1942), AAR Sixteenth CT (November 1942-April 1943), SF-301-INF(16)-0.3; First Ranger Battalion AAR, 1 January 1943, SF-INBN 72-37 R1 F212-15.

[3] First Ranger Battalion AAR, 1 January 1943, SF-INBN 72-37 R1 F212-15; Report of Operations (8-10 November 1942), Report of

Operations Eighteenth CT, SF-301-INF(18)-0.3; First Infantry Division FO No. 3, 2210 9 November 1942, Report of Operations Eighteenth CT, SF-301-INF(18)-0.3.
[4]First Ranger Battalion AAR, 1 January 1943.
[5]Interview with Col. Herman W. Dammer, USA (Ret.), McLean, Virgiania, 15 July 1972.
[6]Dammer interview, 15 July 1972; "Training Guides—Ranger Battalion," SF-INBN-1.3.13; James Altieri, *The Spearheaders* (New York: Popular Library, 1960), p. 149.
[7]"Training Guides—1st Ranger Battalion"; First Ranger Battalion AAR, 5 March 1943, SF-INBN 72-37 R1 F220.
[8]First Ranger Battalion AAR (14-28 February 1943), 5 March 1943, SF-INBN 72-37 R1 F219.
[9]Ibid.
[10]Memo from Allen to Darby, 17 March 1943, First Infantry Division G-3 Journal and File, SF-301-3.2.
[11]G-3 Operations Report First Infantry Division (15 January-8 April 1943), SF-301-3; Dextrous One Unit Journal, 20 March 1943, Report of Operations, Twenty-Sixth Regiment (8 November 1942-8 May 1943), SF-301-Inf(26)-0.3.
[12]First Ranger Battalion AAR, 9 April 1943, SF-INBN 72-37 R1 F221.
[13]Telephone conversation, Mason to Roosevelt, 0730 24 March 1943, First Infantry Division G-3 Journal and File, SF-301-3.2.
[14]Altieri, *The Spearheaders*, p. 202.

Notes to Chapter IV

[1]AFHQ Incoming Message No. 6300, 19 April 1943, from Marshall to Eisenhower, SF-INBN 72-37 R1 F287.
[2]Letter, 22 April 1943, from HQ North African Theater of Operations to Darby, SF-INBN 72-37 R1 F286; subject letter "Volunteers for Ranger Battalions," 17 May 1943, from HQ Atlantic Base Section by command of Brigadier General Wilson to Darby, SF-INBN 72-37 R1 F228.
[3]Memorandum, 29 April 1943, from the Office of the G-1, Fifth Army, to Darby, SF-INBN 72-37 R1 F294.
[4]Ibid.
[5]Fifteenth Infantry Regiment FO No. 1, 22 June 1943, Regimental Field Orders, SF-303-Inf(15)-3.9.
[6]James Altieri, *The Spearheaders* (New York: Popular Library, 1960), p. 207; James Altieri, *Darby's Rangers: An Illustrated Portrayal of the*

Original Rangers (Durham, North Carolina: The Seeman Printery, Inc., 1945), p. 46.

[7]William O. Darby, "U. S. Rangers" (lecture given at the Army and Navy Staff College, Washington, D. C., 27 October 1944), SF.

[8]Provisional Corps FO No. 2, 20 July 1943, SF-INBN 72-37 R1 F588-89; Provisional Corps Report of Operations (15 July-20 August 1943), SF-200-0.3; Fourth Ranger Battalion AAR, 9 August 1943, SF-INBN 72-37 R4 F121.

[9]Subject letter "Status of RANGER Battalions," 10 August 1943, from Darby to CiC AFHQ, SF-INBN 72-37 R1 F290-91.

[10]First endorsement to letter from Darby to CiC AFHQ, 12 August 1943, SF-INBN 72-37 R1 F297.

[11]Note from "AWG" to Gen. Mark W. Clark, 14 October 1943, SF-INBN 72-37 R1 F303.

Notes to Chapter V

[1]Ranger Force FO No. 1, 1 September 1943, SF-INBN 72-37 R1 F826.

[2]Ibid.

[3]Interview with Stan Zaslaw, Deerfield, Illinois, 19 June 1972.

[4]Memorandum for General Clark, commanding general, Fifth Army, from Lieutenant General McCreery, commanding Ten Corps, 12 September 1943, Clark.

[5]Mark Wayne Clark, *Calculated Risk* (New York: Harper & Brothers, 1950), pp. 208-9; message from Clark to Eisenhower, 16 September 1943, Clark.

[6]Ten Corps Operations Instructions No. 4, 18 September 1943, Fifth Army G-3 Journal and File (9 September 1943-15 February 1944), SF-105.3.2; Message No. 369 from Fifth Army to CG Eighty-second Airborne Division, 20 September 1943, Eighty-second Airborne Division G-3 Message File, SF-382-3.3; Eighty-second Airborne Division History of Operations, Italy (September-October 1943), SF-382-0.3.

[7]VI Corps Memo, 3 November 1943, from L. B. Keiser to CG Fifth Army, Fifth Army G-3 Journal and File (9 September 1943-15 February 1944), SF-105-3.2.

[8]Telephone message from Martin to Colonel Arnote, 091145 November 1943, Forty-fifth Infantry Division G-3 Journal and File (1 November-14 December 1943), SF-345-3.2.

[9]Fourth Ranger Battalion subject letter "Ranger Infantry Battalions,"

28 November 1943 from Murray to commander in chief, Ground Forces, War Department, US Army, SF; subject letter "Commando Organization," 1 June 1942 by command of Maj. Gen. James E. Chaney to CG USANIF, SF-INBN 72-37 R1 F4-6.

Notes to Chapter VI

[1] VI Corps FO No. 19, 15 January 1944, VI Corps Outline Plan— Operation SHINGLE, SF-206-0.13.

[2] Ranger Force Outline Plan—Operation SHINGLE, Changes, Plans, Supplements, and Annexes to Operation SHINGLE (December 1943–May 1944), SF-105-0.13.

[3] Message from Lucas to CG Third Infantry Division, 23 January 1944, VI Corps G-3 Journal and File (1 November 1943–20 February 1944), SF-206-3.2; Third Infantry Division G-3 Report No. 2, 23 January 1944, Fifth Army G-3 Journal and File, SF-105-3.2; Third Infantry Division G-3 Report No. 3, 24 January 1944, Third Infantry Division Report of Operations (22–31 January 1944), SF-303-0.3.

[4] VI Corps Historical Record—The Mounting and Initial Phase of Operation SHINGLE (January 1944), VI Corps AAR, SF-206-0.3.

[5] Ibid.; interview with Col. William S. Hutchinson, Jr., USA (Ret.), Jacksonville, Florida, 14 June 1973.

[6] Ranger Force Journal entry, 291835 January 1944, SF-INBN 72-37 R1 F528; Third Infantry Division G-2 Estimate, 29 January 1944, SF-INBN 72-37 R1 F521-22.

[7] Fifth Army G-2 Report No. 142, 26 January 1944, SF-105-3.2.

[8] Martin Blumenson, *Salerno to Cassino: The United States Army in World War II* (Washington, D.C.: Office of the Chief of Military History, United States Army, 1969), p. 387; Third Infantry Division G-2 Estimate, 29 January 1944.

[9] VI Corps Historical Record—The Mounting and Initial Phase of Operation SHINGLE (January 1944).

[10] Fifth Army G-2 Special Report, 9 March 1944, SF-INBN 72-37 R1 F751.

[11] Ranger Force AAR (22 January–5 February 1944), SF-INBN 72-37 R1 F681.

[12] Hutchinson interview, 14 June 1973.

[13] Blumenson, *Salerno to Cassino*, p. 391.

[14] Interview with Gen. Mark W. Clark, USA (Ret.), Leland, Michigan, 8 September 1973.

[15] Blumenson, *Salerno to Cassino*, p. 423.

[16] Message from Darby to Colonel Martin, 181748 February 1944, Forty-fifth Infantry Division G-3 Journal and File (11 November 1943-30 April 1944), SF-345-3.2.
[17] Hutchinson interview, 14 June 1973.
[18] Clark interview, 8 September 1973.

Notes to Chapter VII

[1] Interview with Gen. Mark W. Clark, USA (Ret.), Leland, Michigan, 8 September 1973; Mark Wayne Clark, *Calculated Risk* (New York: Harper and Brothers, 1950), p. 436.
[2] Clark, *Calculated Risk*, pp. 435-36; Clark interview.
[3] HQ Eighty-sixth Mountain Infantry "Statement" by Lt. Col. Robert L. Cook, 10 May 1945, TAGO 201; HQ Tenth Mountain Division Artillery "Certificate" signed by David L. Ruffner, 10 May 1945, TAGO 201; HQ Tenth Mountain Division Artillery "Certificate" signed by 1st Lt. Rawleigh Warner, Jr., 10 May 1945 TAGO 201; Brig. Robert L. Cook, USA (Ret.), to author, 23 November 1972.
[4] "Memorandum for the President" from Secretary of War Henry L. Stimson, 2 May 1945 TAGO 201; Maj. Gen. J. A. Ulio, the adjutant general, to Mrs. Percy W. Darby, 17 May 1945, TAGO 201. Stimson's memorandum invalidates the account of Darby's promotion which until now has been generally accepted. That account cited only the fact that Darby's promotion had been posthumous and implied that, because it was posthumous, it was honorary. Gen. Mark W. Clark gave support to that account in his book *Calculated Risk*, writing that he had "asked General Marshall to promote [Darby] to Brigadier-General posthumously, and he did...." When I showed a copy of Stimson's memorandum to Clark during an interview on 8 September 1973 he appeared to be genuinely surprised, and said that he had always thought Darby's promotion was the result of his own recommendation.

Notes to Chapter VIII

[1] Headquarters, Department of the Army, *FM 21-50: Ranger Training and Ranger Operations* (Washington, D.C.: Department of the Army, 1962), p. i.
[2] Interview with Gen. Mark W. Clark, USA (Ret.), Leland, Michigan, 8 September 1973.

The Sources

DOCUMENTS

Theater, Base and Invasion Force Headquarters

AFHQ Administrative Papers—Letters & Memos—Operation TORCH. SF-95-AL1-1.1.

AFHQ Circulars, October-December 1942. SF-95-AL1-1.12.

AFHQ Commander-in-Chief's Dispatch—North African Campaign. SF-95-AL1-0.5.

AFHQ—Compilation of Reports on Operation TORCH submitted by Assault and Task Force Commanders. SF-95-AL1-0.4.

Allied Forces HQ Memos (18 October 1942–12 August 1943). SF-202-3.9.1.

History of AFHQ, Part One (August-December 1942). SF-95-AL1-0.1.

Operations of British Troops, Invasion of Italian Mainland (9 September–20 December 1943). SF-105-0.3.0.

Center Task Force G-3 Journal File (7 November-31 December 1942). SF-TF1-3.3.

Field Order No. 1, HQ Center Task Force—October 1942. SF-301–3.9.1.

Administrative History—An Outline of HQ ETOUSA, June 1942. SF-97-USF1-0.1.

197

History—U.S. Army in the European Theater of Operations. SF-97-USF1-0.1.

Amphibious Operations in North Africa, 1942-1943. SF-301--0.13.1.

A History of Northern Ireland Base Command (Provisional) and Northern Ireland Base Section (1 June-20 December 1942). SF-97-BC3-0.2.

History—United States Army Forces in Northern Ireland (January-May 1942). SF-97-USF7-0.2.

Outline Plan—Operation SHINGLE (November 1943-January 1944). SF-105–0.13.

Changes, Plans, Supplements, and Annexes to Operation SHINGLE (December 1943-May 1944). SF-105–0.13.

Operation Plan TORCH, HQ Allied Force (September-October 1942). SF-301–0.13.1.

Western Naval Task Force Operation Plan No. 2–43, 1943. SF-301–0.13.1.

Armies

Memorandum for Gen. Mark W. Clark, commanding general, Fifth Army, from Lieutenant General McCreery, commanding Ten Corps, 12 September 1943. Clark.

Message from Clark to Eisenhower, 16 September 1943.

Field Orders of VI Corps, Ten Corps, Fifth Army, for December 1943. SF-105–3.9.

Fifth Army Field Order No. 4. SF-105–3.9.

Fifth Army G-3 Journal and File (9 September 1943–15 February 1944). SF-105–3.2.

Fifth Army Invasion Training Center—History 1943–1944. SF-105-TC-O.1.

G-3 Fifth Army Outline Plan "Operation SHINGLE" (1–12 January 1944). SF-105–3.5.

G-3 Incoming Messages (Operation BIGOT) Fifth Army (23 July-25 August 1943). SF-105–3.4.

G-3 Messages—Movement Orders—Fifth Army (19 October-30 November 1943). SF-105-3.4.
G-3 Operations Instructions No. 4, 5A (29 September 1943). SF-105-3.17.
G-3 Operations Instructions, 5A (4 November 1943-5 October 1944). SF-105-3.17.
G-3 Operations Journal "SHINGLE Log" (18 November 1943-4 February 1944). SF-105-3.2.
G-3 Operations Memos—Fifth Army (21 August 1943-31 March 1944). SF-105-3.16.
G-3 Operations Reports—Fifth Army (9 September 1943--February 1944). SF-105-3.
G-3 Outgoing Messages (Operation BIGOT) Non-Movement Fifth Army (20 July-25 August 1943). SF-105-3.4.
Map—Salerno Beachhead—Advance to the Volturno, 5A (15 September-6 October 1943). SF-105-3.7.
Seventh Army—G-3—Notes on the Sicilian Campaign (10 July-18 August 1943). SF-107-3.0.
Seventh Army—G-3 Operation Report—Sicilian Campaign (Operation HUSKY) (July-August 1943). SF-107-3.0.
Seventh Army—Overlays (G-3 Periodic Reports No. 18-41) (27 July-19 August 1943). SF-107-36.
Seventh Army—Overlays of 1st Infantry Division G-3 Reports (4 July-6 August 1943). SF-107-3.6.

Corps

Center Task Force—II Corps—G-2 Journal and File (January 1943). SF-202-2.2.
Center Task Force—II Corps—G-2 Journal and Overlay (February 1943). SF-202-2.2.
II Corps Field Orders. SF-202-3.9.
II Corps—Field Orders and Operational Orders from HQ under the control of II Corps. SF-202-3.9.1.
II Corps G-2 Intelligence Report—The El Guettar Operation. SF-202-2.

II Corps G-2 Message File (10 December 1942–1 January 1943). SF-202–2.4.
II Corps G-2 Plans and Personnel (4 September-27 December 1942). SF-202–2.5.
II Corps G-2/G-3 Journal (9–10 July 1943). SF-202–0.7.
G-3 Journal and File—II Corps. SF-202–3.2.
G-3 Periodic Reports—II Corps (24 November-7 December 1943). SF-202–3.1.
II Corps Messages. SF-202–0.12.
II Corps Periodical Reports. SF-202–3.1.
Report of Operations of II Corps in the Sicilian Campaign (10 July-17 August 1943). SF.
II Corps Report of Operations—Tunisia (1 January-15 March 1943). SF-202–0.3.
Operation Plan "WOP" (March 1943) II Corps. SF-301–0.13.
VI Corps After Action Report (November-December 1943). SF-206–0.3.
VI Corps Field Orders (1943–1945). SF-206–3.9.
VI Corps G-3 Journal and File (1 November 1943–20 February 1944). SF-206–3.2.
G-3 Reports—Italy VI Corps. SF-206–3.1.
VI Corps Operation Report—Crossing the River Volturno (October-November 1943). SF-206–0.3.0.
VI Corps Outline Plan—Operation "AVALANCHE" (19 August 1943). SF-206–0.13.
VI Corps Outline Plan—Operation SHINGLE. SF-206–0.13.
Mounting/Initial Phase of Operation SHINGLE VI Corps. SF-206–3.0.
VI Corps Unit History Report (January 1941-February 1945). SF-206–0.1.
Provisional Corps Report of Operations (15 July-20 August 1943). SF-200–0.3.

Divisions

History—First Cavalry Division (12 September 1921-December 1944). SF-901-0.1.
Amphibious Operations—CARIB—First Infantry Division 1941. SF-301-0.3.
First Infantry Division Final Report—Army and Navy Joint Exercise No. 7—First Division Task Force 1940-1941. SF-301-0.3.0.
G-3 Journal and File—First Infantry Division. SF-301-3.2.
G-3 Operations Report—First Infantry Division (8-10 November 1942). SF-301-3.
G-3 Operations Report—First Infantry Division (15 January-8 April 1943). SF-301-3.
Second Armored Division—G-3 Journal and File (25 July-20 August 1943). SF-602-3.2.
Second Armored Division Maps. SF-602-3.7.
Second Armored Division—Operations Reports (22 April-September 1943). SF-602-0.3.
Third Infantry Division—G-2 Journal (10 July-17 August 1943). SF-303-2.2.
Third Infantry Division—G-2 Periodic Reports (20 July-18 August 1943). SF-303-2.1.
Third Infantry Division G-3 Journal (10 July-19 August 1943). SF-303-3.2.
Third Infantry Division G-3 Journal and File. SF-303-3.2.
Third Infantry Division G-3 Journal and File (10 July-19 August 1943). SF-303-3.3.
Third Infantry Division Reports of Operations (10 July-17 August 1943). SF-303-0.1.
Third Infantry Division Report of Operations (22 January-31 January 1944). SF-303-0.3.
Third Infantry Division FO Operations SHINGLE. SF-303-3.9.
History of the Sixth Infantry Division, "Those Who Walked" (November 1917-January 1941). SF-306-0.
Field Orders 3-5, Tenth Mountain Division (April 1945). SF-310-3.9.

Tenth Mountain Division History (1943-1945). SF-310-0.

Thirty-sixth Infantry Division Field Orders (6 November 1943-30 January 1944). SF-202-3.9.1.

Thirty-sixth Infantry Division G-3 Journal and File (27 November-14 December 1943). SF.

Report of Operations, Thirty-sixth Infantry Division (November-December 1943). SF-336-0.3.

Forth-fifth Division G-3 Report (November-December 1943). SF-345-3.

Forty-fifth Infantry Division G-3 Journal and File (1 November-14 December 1943). SF-345-3.2.

Forty-fifth Infantry Division G-3 Periodic Reports (1-30 November 1943). SF-345-3.1.

Operations of the Forty-fifth Infantry Division in Italy (1-30 November 1943). SF-345-0.3.

Eighty-second Airborne Division Commanding General's Journal, Sicilian Campaign (2 July-19 August 1943). SF-382-0.7.

Eighty-second Airborne Division G-3 Journal, Italy (September-October 1943). SF-382-3.2.

Eighty-second Airborne Division G-3 Message File (September-October 1943). SF-382-3.3.

Eighty-second Airborne Division G-3 Periodic File, Sicily (12 July-18 August 1943). SF-382-3.1.

Eighty-second Airborne Division History of Operations, Italy (September-October 1943). SF-382-0.3. .

Eighty-second Airborne Division Journal File—Sicily (17-29 July 1943). SF-382-0.8.

Eighty-second Airborne Division Message Books (5 July-8 August 1943). SF-382-3.3.

Eighty-second Airborne Division in Sicily and Italy (9 July 1943-22 January 1944). SF-382-0.3.0.

Eighty-second Airborne Division Synopsis of Operations in Sicilian Campaign (16 July-21 August 1943). SF-382-0.3.

Regimental and Smaller Headquarters

1st Ranger Battalion—Historical Information (1942–44) through Unit Journal (November-December 1943). SF-INBN 72–37 R1.
1st Ranger Battalion—Messages (February-December 1943) through Training Guides (8 July 1943). SF-INBN 72–37 R2.
3rd Ranger Battalion—Report of Action (10–18 July 1943) through Special Orders (June 1943-January 1944). SF-INBN 72–37 R4.
Report of Operations—7th Infantry (10 July-25 August 1943). SF-303-Inf(7)-0.3.
Regimental Field Orders—15th Infantry (14 November 1942–30 December 1943). SF-303-Inf(15)-3.9.
Journal and File—15th Infantry (7 July-18 August 1943). SF-303-Inf(15)-0.7.
Unit Journal and File—15th Infantry (31 July-18 August 1943). SF-303-Inf(15)-3.2.
Report of Operations—15th Infantry (7 July-18 August 1943). SF-303-Inf(15)-0.3.
After Action Report—16th Combat Team (November 1942-April 1943). SF-301-Inf(16)-0.3.
Report of Operations—18th Combat Team. SF-301-Inf(18)-0.3.
Report of Operations—26th Infantry Regiment (8 November 1942–8 May 1943). SF-301-Inf(26)-0.3.
39th Infantry Report of Operations (13 July-15 August 1943). SF-309-Inf(39)-0.3.
Report of Operations—Combat Command "A" (2nd Armored Division), Sicily. SF-602-CC(A)-0.3.
History—80th Field Artillery Battalion—6th Infantry Division (17 June-5 December 1942). SF-306-FA(80)-0.1.
Unit History File—80th Field Artillery, OCMH-80FA.
Annual Histories—82nd Field Artillery Regiment (1926–1939). SF-FARG-82-0.1.
History—82nd Field Artillery Regiment (1917–1941). SF-FARG-82-0.1.

Unit History File—82nd Field Artillery, OCMH-82FA.
History—84th Field Artillery Battalion—9th Infantry Division (1934-March 1938). SF-309-FA(84)-0.1.
Unit History File—84th Field Artillery, OCMH-84FA.
86th Mountain Infantry Regiment History (10 December 1944–30 June 1945). SF-310-Inf(86)-0.1.
86th Mountain Infantry Regiment Journal and File (February-April 1945). SF-Inf(86)-2.2.
History—99th Field Artillery Battalion (1 June 1940–30 April 1944). SF-901-FA(99)-0.1.
Unit History File—99th Field Artillery, OCMH-99FA.
History—179th Infantry Regiment—45th Infantry Division (1943–1945). SF-345-Inf(179)-0.
S-3 Journal—179th Infantry Regiment. SF-345-Inf(179)-3.2.
504th Parachute Infantry—Action in Italy (13–30 September 1943). SF-382-Inf(504)-0.3.
504th Parachute Infantry—Staff and S-3 Journal, Italy (October-December 1943). SF-382-INf(504)-0.3.

Nonunit Documents

Darby, William Orlando.
———. "U.S. Rangers,"(Lecture given at the Army and Navy Staff College, Washington, D. C., 27 October 1944). A copy is in the author's possession.
———. Official Transcript of United States Military Academy Record. A copy is in the author's possession.
———. United States Military Academy Personnel File (USMA 201 File), United States Military Academy Archives. West Point, New York.
HQ Army Ground Forces Notes on Interview with Colonel William O. Darby, 18 May 1944. Infantry Hall Library, Fort Benning, Georgia.
Memorandum for General Clark, commanding general, Fifth Army, from Lieutenant General McCreery, commanding Ten Corps, 12 September 1943.

Message from Clark to Eisenhower, 16 September 1943. Clark.
Remarks made to Colonel R. F. McEldowney by Lt. Col. William O. Darby, 18 October 1943. Infantry Hall Library, Fort Benning, Georgia.
United States Military Academy. General Orders, Special Orders, Special and General Court-Martial Rules, and Memoranda. United States Military Academy Archives. West Point, New York.

LETTERS

Ashworth, Col. Edward T., USA (Ret.), to author, 4 December 1977.
Bernard, Col. Lyle W., USA (Ret.), to author, 6 December 1977.
Boswell, Brig. Gen. James O., USA (Ret.), to author, 28 November 1977.
Cleveland, Col. John A., Jr., USA (Ret.), to author, 29 November 1977.
Cunin, Col. Kenneth A., USA (Ret.), to author, (undated) 1977.
Dodge, Melvin, to author, (undated) 1978.
Donnelly, Lt. Gen. Harold C., USAF (Ret.), to author, (undated) 1977.
Downing, Col. Walter A., USA (Ret.), to author, 12 January 1978.
Edwards, Brig. Gen. Morris O., USA (Ret., to author, 9 January 1978.
Ehalt, Robert, to author, (undated) 1978.
Ehlen, Brig. Gen. Edward S., USA (Ret.), to author, 2 December 1977.
Gray, Maj. Gen. David W., USA (Ret.), to author, 28 January 1973.
Hummer, Maj. John F., AUS (Ret.), to author, 6 September 1978.
Hutchinson, Col. William S., Jr., USA (Ret.), to author, 27 December 1972 and 1 August 1973.

Johnson, Gen. Harold K., USA (Ret.), to author, 18 January 1978.
Jones, Col. Beverly D., USA (Ret.), to author, 23 January 1978.
King, Col. Harrison, USA (Ret.), to author, 1 February 1973.
Kopveiler, Eugene N., to author, 23 September 1978.
Leavey, Maj. Gen. Edmond H., USA (Ret.) to James Altieri, 3 August and 14 October 1965. James Altieri.
Lehmann, Carl Harrison, to author, 8 September 1978.
Lincoln, Lt. Gen. Lawrence J. USA (Ret.), to author, 1 February and 11 March 1973.
Lothrop, Col. Guy C., USA (Ret.), to author, 19 January 1978.
Mahoney, Ed, to author, 28 August 1978.
Markham, Ken, to author, (undated) 1978.
Marshall, Col. Edward D., USAF (Ret.), to author, 22 January 1978.
Peterson, Col. Charles A., USA (Ret.), to author, 23 November, 1 and 12 December 1972.
Prudhomme, Thomas, to author, tape (undated) 1978.
Rensinck, Gerritt, to author, (undated) 1978.
Rudolph, Col. Jack W., USA (Ret.), to author, 18 January 1978.
Ryan, Brig. Gen. William F., USA (Ret.), to author, 20 January 1978.
Schuder, Raymond (Jack), to author, 14 September 1978.
Sommers, Sheldon C., M.D., to author, 11 September 1978.
Swank, Lt. Col. Marcell G., USA (Ret., to author, (undated) 1978.
VanArtsdalen, Donald W., to author, 18 October 1978.
VanWay, Col. George L., USA (Ret.), to author, 19 January 1978.

INTERVIEWS

Beasley, Natalie Darby. Telephone interview, 13 April 1979.
Buck, Lt. Col. Peer, USA (Ret.). Plover, Wisconsin, 18 November 1972.

Clark, Gen. Mark W., USA (Ret.). Leland, Michigan, 8 September 1973.
Dammer, Col. Herman W., USA (Ret.), and Elizabeth. McLean, Virginia. Interview 15 July 1972.
Darby, Lena. Fort Smith, Arkansas, 12 August 1973.
Gardner, Carnall (Tiny). Fort Smith, Arkansas, 13 August 1973.
Hogan, Bill and Ruby. Fort Smith, Arkansas, 11 August 1973.
Hutchinson, Col. William, USA (Ret.). Jacksonville, Florida, 14 June 1973.
Lemuth, Ruth Tumblin. Fort Chaffee, Arkansas, 13 August 1973.
Murray, Col. Roy, USA (Ret.). Fort Bliss, Texas, and Ciudad Juarez, Mexico, 3 March 1973.
Olesen, Robert H. Racine, Wisconsin, 24 March 1979.
Van Skoy, John. Columbus, Ohio, 20 May 1972.
Watkins, Doris Nell Darby. Cleveland, Mississippi, 23 April 1973.
Zaslaw, Stan. Deerfield, Illinois, 19 June 1972.

BOOKS

Altieri, James J. *Darby's Rangers: An Illustrated Portrayal of the Original Rangers*. Durham, North Carolina: The Seeman Printery, Inc., 1945.
_____. *The Spearheaders*. New York: Popular Library, 1960.
Blumenson, Martin. *Salerno to Cassino: United States Army in World War II*. Washington, D.C.: Office of the Chief of Military History, United States Army, 1969.
Clark, Mark Wayne. *Calculated Risk*. New York: Harper and Brothers, 1950.
Cline, Ray S. *Washington Command Post: The Operations Division: United States Army in World War II*. Washington, D.C.: Office of the Chief of Military History, United States Army, 1951.
Department of the Army, Headquarters. *FM 21-50: Ranger*

Training and Ranger Operations. Washington, D.C.: Department of the Army, 1962.

_____. *FM-21-100: Soldier's Handbook.* Washington, D.C.: United States Government Printing Office, 1941.

Eisenhower, Dwight D. *Crusade in Europe.* New York: Avon Books, 1968.

Fort Smith Senior High School. *The 1929 Bruin.* Fort Smith, Arkansas: Fort Smith Senior High Garland, Lt. Col. Albert N., ting Department, 1929.

and Smyth, Howard McGaw. *Sicily and the Surrender of Italy: United States Army in World War II.* Washington, D.C.: Department of the Army, 1965.

Gregory, Jack, and Strickland, Rennard. *Hell on The Border.* Muskogee, Oklahoma: Indian Heritage Publications, 1971.

Hicks, Edwin P. *Belle Starr and Her Pearl.* Little Rock, Arkansas: Pioneer Press, 1963.

Howe, George F. *Northwest Africa: Seizing the Initiative in the West: United States Army in World War II.* Washington, D.C.: Office of the Chief of Military History, United States Army, 1957.

Huntington, Samuel P. *The Soldier and the State.* New York: Vantage Books, 1957.

Jackson, W. G. F. *The Battle for Italy.* New York: Harper & Row, 1967.

Janowitz, Morris. *The Professional Soldier.* New York: The Free Press, 1960.

Link, Arthur S. *American Epoch.* New York: Alfred A. Knopf, 1961.

Millis, Walter. *Arms and Men.* New York: Mentor Books, 1958.

Morrison, Olin Dee. *New Historical Atlas of Illinois.* Athens, Ohio: E. M. Morrison, 1966.

Otto, S. E., ed. *The Howitzer.* Privately printed, 1933.

Taggart, Donald G., ed. *History of the Third Infantry Division in World War II.* Washington, D.C.: Infantry Journal Press, 1947.

Truscott, Lt. Gen. Lucian King, Jr. *Command Missions: A*

Personal Story. New York: E. P. Dutton and Company, 1954.
United States Military Academy. *Information Relative to the Appointment and Admission of Cadets to the United States Military Academy, West Point, N.Y. 1930 edition.* Washington, D.C.: United States Government Printing Office, 1929.

───. *Official Register of the Officers and Cadets: United States Military Academy for 1930.* West Point, N.Y.: United States Military Academy Printing Office, 1930.

───. *Official Register of the Officers and Cadets: United States Military Academy for 1931.* West Point, N.Y.: United States Military Academy Printing Office, 1931.

───. *Official Register of the Officers and Cadets: United States Military Academy for 1932.* West Point, N.Y.: United States Military Academy Printing Office, 1932.

───. *Official Register of the Officers and Cadets: United States Military Academy for 1933.* West Point, N.Y.: United States Military Academy Printing Office, 1933.

Watson, Mark Skinner. *The War Department: Chief of Staff: Prewar Plans and Preparations.* Washington, D.C.: Historical Division, Department of the Army, 1950.

Weigley, Russell F. *Towards an American Army.* New York: Columbia University Press, 1962.

NEWSPAPERS AND PERIODICALS

Boyle, Harold V. "Fort Smithian Leads Rangers in Tunisian Raid." *Southwest Times Record* (Fort Smith, Arkansas), 23 February 1943, p. 1.

"Darby Parade." *Southwest American* (Fort Smith, Arkansas), 26 April 1944, p. 1.

Hicks, Edwin P. "Story of Bill Darby—A Fort Smith Boy Who Has Gained National Fame as Outstanding Soldier in World War 2." *The Fort Smithian*, 11 November 1943, pp. 1-2.

"Lessons from the Maneuvers: Extracts from the Reports of Field Artillery Official Observers at the Second Army-First

Army exercises." *Field Artillery Journal* 31 (1941):914–17.
"Parade Planned for Darby Visit." *Southwest American* (Fort Smith, Arkansas), 25 April 1944, p. 1.
"Ranger Organizer Sees the Infantry School, Old Buddies."*The Bayonet* (Fort Benning, Georgia), 25 May 1944, p. 5.
Underhill, Garrett. "Louisiana Hayride." *Field Artillery Journal* 31 (1941):907–13.
Williams, Col. R. C., Jr. "Amphibious Scouts and Raiders." *Military Affairs* 13 (1949):157.

Index

The index includes references to military units only when Darby was attached to their command, they were attached to his command, or they and he fought for the same immediate objective.

Achnacarry, 36, 39, 168
Adige River, 173
Agerola, 125
Alban Hills, 139, 148, 152, 154
Alexander, Gen. Sir Harold R. L. G., 63
Allen, Maj. Gen. Terry de la Mesa, 40, 44, 53-55, 62, 64, 69, 77, 79
Allied Forces Headquarters (AFHQ), 41
Altieri, James J., 52, 54, 66
Amalfi, 114
Anzio, 137, 139-49, 184
Army Air Force, 29
Army and Navy Staff College, 169
Army Ground Forces (AGF), 28, 29
Arzew, 42-55, 71, 108, 184
Ashworth, Edward T., 169
AVALANCHE, 99-113
Avellino, 122, 126

Bachle, Pearle, 8, 11

Batterie Superieur, 46-52
Bayonets and knives, 58, 147, 153, 156-57
BAYTOWN, 100, 108, 113
Beeler, George Wood, 13, 18
Bernard, Lyle W., 16
Boswell, James O., 17
Bradley, Maj. Gen. Omar, 77, 88
Brady, Lt. Col. Brookner W., 80
Brann, Brig. Gen. Donald W., 130
Buck, Sgt. Maj. Peer, 35, 106, 118
Butera, 88-89

Camp Beauregard, Louisiana, 21
Camp Butner, North Carolina, 161, 165, 168
Camp Chaffee, Arkansas, 165
Camp Croft, South Carolina, 165
Camp Fannin, Texas, 167
Camp Forrest, Tennessee, 135
Camp Hood, Texas, 167
Camp Ritchie, Maryland, 168
Camp Robinson, Arkansas, 167

Camp Wheeler, Georgia, 165
Camp Wolters, Texas, 167
Campbell, Lt. Raymond F., 90
Cannavinelle Hill, 127
Carib Force, 24
Carrickfergus, 34-35
Castellammare, 117, 126
Casualties
 French, 44-45, 50, 51, 53
 German, 63, 90, 110, 113-14, 116, 147-49, 153, 159
 Italian, 60, 63, 66, 84-87, 89-90
 Ranger, 39, 40, 50, 51, 52, 54, 58-59, 63, 66, 68, 71, 86, 90, 103, 114, 121, 130, 133-35, 153, 156-57
Cava Gap, 101, 105-7, 123
Center Task Force, 42, 52
Ceppagna, 129, 131
Chaney, Maj. Gen. James E., 26, 29-31, 33, 36
Chiunzi Pass, 101-21, 123-25, 127, 137, 184
Cisterna di Littoria, 137, 149-59, 165, 168, 184, 185
Civilian Conservation Corps (CCC), 19
Clark, Lt. Gen. Mark W., 28, 100-103, 114, 116, 118-19, 122, 124-25, 137-40, 149, 158, 161-62, 168, 170-71, 185
Cleveland, John A., 16
Combined Operations Headquarters (COHQ), 30
Commandos
 as model for Rangers, 30-32
 train First Ranger Battalion, 36-40

Communications and control, 50-52, 57, 58, 83, 85, 108-9, 152-53, 156, 166-67
Conca, 151-52, 154
Contrera, Sgt. Carlo, 157
Control. *See* Communications and control
Cook, Lt. Col. Robert L., 174-75
Corleone, 93-94, 103
Cowes, 35
Cunin, Lt. Col. Kenneth A., 82

Dammer, Elizabeth, 169
Dammer, Maj. Herman W., 10, 34-35, 45-49, 54-55, 74, 80, 86, 89, 103, 106, 145, 150, 169-70, 185
Darby, Doris Nell, 6, 11, 164
Darby, Edgar, 8
Darby, Lena Godt, 8
Darby, Nell, 6, 7, 164-65
Darby, Percy, 6, 7, 9, 11, 164-65
Darby, Thelma May, 6, 9
Darby, Brig. Gen. William Orlando
 artillery background, influence of, 51, 82, 106-7, 115, 160-61, 185-86
 assignments, peacetime, 18-26
 assistant division commander, Tenth Mountain Division, appointed, 171
 birth, 6
 brigadier general, promoted to, 175
 Cisterna, attitude toward attack on, 150
 colonel, promoted to, 136, 178-82; recommended for pro-

Index

motion to by Clark, 119; refuses promotion to, 68-69, 88
as commander: of combined arms team, 70, 88, 91-92, 114, 171-73; of First Ranger Battalion, 32, 36; of Force "X," 79-87, 180; of 179th Infantry, 159-62; of TF Darby, 171-73; of TF "X," 91-92, 180
commissioned, 18
confidence, 14, 160, 177
death of, 174-75
Distinguished Service Cross, awarded, 68
Distinguished Service Order, recommended for by British, 121
education, primary, 8
education, secondary, 9-10
efficiency reports, 46, 168, 170, 177-78
Field Artillery School, attends, 20
Hartle, Maj. Gen. Russell P., serves as aide to, 26-32
intelligence, 46, 177
leadership, 7, 16, 46, 60-61, 68, 85-86, 95-96, 134, 138, 177, 183
180th Infantry, refuses command of, 88
personality, 7, 16-17, 46, 168, 177
persuasiveness, 10
Ranger battalions: commands all three, 92, 137; no control over, 75-76, 133

Ranger Force, relieved as CO of, 160
Rangers: and conventional use of, 54, 87-88, 96-98, 106-7, 185-86; as senior battalion commander of, 136
Silver Star, awarded, 61
training, inspects, 165-68
troops, concern for, 69, 95
West Point, wins appointment to, 11-12; attends, 12-18
Dieppe, 39-40, 96
Djebel el Ank, 65-66, 71, 184
Dobson, Maj. Jack, 145-46, 154, 156
Dodge, Melvin, 138
Donnelly, Harold C., 17
Downing, Walter A., 16
Duff, Brig. Gen. Robinson E., 170

Eagles, Maj. Gen. William W., 132, 160
Eddy, Maj. Gen. Manton S., 62
Edwards, Morris O., 169
Ehalt, Sgt. Maj. Robert, 157
Ehlen, Edward S., 16
Eisenhower, Gen. Dwight D., 28, 41, 55, 63, 97-98, 100
El Guettar, 57, 121
Evans, M. Sgt. John T., 174-75

Femina Morta. *See* Isola Bella
Fort Benning, Georgia, 165-67
Fort Bliss, Texas, 18-19, 21, 82
Fort Bragg, North Carolina, 15, 22, 24
Fort de la Pointe, 46-52
Fort du Nord, 52

Fort Hoyle, Maryland, 21-26, 82
Fort Lewis, Washington, 21
Fort McClellan, Alabama, 165, 166
Fort Meade, Maryland, 165
Fort Monroe, Virginia, 15
Fort Riley, Kansas, 21
Fort Sill, Oklahoma, 21
Fort Smith, Arkansas, 5-12, 163-165, 168
Fowler, Lt. James G., 153
Fredendall, Maj. Gen. Lloyd R., 42, 51, 54-55, 61
French Foreign Legion, 52

Gaffey, Maj. Gen. Hugh J., 88
Galita, 55
Garrison, Pfc. Elmer W., 58
Gela, 77, 79-87, 95, 96, 106, 108, 143, 183, 184
Glendenning, Lt. Col., 36
Gragnano, 115, 117, 125
Grissamer, Pfc. George G., 52
Gun, 75mm self-propelled, 53, 106-7, 115
Gustav Line, 122

Hartle, Maj. Gen. Russell P., 26, 27, 31, 35, 39
Hays, Maj. Gen. George P., 22, 24, 170, 173-74, 182
Highway 6, 127, 129, 139
Highway 7, 139, 149-50
Hogan, Bill, 7
Holland, Chester, 164
Hummer, John F., 94-95
Hunt, Capt., 36
HUSKY, 73-87, 108

Hutchinson, William W., Jr., 82, 134

Isola Bella, 151-52, 154, 156

Johnson, Harold K., 17
Jones, Beverly D., 16

Kasserine, 61-63, 67
Kenny, Lt. Col. Roy W., 144
Keyes, Maj. Gen. Geoffrey T., 91-92, 132
Kopveiler, Eugene, 94

La Macta, 53-54, 67, 184
La Molina Defile, 101, 110
Ladd, Cpl. Garland S., 60
Lake Garda, 173-75
Laycock, Brigadier R. E., 36
Leavy, Maj. Gen. Edmond H., 27, 32
Leppert, Capt., 81
Lewis, Capt., 143-44, 146-47
Licata, 96
Lincoln, Lawrence J., 169
Lothrop, Guy C., 169
Louisiana Maneuvers, 21, 168
Lucas, Maj. Gen. John P., 140, 147-49, 154
Lucrino, 137
Lurgen, 33
Lyle, Lt. Jim, 62

McCreery, Lt. Gen. Sir Richard L., CG 10 Corps, 117-18, 120, 122-23, 171
McLellan, Lt. James H., 174-75
Mahoney, Sgt. Ed, 96

Index

Maiori, 100-101, 103, 105, 110, 118, 123
Marsala, 91-92
Marshall, Edward D., 17, 169
Marshall, Gen. George C., 28, 30, 74, 162
Messina, 92-94
Middleton, Maj. Gen. Troy H., 77, 88, 132
Mignano Gap, 127, 129, 132
Miller, Maj. Alvah, 145
Monte Camino, 127
Monte Cassino, 122
Monte Corno, 133
Monte di Chiunzi, 105-6, 133-14
Monte la Difensa, 127
Monte Lungo, 127, 129
Monte Maggiore, 127
Monte Pendolo, 114, 117
Monte Rotondo, 127, 129
Monte Sammucro, 127, 131, 136
Monte San Angelo di Cava, 105-6, 123
Mortars, 60mm, 38-39, 48, 58, 82, 116
Mortars, 81mm, 48-51, 82
Mortars, 4.2-inch, 25, 82, 87, 186
MOSSTROOPER, 45
Mountbatten, Lord Louis, 28
Mulholland, Paige, 7
Murray, Maj. Roy A., 46, 74-75, 103, 106, 129-32, 134-36, 154, 161

Nago, 174
Naples, 100-101, 114, 121-26
Naples, Plain of, 101, 105, 110, 115, 118, 122-23
Naval gunfire, 44, 48, 84-85, 87, 110, 115-16

Nettuno, 140, 147
Nocera, 103, 105, 106, 113, 120, 123-25
Nye, Lt. Walter F., 133

Omagh, 33

Padiglione Woods, 149, 159
Pagani, 103, 105, 113, 120, 123, 125
Palermo, 91-92, 108
Patton, Maj. Gen. George S., Jr., 42, 63, 64, 68-69, 70, 76-77, 86-89, 90-93, 97
PEASHOOTER, 55
Piccolo Peak, 116, 137
Po River, 171-72
Porto Empedocle, 90
Pozzuoli Bay, 144
Presenzano, 127, 129
Prudhomme, Thomas, 138

Ranger Battalion, First
   Achnaccary, at, 36-39
   activated, 34, 36
   Anzio, at, 140-49
   Arzew, in capture of, 49-52
   Carrickfergus, at, 34-36
   Cisterna, in battle for, 149-59
   Clyde, at, 45, 48-49
   Corkerhill Camp, at, 40, 45
   designated, 32
   Distinguished Unit Citation, awarded, 121
   Djebel Berda, at, 67-68
   Djebel el Ank Pass, captures, 65-66
   Dorlin House, Argyle, at, 39
   Dundee, at, 40
   El Guettar, at, 67-68

Fifth Army Invasion Training Center, at, 55-57
Gafsa, attacks, 64
Gela, at, 80, 83-87
Gourock, at, 45
inactivated, 161
Kasserine, at, 61-63
Loch Linnhe, at, 45
morale, declining, 56
Salerno, at, 103-21
Sened raid, on, 57-61
train selves, 56-57
training, and organization, 33-40; preinvasion, 81-82; reveals deterioration of fighting skills, 144
Winter Line, on, 126-38
Ranger Battalion, Second, 135
Ranger Battalion, Third
activated, 81
Anzio, at, 140-49
Cisterna, in battle for, 149-59
Darby's control, out of, 91
Dintinguished Unit Citation, awarded, 121
formation of, 73-74
inactivated, 161
Licata, at, 80, 86
Porto Empedocle, captures, 90
Salerno, at, 103-21
training demonstrates maintenance of fighting skills, 145
Winter Line, on, 126-38
Ranger Battalion, Fourth
activated, 81
Anzio, at, 140-49
Cisterna, in battle for, 149-59
formation of, 73-74
Gela, at, 80, 83-87
inactivated, 161
Salerno, at, 103-21
Winter Line, on, 126-38
Ranger Battalion, Fifth, 135
Ranger Cannon Company, 106, 151, 180
Ranger Force
Cisterna, at, 149-59
conventional use of, 111, 137, 148
formation of, 73-74
headquarters, authorized, 145; not authorized, 75-76, 97-98, 135-36
redesignated 6615th Ranger Force (Provisional), 140
replacements, difficulty getting, 129-31
Ridgway, Maj. Gen. Matthew B., commander of, 124-25
training reveals deterioration of fighting skills, 144-45
unit, seldom fought as, 76
Rensinck, Cpl. Gerrit, 34
Ridgway, Maj. Gen. Matthew B., 92, 124-25, 126
Ripley, Cpl. Charles, 84
Roosevelt, Brig. Gen. Theodore, Jr., 67
Rudolph, Jack W., 169
Ruffner, Brig. Gen. David, 174
Ryan, William F., 16

S. Agata, 94
Saint Cloud, 53-54, 67, 71, 184
Sala, 125
Salerno, 100-103, 107-21, 126, 137, 183, 184
San Egidio, 125

Index

San Pietro Infine, 131, 136, 184
Sanseverino, 101, 120, 123, 126
Schuder, Raymond, 95
Schuster, Capt. Emil, 117
Security, 48
Sened, 57-61, 71, 167, 184
Service of Supply, 29
Sesto Campana, 130
Shinberger, John Baird, 13, 18
SHINGLE, 139-46
Shunstrom, Capt. Charles, 106, 115, 153-54, 156
Sommers, Capt. Sheldon C., 95-96
Surprise, 46-49, 66, 84-85, 86, 107, 110-11
Swank, Sgt. Marcell G., 96

Thorn, Lt. Gen., 36
Torbole, 173-75
TORCH, 41-55, 108
Trapani, 92
Truscott, Maj. Gen. Lucian K., Jr., 28, 29, 30, 32, 77, 80, 90, 149, 171
Tumblin family, 8

Units and Commands, Axis
  Herman Goering Panzer Division, 87, 113-14, 116-17, 148, 152
  Tenth Bersaglieri Regiment, 60
  Sixteenth Panzer Division, 109-10, 113
Units and Commands, British and Commonwealth
  Commando Depot, 36
  Scottish Command, 36
  Special Services Brigade, 31, 36, 38

First Division, 140, 147-49
Second Canadian Division, 35
Second Royal Marine Commandos, 107, 110
Seventh Armoured Division, 123
Ten Corps, 100-101, 107-11, 115, 123-34
Twenty-third Armoured Brigade, 120, 123, 125
Forty-first Royal Marine Commandos, 107, 110
Forty-sixth Division, 101, 111, 113, 118, 123
Fifty-sixth Division, 101, 111, 123, 126
Units and Commands, United States' and Combined
  Atlantic Base Section, 74
  Combined Chiefs of Staff, 73, 100
  Force "X," 79, 81-87, 180
  Force 141, 73
  Force 343, 76-77
  Provisional Corps, 91-92
  Task Force Darby, 171-73
  Task Force "X," 91-92, 180
  United States Army Forces British Isles (USAFBI), 29, 30
  United States Army Northern Ireland Forces (USANIF), 27, 30, 33
  First Army, 61
  I Armored Corps, 76-77
  First Armored Division, 30, 34, 102, 132, 140
  First Cavalry Division, 18-20
  First Infantry Division, 23, 24, 40, 42, 52-54, 67-69, 77, 87

First Special Service Force (Canadian-American), 161
II Corps, 40, 42, 54, 57, 61-64, 68-70, 73, 77, 80, 89, 93-94, 132
Second Armored Division, 88-89
Second Motorized Chemical Battalion, 114
Third Infantry Division, 22, 77, 86, 88-91, 102, 120, 128-29, 132, 140-41, 143-44, 147-51, 158, 185
Third Reconnaissance Troop, 154
Fourth Field Artillery Battalion (Pack), 24
Fifth Army, 100, 103, 111, 120, 122, 132-33, 137, 158, 171
V Corps (Reinforced), 27, 33
VI Corps, 100-101, 107, 111, 113, 115-116, 122, 127-29, 137, 140, 147-49, 151, 158-59
Seventh Army, 77, 90, 93, 97
Seventh Infantry, 150
Seventh RCT, 80
Ninth Infantry Division, 62, 68
Tenth Mountain Division, 170-75
Tenth Medical Battalion, 171
Thirteenth Tank Battalion, 171
15 Army Group, 73
Fifteenth Infantry, 80-81, 86, 150
Sixteenth Infantry, 52-53
Sixteenth RCT, 80
CT 16, 64
18 Army Group, 63, 73
Eighteenth Infantry, 53-54, 68
CT 18, 64, 67
Twenty-sixth Infantry, 65-66
Twenty-sixth RCT, 80
Thirtieth Infantry, 130
Thirty-fourth Infantry Division, 27, 29-31, 33-34, 102, 128-29
Thirty-sixth Infantry Division, 101-02, 116, 132
Thirty-sixth Combat Engineers, 114, 126, 140, 143, 147-48
Thirty-ninth RCT, 91
Thirty-ninth Combat Engineers, 79-80, 84-85
Forty-first Infantry, 88
Forty-fifth Infantry Division, 77, 87, 88, 101, 113, 116, 128-34, 140, 159
Fifty-seventh Signal Battalion, 140
Seventy-seventh Artillery, 91
Seventy-eighth Armored Field Artillery Battalion, 88
Eightieth Field Artillery, 21
Eightieth Antiaircraft Battalion, 125
Eighty-second Airborne Division, 92, 120, 125-26
Eighty-second Field Artillery, 18-19, 21, 82
Eighty-second Reconnaissance Battalion, 88
Eighty-third Chemical Battalion, 79, 82, 84-85, 106, 126, 131, 140, 143, 151, 180-81
Eighty-fourth Field Artillery, 20-21
Eighty-fifth Mountain Infantry Regiment, 171-72
Eighty-sixth Mountain Infantry, 171, 173-74
Eighty-seventh Mountain Infantry, 171

Index

Ninety-ninth Field Artillery (Pack), 21-26, 82, 170
120th Engineer Battalion, 131
126th Engineer Battalion, 171
133rd Field Artillery Battalion, 114
143rd Infantry, 114
163rd Signal Photography Company, 140
179th Infantry, 159-62, 183
180th Infantry, 88, 131-32, 136-37
250th Motor Transport Company, 20
319th Glider Field Artillery Battalion, 120
325th Glider Infantry, 120
504th Parachute Infantry, 120, 125, 140
509th Parachute Infantry, 131, 140, 143, 147
531st Engineer Shore Regiment, 79, 84
601st Tank Destroyer Battalion, 114, 151
701st Tank Destroyer Battalion, 171
751st Medium Tank Battalion, 114
1125th Field Artillery Battalion, 171

Vaccaro, 105
Vallecupa, 129
VanArtsdalen, Sgt. Donald W., 60
VanWay, George, 16
Vaughan, Col. Charles A., 36, 38-39
Venafro, 129, 136
Verona, 171-73
Vietri, 101, 103, 107, 111, 117, 120, 123-34
Villafranca, 172-73
Volturno River, 127, 129-31

War Department, 29, 97, 136, 162-70
Weems, Brig. Gen. George H., 166
West Point, 8-9, 11-18, 35, 46, 82, 145-46, 169, 177-78, 182-83
Wilmont, 27, 33
Wingo, Otis, 11
Winter Line, 122, 126-38, 184-85
Woodruff, Kellum, 7
WOP, 64

Zaslaw, Lt. Stan, 85